Griffin
W9-CNN-990

Reading–Writing Classroom

Grades 3–6

Reading–Writing Classroom

Grades 3–6

Strategies for Extraordinary Teaching

Leslie Blauman

foreword by Stephanie Harvey

Heinemann
361 Hanover Street
Portsmouth, NH 03801–3912
www.heinemann.com

Offices and agents throughout the world

© 2011 by Leslie Blauman

All rights reserved. No part of this book may be reproduced in any form or by any electronic or mechanical means, including information storage and retrieval systems, without permission in writing from the publisher, except by a reviewer, who may quote brief passages in a review, and with the exception of reproducible pages (identified by the *Inside Guide to the Reading–Writing Workshop, Grades 3–6* copyright line), which may be photocopied for classroom use only.

"Dedicated to Teachers" is a trademark of Greenwood Publishing Group, Inc.

The author and publisher wish to thank those who have generously given permission to reprint borrowed material:

Cover of *Tracks in the Snow* by Wong Herbert Yee. Copyright © 2003 by Wong Herbert Yee. Reprinted by arrangement with Henry Holt and Company, LLC.

Acknowledgments for borrowed material continue on page viii.

Library of Congress Cataloging-in-Publication Data
Blauman, Leslie.
The inside guide to the reading–writing classroom, grades 3–6 : strategies for extraordinary teaching / Leslie Blauman ; foreword by Stephanie Harvey.
p. cm.
Includes bibliographical references and index.
ISBN-13: 978-0-325-02831-6
ISBN-10: 0-325-02831-1
1. Language arts (Elementary). 2. Effective teaching. I. Title.

LB1576.B4983 2011
372.6'044—dc22 2010049806

Editors: Harvey Daniels and Wendy Murray
Production: Vicki Kasabian
Tech developer: Nicole Russell
Interior text and cover designs: Lisa Fowler
Photographer: Barry Staver
Typesetter: Publishers' Design & Production Services, Inc.
Manufacturing: Steve Bernier

Printed in the United States of America on acid-free paper
15 14 13 12 11 VP 1 2 3 4 5

To my two children—Carolynn and John.

And to all the amazing students I've been lucky enough to teach.
Your voices and brilliance shine through
in the pages of this book.

CONTENTS

Credit lines continued from page iv:

Excerpt from *Colorado Nature Almanac: A Month-By-Month Guide to Wildlife and Wild Places* by Stephen R. Jones and Ruth Carol Cushman. Copyright © 1998. Published by Pruett Publishing Company. Reprinted by permission of the publisher and authors.

"Cruel as it is, we somehow go on" by Leonard Pitts Jr., published January 14, 2010. © The Miami Herald, 2010. Reprinted by permission of the publisher.

"Regie Routman's Reading Strategies for Unknown Words" from *Literacy at the Crossroads* by Regie Routman. Copyright © 1996 by Regie Routman. Published by Heinemann, Portsmouth, NH. Reprinted by permission of the publisher.

Excerpt from *Daily Language Instruction: Grade 4* by Barbara Anderson. Copyright © 2004 by Hogback Press. Reprinted by permission of the publisher. www.dailylanguage instruction.com.

FOREWORD

Writing a foreword is both a true honor and a bit of a challenge. When I was approached to write it for the incredible book you hold in your hands, I agreed instantly. I've had the great fortune of knowing Leslie Blauman for more than twenty years. I have spent many hours over these years in her mesmerizing classroom. We have participated in innovative study groups, worked side by side in lab classrooms, marveled at conversation-rich, student-led book clubs, reveled in kids' work, and shared our own family stories. But I still worried that I could not do Leslie and her teaching justice. How could I craft a foreword that showcased Leslie's extraordinary instinct for teaching, spirit for learning, and passion for kids? Although not insurmountable, the task seemed formidable.

But then I read the first page of *The Inside Guide to the Reading–Writing Classroom*, which includes Leslie's annual welcome letter where she introduces herself to the kids, shares her love of teaching and learning, and invites them to bring in an important book on the first day of school. And I realized that this book speaks for itself. Leslie had me from page one. Oh how I wish I were back in fourth grade on the first day of school. I would have hurried into Leslie's classroom with a copy of Margaret Wise Brown's *The Sailor Dog* tucked under my arm. When my time to share came around, I would have read my all-time favorite lead: "Born at sea in the teeth of a gale, the Sailor was a dog." I would have shown pictures of Scuppers, the Sailor Dog, dressed in ship captain's attire sailing to exotic seaports, and I would have talked about how it made me ache with wanderlust to travel the world. Leslie tells the kids that sharing their most important book is a way for them to see what they have in common as readers. But it goes way beyond that. Sharing our most important books and our thoughts about them shows us what we have in common as human beings—how we are all connected and how that connection leads to a community of thinkers and learners that will make a permanent difference in our lives, the kind of learning community that Leslie inspires every day.

As I find myself lost in a swirl of inviting images from Leslie's classroom, I can't help but think of Frank Smith's Literacy Club metaphor that evokes the social nature of literacy learning. He describes the Literacy Club as a gathering place in which everyone is a member, a classroom where no child is excluded from the abundance of rich reading, writing, talking, and listening experiences that occur across the curriculum as well as throughout the year. Leslie's classroom is a Literacy Club extraordinaire. No one is excluded, ever. No one is made to feel anything but welcome beyond measure. Leslie says it every day with her actions and her words: *Come join us! We are all here for you. Be a part of us. Join this club.*

Some people are led into teaching, others are born to it. Leslie falls into the latter camp. When it comes to kids, her instinct is uncanny. Her expectations are over-the-top high. Her energy is palpable. More than all this, Leslie's generosity extends beyond her students as she shares her secrets so that we too can be insiders. The strategies, techniques, routines, and rituals in this invaluable book are a recipe for good instruction, quality learning, and purposeful interaction. This book gives us the tools to create classrooms that sing with energy, joy, and achievement.

From the very first day, we can see how Leslie almost sneaks in the teaching as she builds community. When sharing important books, Leslie honors kids' thinking first and foremost and carefully listens to learn about each and every child. But she also teaches valuable concepts, vocabulary, and procedures, always nudging kids to make their thinking visible and take it public. As we read on, Leslie unveils a simple yet powerful lesson structure that includes its purpose, the nitty-gritty, and the kids' ownership. Chapters 4 and 5, which describe the Book Lover's Book (BLB), could have been a book in their own right. What a novel idea, these book lover's books: one place to hold all of the literacy thinking and learning over the course of a year. Entries include class thinking, strategy learning, beloved anchor texts, minilesson learning, lit logs, personal booklists, responses and reflections, and my personal favorite, the Someday List—a special place to keep track of friend and family book recommendations so that you don't forget them and may really read them one day. Kids develop a personal attachment to their Book Lover's Books and teachers get the bonus of an entire literacy history on every child easily within reach.

I can't write about Leslie's teaching without mentioning book clubs. Kids getting together regularly in small, peer-led book groups has long been one of the highlights of Leslie's classroom, the payoff for all of the modeling, guiding, and stepping aside that Leslie advocates throughout the book. As Leslie says in Chapter 9, "Book clubs are the ultimate expression of students' rich, self-generated, self-monitored thinking." Leslie's vast experience pays off in this chapter, as she guides us through the rationale, formation, implementation, and management of kids' book clubs. Leslie includes forms, schedules, anchor charts, and scripts of kids' conversations, all of which give us a picture of how her book clubs soar, yet make book club implementation seem manageable and fun.

At the core of this book is Leslie's wholehearted belief that kids can achieve anything if they are shown how and given time to practice. David Perkins says, "Learning is a consequence of thinking." Kids learn heaps in Leslie's room because they are constantly pressed to think expansively and deeply. The comprehension work of P. David Pearson and his colleagues lay a foundation for her teaching along with the work of Donald Graves and his many protégés in the writing workshop world. As you will see, kids spend all their time engaged in meaningful work in Leslie's classroom. They read, write, talk, and listen their way through the day. And Leslie stays focused on good, solid, research-based instruction no matter what the current trends. Year in and year out, through thick and thin, Leslie has never diverged from the tenets of workshop teaching, time, choice, ownership, response, rich text, visible thinking and a foundational belief in the agency of kids. This is a great read. Enjoy!

Stephanie Harvey

ACKNOWLEDGMENTS

My daughter, Carolynn, commented that I'd probably dedicate this book to my dogs, since they had been by my side throughout the entire process. That's not going to happen. However, they *were* the impetus for my climbing out of bed at 5 A.M. to run them and then start the morning early, writing at the computer. If you had walked into my office, you would have found at least one golden retriever at my feet—usually under the desk or directly behind me, draped over the air conditioner. So yes, Gunner, Alie, and Dakota deserve thanks.

That's the flippant acknowledgment; however, there is the serious and heartfelt thank-you to all the people who helped make a dream a reality.

Really, Missy Matthews writing, "Tag, you're it," as she signed my copy of *Put Thinking to the Test* was the final push for me to write. Thank you, Missy.

A month earlier, at the twenty-fifth annual Public Education and Business Coalition (PEBC) luncheon, visiting with Steph Harvey, Ellin Keene, Cris Tovani, Debbie Miller, and Chryse Hutchins, I said, "I want to write, but I don't know where to start." Susan Zimmermann walked by at that moment and said, "I'll start you out." This book began at her house, in Evergreen, on a beautiful summer day. Susan listened to me and wrote down what I said. She captured what I felt passionately about. Susan listens better than anyone I have ever met. I am forever indebted. And she put me in touch with Heinemann and ultimately Wendy Murray. Susan started the journey. Susan, I cannot say thank you enough. Thank you for your mentoring and your friendship. Truly, thank you for making me the teacher I am today.

I believe in serendipity—because I cannot imagine writing this book without Wendy Murray—my editor and my friend. This book wouldn't have happened without Wendy nudging and guiding and holding my hand. And always with humor. We did it! And it's been such a fun (and quick) journey. I hope we have a few more ahead of us!

Smokey Daniels, who jumped in feetfirst for the hand off from Wendy and brought a new perspective to this project and made it even better—and fun! I look forward to many more projects with you. Thank you for your guidance and your never-ending humor.

And the rest of the Heinemann family. So many people have added their expertise and wisdom to this book. Thank you to Stephanie Turner, another patient guide for a new author . . . and to Sarah Fournier for taking over and keeping me organized.

To Alan Huisman, editor extraordinaire—and that is no understatement. I never knew that the editing phase could be so fun. You brought clarity and flair to my writing with your incredible insight and eye for the written word. Thank you.

Vicki Kasabian, who actually put the book together. Wow. Simply wow. You have been such a guide through this. I trusted your vision and I know I was right.

Finally, some Heinemann folks I haven't met but who have been instrumental in the final design and shape of this book. Nicole Russell for tech development of the CD and Lisa Fowler for the interior and cover designs. And Cindy Ann Black for the final edits. Thank you.

To Ellin Keene, Chryse Hutchins, Lori Conrad, Bruce Morgan, Barb Smith, Kristin Venable, Susan Zimmermann, and Trina Hayden. Thank you, thank you, thank you! You read my drafts and offered your insights and wisdom in such caring ways. You helped me clarify and reorganize. Thank you for your time and for making this a better book. I listened to you—and you were right!

The working title of this book was *How Did You Get the Kids This Far?*—the question the PEBC lab visitors invariably asked me. How can I ever begin to thank the PEBC? I am the teacher I am because of the PEBC. Susan Zimmermann and Gail Klapper founded it, and I was fortunate enough to be in on the ground floor. What visionaries. Thank you for touching so many teachers' and students' lives. You have made such a difference.

Thank you to George Mansfield, who mentored and supported a novice teacher and gave me the opportunity to work with the PEBC. I was so fortunate to have you as my first principal. Your encouragement and expectations pushed me to excel.

To Liz Stedem. You were my first teacher trainer. You modeled and showed me what could happen when we had high expectations and taught students to think.

To Ellin Keene. You were there from the start too. Twenty-five years ago you were already grappling with the idea of what it means to understand. You are such a thoughtful, wise mentor. And thank you for continuing to push our professional development. I strive to rise to your level of excellence.

To Steph Harvey. You pushed my thinking. I was so fortunate to have you as a teacher trainer, to learn from you and with you. Thank you for helping launch my professional development. You have been a great friend and mentor. I cannot thank you enough for writing the Foreword—thank you for knowing my class and my teaching the way you do.

To Chryse Hutchins. What can I say? You know my classroom better than anyone. You are wise and observant and a phenomenal mentor, on so many levels. You were there as a facilitator during my labs, transcription after transcription after transcription. And those transcripts are embedded in this book. Thank you for capturing the class. Thank you for asking probing questions. You're the best.

To the rest of the PEBC folks who are always stretching thinking and teaching, and always with the thought of what is best for kids—Suzanne Plaut, Roseann Ward, Anne Goudvis, Debbie Miller, Cris Tovani, Cheryl Zimmerman, Patrick Allen, Karen Anderson Berg, Carla Randall, Annie Patterson, Sue Kempton, Susan Logan, Kim Schmidt, Ilana Spiegel, and Carole Quimby. You are brilliant thinkers and I am privileged to study with you. Thank you. And to Judy Hendricks. Thank you for keeping us all organized.

To my teammates, Jessica Ehrlich and Kelly Kirby, who have put up with me and offered a support system. Thank you. I am lucky to work with you, and your students are fortunate to be in your classes.

To the teachers I worked with when we had "Camelot"—Mary Pfau, Pat Marden, Clay Borchert, Teresa Aye, Terri Poole, and Bev Robin. It was magical.

To my colleagues at Cherry Hills Village Elementary. I am honored to work with such a dedicated and talented staff.

To my fellow administrators and literacy coordinators in Cherry Creek—Denise Campbell, Bonnie Kelly, Lori Ramirez, and Mark Overmeyer. What a gift to work and learn with you.

To the administrators. I have come to realize that they are integral to a school. Their vision can create magic. And I have worked with some of the very best. George Mansfield, you have always set the bar so high.

To Mary Terch, Mary Chesley, and Trina Rich. My teaching has been enriched by your guidance and support. Thank you. You always put kids first.

I also have been fortunate to work with phenomenal leaders around the country. In Nebraska, Amy Hill is leading a consortium of schools to improve literacy. Thank you for your vision about what literacy can be.

One of her schools is Covington Elementary, in South Sioux City, Nebraska. The principal is Sue Galvin. I wish we could all have principals like Sue. Truly. Education would be different. Two of her teachers, Lori Hasselquist and Becky Hansen, took my book lover's book and formatted it beautifully. Their work is on the CD-ROM. What talented teachers. They made it their own and they were willing to share. Thank you.

Then there's Clinton Elementary School, in Lancaster, South Carolina. Amazing. I cannot begin to say thank you to the staff (and students) for allowing me to be a part of their school. These teachers are working so hard for their students. I have never seen a school undertake so much and do it so well. I love you.

To Rachel Ray and Shirnetha Stinson, Clinton's principal and assistant principal. Again, vision. Change is hard, but when it's good for kids (and done with humor), it works.

Go see these schools. See what they are doing. And there are so many other schools. Thank you for allowing me to visit and to work with your children. Our children are brilliant.

With that, how can I not thank my children, my students? *All* of them. Almost thirty years of classes in different schools. While I dedicated the book to my two kids, truly this book is for the students. Their voices and thinking are the threads throughout. They are brilliant. They are beautiful. They always rise to the challenge. To all of my kids—and I'd love to list you all—this is for you. I couldn't have done this without you. I could have put in words and stories from each and every child who has been in my room (but Wendy wouldn't let me!). Thank you. You know I love you—so much.

To my friends. My friends who have waited while I've written. Thank you. To my Yia Yia's girls—Trina Hayden, Kate Blanchard, and Sue Beman. You're the best. You are true friends and I love you.

To my other friends who have helped and waited—those near and far. You know who you are. Some of you have been an integral part of the journey. You were always there. Always. I think you know how I feel—and thank you doesn't begin to capture it.

To my brother, Andy, and his wife, Jill, and their children, Allison and Mark. I love you guys. Thanks for your support.

To Mom. I love you. Thank you for believing and instilling the love of reading and writing in me. Your love of literacy flows through me.

To Dad. You are my rock. When life got hard, you were always there. You have always believed and I love you so incredibly much. Thank you.

And finally, the best of the best. Don't you always save the best for last? To my kids, Carolynn and John. You truly are the light of my life. It's been a journey, huh? And you've been there to support me this past year—with patience. Thanks for waiting for me. I love you both more than you know, and I couldn't ask for better. I am so incredibly proud of you. You both are amazing and I am truly blessed. This one's for you. Cheers!

HOW TO USE THIS BOOK

A group of teachers from around the United States is visiting my classroom for two consecutive mornings in April as part of a national lab hosted by the Denver-based Public Education and Business Coalition (PEBC), which, in its twenty-five-year history, has spearheaded numerous projects to increase community involvement and improve the quality of public education in the Denver metro area. My classroom is a frequent destination spot for visiting educators. I like to joke that it's like being out on the skating rink at Rockefeller Center—I've become very used to having visitors watch me glide about the room.

Jest aside, my connection with the PEBC has been central to my growth as a teacher. When the coalition was first started as a way to bridge public education with the private sector, none of us could have predicted how it would rock the reading world. Early on, it began a staff development initiative focused on quality writing instruction, specifically writing workshops. Quickly that focus grew and expanded into thinking about the strategies that proficient readers use, centered on the body of research on comprehension instruction.

As a result, groundbreaking books on reading comprehension strategies were published, beginning with Ellin Keene and Susan Zimmermann's *Mosaic of Thought*, followed by Stephanie Harvey's *Nonfiction Matters* and Harvey and Ann Goudvis' *Strategies That Work*. Professional books extending this work continue to be published by authors associated with the PEBC (Tovani, Miller, Kempton, Hutchins and Zimmermann, Morgan, Bennett, to name a few), most recently Conrad, Matthews, Zimmermann, and Allen's *Put Thinking to the Test*. These authors and teachers are my mentors and my colleagues. They have taught in my room, and my teaching has been captured in their books and on their instructional tapes. Studying and learning together, we have discovered what *really works in the classroom*.

At times I've asked myself, Who am *I* to write a book on reading and writing for other teachers? And then I think of the PEBC lab, where I teach, and all the many other schools I've taught this same way: schools with a mobility rate of more than 60 percent and the impact of low socioeconomics. Schools with both high ESL and gifted and talented populations. Schools with diverse needs. I've been fortunate to work with schools around the country. Schools where the majority of students speak a second language. Schools with 95 percent free–reduced lunch and more than 90 percent minority. And schools outside the country—for example, international schools in Central America in which English is the second language. And always—always—in my experience, kids rise to the expectations we have for them.

Because of this background and expertise, teachers visit my room throughout the year. And they ask the same awestruck question every time:

"How did you get your kids this far?"

Their goal is to return to their own classroom and implement or replicate what they see happening in my students' and my classroom.

What are they really asking? I believe it's this: How I can take a heterogeneous class of students and get them to perform as well or better in reading and writing than students in any district in the United States? The answer is simple: Kids know instinctively whether you really care about them and are genuine and honest. When they know that you do and are, they excel.

But it's more than that. In this book, I give a fuller, more complete answer. I've only recently been able to clarify for myself how I might bottle what I've discovered for other teachers to sample—*and make their own*. I want every student in America to get as far as my kids. And my methods are "kid approved," because my students are invested in my sharing them with you. Because they can't imagine anything better. Because they've sat in classrooms where their abilities are underestimated and they're *bored*. Who wants to teach like that? Who wants to learn like that?

Enjoy this book, underline it, dog-ear it, scribble in the margins—I am confident that it will help you teach reading and writing with greater playfulness and precision. As you will discover in Chapter 1, this book also brings the PEBC quest full circle, in that I show you a new generation of reading and writing workshop—an iteration that makes much more of the natural rapport between the literature we love and the writing we do in and out of school. I am a full-time teacher, so you can count on me to keep it real on every page. Yes, many of the practices are backed by research, but what makes this book unique is that you get my real teaching practices, lessons, and management ideas as influenced by the incredible PEBC "think tank."

CHAPTER 1

"It's 9:00 A.M. Do You Know Who Your Readers and Writers Are?"

August 18. Summer is over and I'm in high gear. Desks are arranged, bulletin boards hung, and I've just received my official class list in the morning mail. It's what I've been waiting for—names to attach to letters. I head eagerly to the post office, twenty-five envelopes stuffed in my purse.

The letter I send to students before school starts each year reflects the planning I've done and the expectations I have before the students walk through the door. It welcomes kids and emphasizes that we'll be hitting the ground running. It goes something like this:

Dear __________,

Welcome to fourth grade! I'm sure summer has flown by for you and it's hard to believe that Monday we come back to school. I am looking forward to a fantastic year of learning with you. Although I've been teaching for more than twenty years, I still get excited about meeting a new group of students! We'll be spending time next week settling in and becoming a learning community, but before then I'm going to ask you to do a little homework so that we're all ready on the first day. Mainly, enjoy the weekend, but if you would collect the following items for Monday, that would be terrific!

1. Your school supplies. Please label them with your name. In addition to the supplies we had listed for the term, you *may* want to purchase an expandable file folder or a "student backpack filer" to help you keep the year organized. This is totally optional.
2. A healthy snack and a water bottle. We have a long morning (lunch is at 11:35), so you may get hungry and thirsty.
3. **Your favorite book. This can be any book that you love. Please be prepared to tell me and your classmates why it's your favorite book.**
4. A book to read in class. If you're in the middle of a book right now, bring that, or bring one you'd like to read.
5. A sense of wonder and curiosity. What have you always wanted to learn? What makes you ask questions? This year we'll be working on research and following our wonders and interests.

I know it's going to be a great year; I could tell when I met most of you on the last day of school last year. I can't wait to get to know you and share stories with you. We'll be starting right away on Monday! Enjoy the weekend, and I'll see you at 7:50 Monday morning!

As I type the words *hitting the ground running,* an image of Olympic long-distance runners superimposes itself on the image of fourth graders reading, writing, and thinking at the top of their game as the result of all we as teachers do. This book is a compilation of "all we do." Think of it as my long letter to you in which I answer the question I've been most often asked by fellow teachers over the years: "So how did you get your kids this far?" The short answer? I get my kids this far via reading–writing workshop.

In these pages, I'll show you how to create this rapport between teaching reading and teaching writing. You'll walk through my days with me, internalizing the pacing, the spirit of teaching and learning reading and writing. This active, forward motion begins with the letter I mail to students and continues on day 1 with a lesson that sets the bar high. My students learn that in my classroom they will experience high involvement, deep engagement, humor, and trust and come to see that books and writing *are* the be-all and end-all.

Camaraderie and Intellectual Engagement from Day 1

It's now August 25; twenty-five fourth graders traipse into my classroom. I sit in my director's chair, several books on my lap, favorites from different phases of my life. The curiosity of the kids sitting around me in a circle is palpable. No teacher before has written to them over the summer and asked them to bring in a favorite book.

"Listen to this dialogue!" I say, reading aloud from my childhood copy of *Dick and Jane*. "'Look, Dick. See Jane help Spot. Oh, see something funny. See little Spot. Funny little Spot.' And would you believe we actually dressed like that when I was a kid!" I show my students the pictures of Jane in a gingham dress and Mary Janes, Dick in collared shirt, khaki shorts, and Buster Browns. My students are laughing hysterically.

"I loved Dick and Jane because of the pictures and they had a dog named Spot and I desperately wanted a dog when I was a kid." I pause. "You're probably wondering why I'm doing this." Many heads nod in agreement. "Here's why: I asked you to bring in a book that's a favorite or has been important to you because it's a wonderful way for me to get to know you, and for you to learn about one another. It's a way to see what we have in common as readers. I'm going to start by showing you the kind of details I want to hear from you when it's your turn."

I hold up Dr. Seuss' *Thidwick the Big-Hearted Moose* (1948). "I couldn't get enough of Dr. Seuss, and this story was a favorite. I was about six when I was at the height of my Seuss addiction."

My students lean forward. They did *not* expect their grown-up teacher to be effusing about a kind moose.

THE LANGUAGE OF LEARNING

From the first day of school I want my students to hear the word *mentor* in relation to reading and writing. Mentor texts teach about craft, genre, inspiration, to name a few attributes. Just as we use mentors to guide us, mentor texts inform our writing—and our reading.

"Now *Good Night Moon* (Brown 1991)—what can I say? I'm mushy hearted. This will always be a cherished book because I read it to both my children. I know it by heart, plus I love the mouse." This time, my students are fairly bouncing up and down in agreement. They, too, remember this book and love it.

"Notice, kids, that I'm not summarizing the plot of any of the books here. Instead I'm telling you *why* I like it. This is what I want you to do, too, with your books."

At this point, we discuss the difference between telling *about* the book (a summary) and telling *why* it's a favorite. I ask, "Which requires more thinking? Could we just read the blurb on the back to get the summary?"

This year we will be *thinking,* and I want the students to hear on the first day of school that we're pushing beyond the literal; this year we're going deep with our thinking. Pushing the *why* versus simply summarizing nudges my students away from retelling, toward bringing their own thoughts and perspectives to the text. I want my students *talking about their thinking.*

I go on to share some of my adult favorites. I tell them that I love mystery and suspense. I share an "out of the box" book, *The World Is Flat* (Friedman 2005)—a book friends have recommended that I normally wouldn't read but that takes me out of my comfort zone and makes me work harder to understand. I share my professional reading and my mentor books. And I share books that reflect my passions, books like *Marley and Me* (Grogan 2005) and Cesar's Way (Milan 2007) (I have three golden retrievers and a crazy household). I talk about my "beach reads," books I can read quickly, don't have to think about, and forget about almost immediately—books I take on vacation.

Next I stand up, write *fiction* and *nonfiction* on the chalkboard at the front of our meeting area, and ask, "What do you see in these two words that's different?" Dexter immediately answers, "The *non*, and that means *not*!"

"Absolutely right. We call that part a *prefix*, and the prefix *non* means *not.* So *nonfiction* means *not fiction.* Who knows what *fiction* is?" I'm not only going to teach the literary terms, I'm also going to take every opportunity to teach about words.

Rachael answers that fiction is a made-up story; that it's not true. Hayden adds that there's fiction that sounds real, and I explain that that's realistic fiction. We continue to discuss exactly what fiction and nonfiction are, then I add the word *genre* to the board and ask the students to pronounce it. Hands go up in the air and students make attempts at pronouncing it phonetically. Finally I give the correct pronunciation and briefly describe its French origin.

We all repeat it and I explain, "*Genres* are how books are grouped. If you go into Barnes and Noble and look in different sections of the store, you're looking at genres. You might see shelves labeled *mystery* or *romance* or *nonfiction*." Heads nod in understanding. I will return to this same concept as we begin writing instruction; it's integral to interlacing reading and writing instruction.

"So now it's your turn. You get to share your favorite book and explain to the class *why* it's your favorite. Then you're going to classify your book as fiction or nonfiction and then maybe by a more specific genre. If you need help, we're all here."

I ask for a volunteer; Ryan goes first. He takes my place in the director's chair, his favorite book in hand—*Bugs* (2007), by Susan Barraclough—and explains that he loves to learn about bugs and he doesn't like to read stories or fiction. He holds up the picture of the most terrifying bug in the book for everyone to see. From this brief interaction, I've already learned a lot about this young man.

As Ryan is sharing, I sit on the floor and create a chart headed *name, title, author,* and *why favorite.* This turns into a minilesson: As I write the title of Ryan's book, *Bugs*, I tell the class that just as a book sits on a shelf, the title of a book sits on a shelf, and that's why we underline it. I show and name the correct format. We discuss which words in the title require initial capital letters. I also tell the students that I'm using quotation marks around the exact words Ryan said, so that we will remember that those were his words, and that this is a tool writers use. I want to be as explicit as possible from the very first day.

"You know, guys, even though we're talking about our reading here, we're also beginning to talk about our writing. Because you can be a reader without being a writer, but you cannot be a good writer without being a reader. Think about that. You're already noticing what makes great writing." I want to drive this point home, as it will be a focus for our entire year, just as it's a focus of this book.

Ryan chooses Erin to go next. *Fudge-a-Mania* (2003), by Judy Blume, is her favorite because it's really funny and the older brother is always annoying the little kid. She says she likes the whole series and that Fudge makes it funny. This leads to a brief discussion about how readers often stay with books in a series they enjoy.

On this first day of school, five students share their books. I stop while they're still excited and listening, before they get fidgety—I want them hooked and looking forward to sharing the next day.

We continue through the week until everyone has had an opportunity to sit in the director's chair and share his book. Students love this activity: if they have forgotten their book on the first day, it is definitely on their desk on the second! If they tell me they don't have the book at home, I make sure they have a chance to go to the school library to find their title: accountability in action.

If someone starts summarizing or retelling, just giving an overview of the plot, I nudge them back to *why*. At first I may need to offer a bit more support and ask questions to pull out the *why*, but after a few kids have shared, the discussion moves quickly. Classifying the books by genre turns into a teachable moment, because many of the students don't know specific genre names. We ask, is it funny? (humor), could it have happened? (realistic fiction), do magical things happen? (fantasy), is it scary? (horror), is it fiction but set in an earlier time period (historical fiction), and so on. If they still can't come up with the name of the genre, the class and I help out. Students are already realizing that it's okay if they don't have the right answer, that there's a support system in place to help them *think*.

And of course I record everything on the chart. Their thinking and words are captured and valued from the first day of school.

Each child takes about four or five minutes, and what I gain is invaluable. The lesson is a very informal reading inventory—I get a glimpse of what types of books each student is reading (or hearing read), the level, and how much she comprehends. I type up everything I've written on the chart, copy it, and include it in each child's "book lover's book" (see Chapter 4 under class thoughts (there's an example in Figure 1.1). I also list each child's favorite book on a poster outside our classroom door, so visitors to our room know that we are a room of readers (great for back-to-school night)!

Figure 1.1 Class Thoughts

WHAT ARE OUR FAVORITES?

Ryan–Bugs, by Susan Barraclough

"I like it because I like insects and it's educational. Most terrifying insects in the world. Great pictures." (Nonfiction)

Erin–Fudge-a-Mania, by Judy Blume

"Really funny. Little kid, older brother is annoying. I like the whole series. Fudge makes it funny." (Fiction/humor)

Ellie–The Problem Child (third book of the Sisters Grimm series), by Michael Buckley

"I like the series. Best one of the series. Gets to the best mystery–who kidnapped their parents." (Fiction/fantasy/mystery)

Reed–Diary of a Wimpy Kid, by Jeff Kinney

"The boys do funny stuff. For example, the kid under the table poking him with a broom. Kinney makes the reader see what's happening–makes you laugh. Makes the reader wish they could do some of those things [live vicariously through the story/characters]." (Fiction/humor)

Peyton–Treasure Island, by Robert Louis Stevenson

"When I'm reading it, I feel like I'm in the book with the characters. Feels like I'm there. Pulls me in and it feels like it's real." (Fiction/adventure)

What messages do you send kids if on the first day of school you spend the majority of the time:

Doing This

- Modeling and practicing expectations
- Sharing favorite books and discussing thinking
- Discussing vocabulary in context and making it meaningful to the students
- Having rich discussions in which speaking and listening are modeled and practiced
- Sharing yourself as a learner and member of the classroom community–trusting and respecting the students

Versus Doing That

- Going over rules you've formulated, especially using the word *no*
- Doing the majority of the talking–talking at the kids rather than letting them do the talking
- Having them read a basal story and answer the questions at the end
- Handing out an assessment worksheet and having students complete it by themselves
- Making them work in silence
- Being in complete control

▶ THE NITTY-GRITTY

In this lesson, I:

- Introduce or reinforce literacy vocabulary (*fiction*, *nonfiction*, *genre*, *prefix*, etc.).
- Show how to underline and correctly capitalize titles.
- Demonstrate that writers put quotation marks around a speaker's exact words.
- Create a community of readers and writers: students notice who in the class has similar interests.
- Introduce the joy of recommending books: as students read books from the classroom library, ask them to include a sticky note inside the front cover with their name and a sentence recommending the book (or not) and why.

Where the First-Day Lesson Leads

Fast-forward to April: this same group of students seven months later. Remember Erin, who brought in *Fudge-a-Mania* on that first day? She just finished *The Invention of Hugo Cabret* (Selznick 2007) and can't wait to discuss it with Conor, who has also finished it. Erin wants to clarify what happened to the mother because that question wasn't resolved for her and she knows that talking with Conor will help. She's also going to google "Hugo Cabret" to get more information; even though she finished reading the book, she's not finished enjoying it and understanding it at a much deeper level.

Then there's Ryan, the reluctant reader, who only read nonfiction at the beginning of the year. Now he's immersed in The Hardy Boys. His current book is *Running on Fumes* (Dixon 2005) and he comments, "I love the new Hardy Boys, but not the old ones. The old ones aren't as good, the new ones have more action." Yes, he's still at a literal level in his reading—summarizing—but he's branching out to fiction and enjoying it. Ryan still loves to go back to nonfiction, though, and has done research reports on space and butterflies (can't break the bug fixation or his love of the Discovery Channel!). But he has taught the class more about these topics than I could begin to.

Finally there's Trinity, who brought in *Where the Sidewalk Ends* (Silverstein 1994) at the beginning of the year. In her current novel reading, she mixes the humor of Roald Dahl with the poignancy of Karen Hesse. However, Trinity still loves poetry, especially the poems of Emily Dickinson. I can't keep enough poetry books in the room for her. Trinity is the epitome of someone who reads like a writer, and her poetry is beautiful. She writes about her inspiration: "I get a lot of my ideas from outdoors. There are a lot of brilliant colored leaves. And in the afternoons the sun hits the water magnificently. I also like to examine my backyard because it is filled with trees. I also get a lot of my ideas from the books I'm reading. I think poetry has such great emotion and that's why I'm drawn to it. I think I like more of the serious writing, but it is good to have a laugh once in awhile." Such wise words from a ten-year-old! (See her poem "Autumn" on the CD.)

The Architecture of This Book

I talk a lot about helping children "hold their thinking" to develop both a mind-set and concrete strategies for hanging on to their ideas, the vivid images of their learning. So I want you to hang on to this portrait of a first-day lesson as I step back from the classroom to declare the broader goals of this book. The books most memorable for me are those in which I can feel the author's fire and sense the spark that got it all going. The spark that ignites the book is the link between reading and writing. Most professional books focus on *either* reading or writing but not the interplay between the two.

I've built on the work of the Public Education and Business Coalition (PEBC), and drew inspiration from the work of Allington, Harwayne, Elbow, Calkins, and Atwell in reading and from the writing research of Graves, Fletcher, Ray, and a score of others. But in this book I push farther, provide angles on practice that haven't been made clear to teachers before.

- *I show what it looks like to connect reading and writing practices in a workshop setting.* Chapters 4 and 5 introduce the book lover's book (BLB) as a place to keep all student thinking about reading. While the BLB is a reading book, I also push writing there. In Chapter 6, I show how to set up the workshop and begin to interweave instruction, especially using mentor texts. Chapter 7 focuses on rich talk and conferring as the glue that holds the workshop together. Chapter 8 continues to dig into strong reading comprehension instruction. The final chapter circles back to reading, and rich conversations in book clubs.
- *I share some essential introductory lessons in both reading and writing.* These lessons—lessons such as living literate lives, what makes great listening, and phenomenal talk—are models for success. I share scenarios, examples, and techniques to reach and motivate students of all backgrounds and academic levels. Without these lessons, it's really easy for things to go adrift.

- *I invite you to think critically about the intentions of your minilessons.* I share minilessons that combine the *how* and the *why* and show in detail what they look like in the classroom before, during, after. *Following the thread of my decision making reveals the kind of thinking* and sussing out you need to do when planning your own demonstrations and creating your own lessons and extensions based on your beliefs and the needs of your students. (Throughout the book, a repeating "Owning the Lesson" feature highlights practices and desired outcomes.)
- *I provide a daily reading instruction framework and a daily writing instruction framework and show you how to manage the two simultaneously.* Time is precious, and you need to use it wisely. I describe what typical days and weeks look like and how to incorporate reading and writing into the day without feeling overwhelmed. How do you do it all? And with children with a wide range of interests and abilities? "There's not enough time in the day!" *Yes, there is*—and here's the way to do it and then make it yours.
- *I show what it looks like to bring the goal of students' independence and high-level thinking to the forefront of all your instruction.* What does it look like to blend the "best of the best," to hone ideas and synthesize research encountered during twenty-five years of teaching? I show what happens when teaching each day arises from the belief that all students have the ability and capacity to achieve. A lot of books hold this up as an ideal—I show you what it looks and sounds like, from conversations to excerpts from phenomenal student writing.
- *I share a reading/writing assessment tool that allows you to keep everything in one place.* How do you keep track of it all without going crazy? How do you know and report how the kids are doing? Holding the thinking and assessing student progress in the book lover's book (see Chapters 4 and 5) is an authentic way to assess and provide feedback to students, parents, and administrators and may even be this book's chief calling card.
- *I provide an overview of how to implement the gradual release model into classroom instruction.* From setting up overarching unit plans to presenting individual lessons, I show how you set the foundation for student success. *Gradual release* and *scaffolding* are integral aspects of a successful classroom. These techniques are explained especially

in Chapters 2 and 8, along with specific examples of how to incorporate them into the literacy classroom. Success begins with the expectation that *all students* have the ability and capacity to achieve at the highest levels, and it's your job to convey this to your students. Children are smart; when they know you honestly believe that, *they* begin to believe—and excel. That's where the magic of incredible achievement starts.

- *I share my philosophical stance as a teacher to help you be metacognitive about your own beliefs.* Just as you want your students to be metacognitive in their learning, you need to be metacognitive about your instruction. In the second edition of *Mosaic of Thought* (2007), Ellin Oliver Keene and Susan Zimmermann write about their game-changing realization that by "thinking about our own thinking—that is, by being *metacognitive*—we could actually deepen and enhance our comprehension of the text" (16). Being metacognitive about your instructional practices can only deepen and enhance the learning that happens in your classroom. The repeating "Language of Learning" feature examines how your language affects your students and how you can create bonds with them that push the learning forward.

My Core Beliefs and the Stances They Engender

Many recent professional books encourage teachers to reflect on and articulate their beliefs. I agree. This is critical to creating a literacy classroom that works. My beliefs, which emphasize *time* and *talk*, have evolved and solidified from years of practice. Many of them stem from the work of Allington (*What Really Matters for Struggling Readers*, 2001). My beliefs infuse every practice, every interaction, in my classroom. Together they form the stances I take in my daily teaching.

Teachers know and connect with their students.
I genuinely like my students.
Sharing, talking, and listening are the cornerstones of my school day.
I know what makes my students "tick," both academically and personally.

Students deserve honest feedback.
I trust the abilities of my students.
My students trust me.
I believe in children's intellectual capacity.

THE LANGUAGE OF LEARNING

My second core belief, that students deserve honest feedback, builds directly on the first. When students know I'm being honest, they trust me. And trust is the cornerstone of success. Creating a classroom in which the teacher and the students are invested in learning together requires absolute trust. It's the key to why students make wise choices. It's the key to why incredible learning and thinking take place. Trust fosters and nurtures independence and the ability to take risks. These qualities in turn create high-level thinkers. Trust is the essential ingredient in all my core beliefs.

I encourage risk taking in my classroom.

I teach talking and listening, and these activities constitute a large part of my classroom day.

I guide my students' growth by giving them honest feedback.

I use authentic assessment to inform and drive my instruction.

Student independence needs to be taught, modeled, and practiced.

I provide explicit instruction using the gradual release method.

I scaffold learning and instruction so that my students can be successful.

I offer students sufficient practice over time at the right pace and level.

I use my time well.

I value lingering–rushing through tasks to "cover" them is a waste of instructional time.

I offer students choice and ownership so that they can become independent.

I provide a safe classroom environment in which students can take risks.

I trust my students to make good choices.

Students are capable of high-level thinking *every day*!

I don't underestimate my students' abilities and potential.

I say, "Yes, my students *can* do that!"

I believe that every single child can work and think at the highest level.

I offer students choice and ownership so that they can become high-level, critical thinkers.

I give my students time to think.

My students and I bring passion to our work.

I teach the *learner*.

▶ QUESTIONS TO THINK ABOUT

- How much time do your students read during the school day? That means *really reading*, in all content areas. (*Reading worksheets doesn't count.*)
- How much time do your students spend writing every day, in all content areas? (Again, *filling out worksheets doesn't count.*)

Students should spend over half of *every* school day immersed in real and meaningful reading and writing.

A Year of Teaching

What might a year of reading and writing look like? While each classroom is different, there are standards and expectations that must be met. Figure 1.2 is an example of an overview planning chart for a typical year in my fourth-grade classroom. Yes, there's a lot on it! And yes, this book will explain all the elements you see. But it reflects how reading and writing can work together in the classroom to deepen achievement, independence, and thinking. It's an example of what you might create with your students in your classroom.

Each year I start with a blank chart, the dates inserted. When I'm putting names on letters in August, the chart remains almost blank, with just my initial foundational lessons penciled in. After twenty-five years of teaching, I know my first three or four weeks will be spent introducing and practicing the lessons you'll find in Chapters 2 and 3. My days will be spent setting up a community of learners and assessing my students—all the "stuff" that has to happen at the beginning of the year. Only as I begin to know my students can I begin to chart out the rest of the year (always in pencil, so I can make changes). My chart begins as a foundation; as I learn about my students—their strengths and needs—I can begin creating the architecture.

As the chart illustrates, setting up an effective workshop takes time. It also requires a great deal of thinking, planning, and anticipating ahead of time, about expectations and logistics. Having clear, explicit expectations, setting high standards, and creating a sense of rigor will facilitate success. Chapter 2 shows you how.

In Kids' Words

Whenever I'm reading, my mind goes to a place that's almost like a factory that takes other writers' great writing and turns it into my own. You really helped me to expand my "factory" with all of the quick-writes and books you shared. What's strange is that before this class, I never viewed my thoughts and mind as a factory, but now I do.

—Fourth-grader Trinity, in her writer's notebook

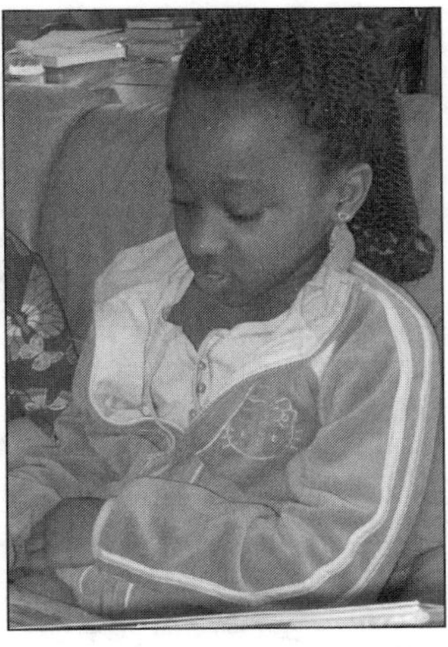

Week	Reading Comp Strategy	Reading	Reading Focus	Ongoing Reading	Ongoing Writing	Writing Focus	Writing Process/Traits	Writing Pieces	Grammar/ Mechanics	Other
Aug 24-28	← SCHEMA → ← WHAT IS LITERACY? monitoring meaning & comprehension VISUALIZING Determining Importance	Reading for purpose ← Assessment → ← Lit Log — RESPONSE to Reading letters) Elements: setting, character, plot, conflict	PURPOSE/self-selected texts ← FOUNDATIONAL LESSONS → Holding/marking thinking	VOCABULARY (yearlong) Tracks in snow — Response to variety of Literature	Descriptive & Narrative Paragraphs (President Pieces – year long) WRITERS NOTEBOOK, QUICK WRITES FIGURATIVE & BEAUTIFUL LANGUAGE	POETRY Letter writing Notetaking	Simile Alliteration onomatopoeia REVISION! What is the Writing Process? Ideas & Content – organization DETAILS! word choice	President Paragraphs (all year long) Poetry	Adj. – NOUNS – VERBS — capitals/ COMMAS ENDMARKS. periods	
Aug 31-Sept. 4										
Sept. 8-11										
Sept. 14-18										
Sept. 21-25										
Sept.28-Oct. 2										
Oct. 5-9										
Oct. 12-16										
Oct. 19-23										
Nov. 2-6	← Questions → (literal & inferential answers) Making Inferences	Elements of Fiction POETRY cause/effect, Drawing Conclusions Etc.	← BOOK CLUBS → ANCHOR TEXT Tiger Rising Holding Thinking	SUMMARIZING.	Yearlong – Ongoing	Language in Fiction and non-fiction	MENTOR TEXTS → VOICE Sentence Fluency	Messy Room "I feel..." "In ___" mentor text In November by Cynthia Rylant Poch- mentor text Piece Barry Lane Reviser's Toolbox	Adverbs ← → (Dialogue) Quotation marks Apostrophes	Grades entered – time for student reflection!
Nov. 9-13										Conferences
Nov. 16-20										
Nov. 23-24										
Nov. 31 – Dec. 4										
Dec. 7-11										
Dec. 14-18										
Jan. 4-8		Non-Fiction								
Jan. 11-										

Figure 1.2 A Year of Reading: My Overview Planning Chart

15										
Jan. 19-22										
Jan. 25-29										
Feb. 1-5										
Feb. 8-12										**Grades entered – time for student reflection!**
Feb. 22-26										
Mar. 1-5										**State testing**
Mar. 8-12										**State Testing**
Mar. 15-19										**State Testing**
Mar. 22-26										

Determining Importance in Text
Questioning
← metacognition ——→ Noticing the strategies in your reading
non-Fiction: Note-Taking
Non-Fiction TEXT Noticing organizational connecting to writing
BOOK CLUBS →
← BOOK CLUBS
Testing As A Genre
Testing As A Genre (Audience) (Purpose)
Poetry
non-Fiction mentor TEXTS.
Punctuation unit of study
Crafting non-Fiction Unit of Study
Punctuation Unit of Study
Poem
Punctuation Piece
Non-Fiction Piece
Paragraphing Dialogue
Using Punctuation correctly

Apr. 5-9										
Apr. 12-16										
Apr.19-23										
Apr. 26-30										
May 3-7										
May10-14										
May 17-21										
May 24-28										
June 1-4										**Reflect, reflect, reflect! Grades entered**
June 7-8										**End of Year!**

← Questioning INFERRING —
— Synthesizing —
Research - Note-taking
← ANCHOR TEXT Bearstone →
← BOOK CLUBS →
Unit of Study Fiction
Unit of Study - Feature Articles
Revision
Fiction Piece
Feature Article - Research Topic
Grammar/mechanics - Use in authentic writing

Figure 1.2 Continued

CHAPTER 2

Reading and Writing Minilessons for the First Weeks of School

The lessons in this chapter are "road-paving" sessions. Remember the sensation when, after riding in a car for miles on bumpy, potholed pavement, you reach a section of brand-new highway? These lessons bring that smooth, new-road sensation to your classroom. They help children stay the course of your high expectations for behavior, engagement in reading and writing, and classroom routines. They lay down the four-lane superhighway on which students will travel as readers, writers, and thinkers.

These minilessons are presented to the whole class, yet as you try them, remember they need to be reinforced individually—during small-group exchanges, or one-on-one (as in the exchange I have with Felix on page 36, in which I give him some anchors to hold on to—he knows to refer back to class anchor charts, and he knows I'll be checking in on him frequently). You also have to go slow to go fast; in

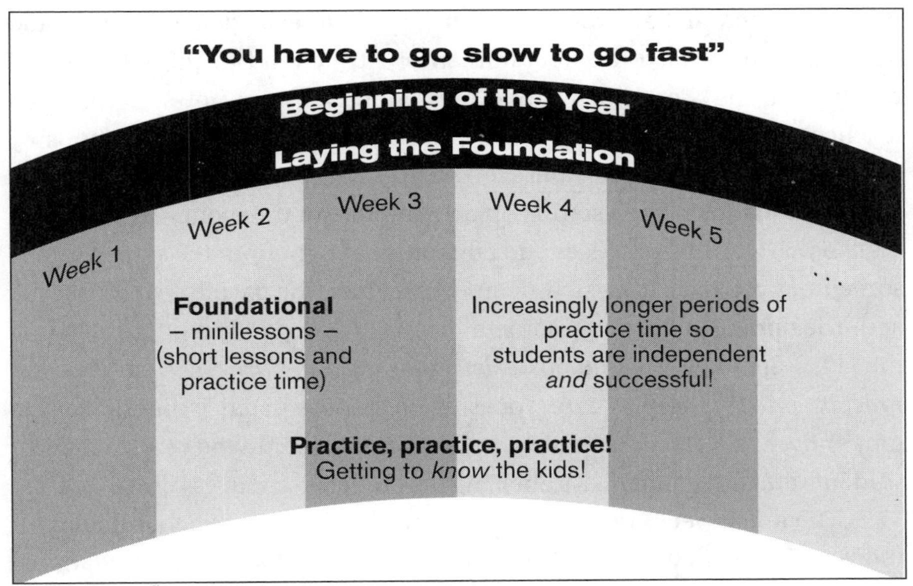

the beginning days of school, you have to provide students with lots of demonstrations and practice.

The minilessons can be presented in about ten minutes. However, a friend of mine once asked teasingly, "Oh, yeah? You really get this done in ten minutes?" and she's right. These lessons are here for you to own, so if one goes from ten minutes to two days, so be it. In fact, my friend advised me to emphasize the idea of minilesson clusters. Often a minilesson "overflows its banks" into another day and by week's end you discover you've delivered a cluster of lessons that go together. The important thing is to keep the phases of the lesson fairly consistent.

When do you teach these lessons? Is there a certain sequence? While these lessons are key components for structure at the beginning of the year, there is no specific order. The lessons in this chapter and the next can be woven in daily during the first few weeks of school.

Initial Minilessons/Practice Combos

As I work with teachers around the country, they often ask, "How do you start?" My off-the-cuff response is, "You hook the kids, and invite them on the journey with you." But that's vague and glib, and when I began writing this book, I realized that answering this question in a really detailed way would help less experienced teachers immensely. They tend to think successful reading–writing workshops arrive mysteriously by way of supertalented teachers and kids—and they don't. You conduct successful workshops by being willing to be very, very basic in the beginning.

It's a matter of both setting up the structure of the room *and* establishing the rich learning practices and environment right from the start. Again—sometimes you have to go slow in order to go fast. The payoffs for taking time at the beginning of the year—sometimes lots of it, depending on the needs of the kids—are huge. That old joke *How do you get to Carnegie Hall? Practice, practice, practice!* applies here. Focusing on student practice during the first four or five weeks leads to student independence later in the year. And when students are independent, it's amazing how much you can get done!

The initial weeks in my classroom focus on setting up a foundation for the year. In the first weeks of school, I present the following foundational minilessons.

- What Exactly Does *Literacy* Mean?
- Living Literate Lives
- Rules and Rituals (and Routines)
- Touring the Room/Managing Movement
- Independent Silent Reading Expectations

These short lessons introduce my expectations, and students then briefly practice what they've learned. This creates stamina—the ability to stay focused for longer and longer periods—which is a goal for independence.

In my minilessons, I always tell kids the purpose, then model, then practice. I present them here in the following format.

- *Purpose*: States how the lesson answers a need or averts a common problem and in turn how it helps facilitate a smoothly running classroom.
- *Here's How It Goes*: Classroom dialogue, intended as a *model*. Just as I want to be explicit with my students, I want to be explicit in these lessons with you. Just as I have created the lesson to reflect my students' needs (and my method of delivery), you need to use my approach as a framework for your own delivery. The goal is student independence.
- *Owning the Lesson*: This section is for you. Besides suggesting how to extend the lesson, it includes questions you may want to reflect on

or simply use as a checklist. It's meant to help you think about your instructional practices and beliefs and how the lessons might fit into your classroom.

The graphs in Figures 2.1 and 2.2 capture an hour of literacy instruction, either the reading block or the writing block. In an optimal world, teachers have a two-hour block for literacy, but that's not always feasible or the way schools allocate instructional time. Therefore, I'm only showing what an hour might look like.

At the beginning of the year, I try to get in three short minilessons and practice sessions during that hour—but that doesn't mean I present three of the lessons detailed in this chapter and the next. I only do one foundational lesson a day, then spend the rest of the time working on all the other essential bits and pieces associated with the beginning of the year—district assessments, inventories, getting-to-know-one-another activities (the CD includes examples), spelling, all the housekeeping "stuff" I need to do.

Figure 2.1 Community and Foundational Lessons Setup: What a Typical Workshop Hour Might Look Like

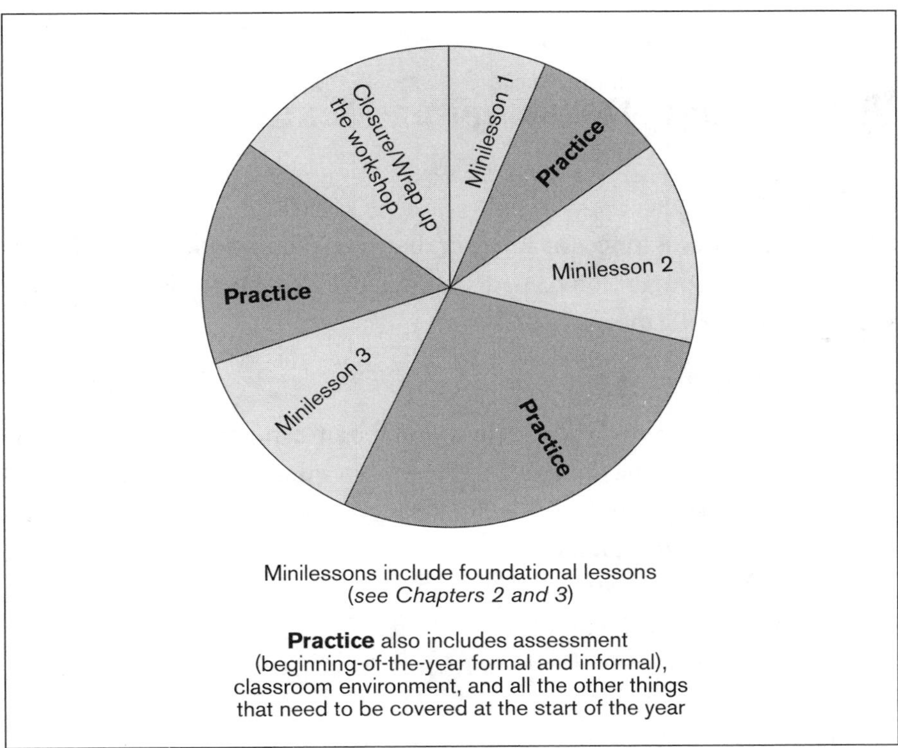

Minilessons include foundational lessons (*see Chapters 2 and 3*)

Practice also includes assessment (beginning-of-the-year formal and informal), classroom environment, and all the other things that need to be covered at the start of the year

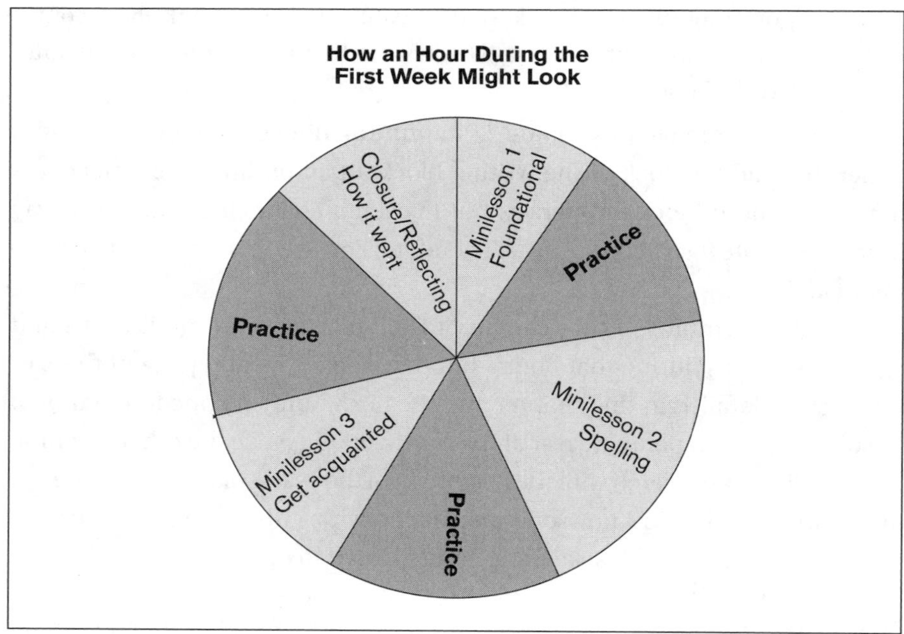

Figure 2.2 A Closer Look

What Exactly Does *Literacy* Mean?

PURPOSE

If I want my students to see the interplay between reading and writing, I need to create a classroom in which literacy is valued. I want my students to understand exactly what it means to be literate.

HERE'S HOW IT GOES

It's 9:00 A.M. on the second day of school and the students are gathered around my director's chair in the group area. Five more students have shared their favorite books, and now I write the word *literacy* on the board. I ask the students what the word is and what it means.

Dexter says, "Writing?"

Emma ventures, "It sounds like literature."

I think, *This could lead to a great discussion.* "Yes, what do you think that means?"

Rather tentatively, Emma says, "To be able to write?"

It's becoming obvious to me that my students are hesitant to take risks or share thinking in front of the entire class. I want to change that—by the end of the first week of school I want students feeling safe taking risks.

"You're sort of on track. Let's keep thinking." I throw the question out to the rest of the class. Each year is different; sometimes the students immediately know the meaning. Not this year! They're stuck on the idea that *literate* means writing. I know what I want them to glean from this discussion, but I may have to do some prompting to get the desired outcome!

I return to yesterday's discussion of genres and where you'd find different books in a bookstore. I write *literature* on the board and say, "You'd find *literature* in a bookstore."

Expressions on children's faces change; lightbulbs are turning on. Matthew makes the connection first. "Does it have to do with reading, too?"

Annie blurts out, "Oh! I've heard the word *illiterate* and that means you can't read."

"You're right, Annie. Some people can't read—or write. The prefix *il* means not. So *illiterate* means not literate. What does *literate* mean?"

Reed says, "I get it! *Literate* means you're able to read. Does it mean writing, too?"

"*Literacy* is both, and this year we are going to live literate lives. We're going to learn exactly what it means to be literate and to become better readers and writers. That's my job as your teacher. Every time I work with you I need to teach you something so that your literacy improves. Your job is to use what I teach you even when I'm not sitting with you, prompting you. We have a lot of work to do, and it's going to be hard, but man is it going to be fun! So let's get back to that original word—*literature*—what is it?"

Hays's hand shoots up in the air. "Well, it has to be books."

"Just books?"

"Oh, it could be all types of writing, right?"

"Nice job, Hays. Yes, it's the writing we read. See how reading and writing combine under literacy? That's what we're studying

▶ THE NITTY-GRITTY

With that invitation, *Are you up for it?*, how can my students not be? The realization that this year is going to be different—ideas and thinking count—is sinking in. Most importantly, students are beginning to grasp the idea that being challenged and pushed to go beyond expectations will be the norm. This is what the start of the year is all about: catching the student's interests, hooking them with that lead, then continuing to reel them in. From day 2, I'm laying the foundation that reading and writing are woven together. I'm getting to know my students as learners and as individuals right away, so I can begin giving them the feedback they need to reach their highest potential. If I don't take my time getting to know my students as learners, a good deal of the beginning of the year is wasted on instruction that skates on the surface.

In Kids' Words

You are right; it is good to be reading so many books. This year is like the best book year. By the way, last year I didn't read so much and since I've been in your class I've really opened up my eyes to books! I just love how you do your magic!

Sincerely,
Claire

this year. And I'm going to teach you the way adults read and write, the way strong readers think and make meaning, and the way authors of all sorts of genres write. Are you up for it?"

Living Literate Lives

I present this lesson on the third day of school, building on the previous lesson about what *literate* means. I use literacy to launch the year because I want to emphasize the connection between reading and writing.

PURPOSE

Students must be aware of how they are measured, scored, and evaluated and also understand the terms and language used in assessment. Teachers cannot underestimate the abilities of students; we should be using the same language with the students as we do to measure and report on student progress. Our words are powerful. When students view themselves as "insiders" privy to the same information teachers use, investment in learning and risk taking increases. Students are doing much of the thinking in this lesson, and it is at a higher level. What is literacy and what does it mean to be literate? That's what I want my students to understand. I want them literate!

HERE'S HOW IT GOES

I take out the picture book *Thank You, Mr. Falker*, by Patricia Polacco (1998). I share that this is one of my favorite books and that I'm using it to launch our study on literacy. I show the cover of the book and ask what it might be about. "What are you *thinking* as you look at this cover? Good readers always think about the book, even before they read."

"It looks like the girl on the cover is really upset," Scott says.

"More like frustrated," says Maddie.

"Who's the guy? Maybe Mr. Falker?" adds Jonny.

"Great questions. Let's read to figure it out. There's always one question I ask before starting a book and that's *what is the story about?* Do you guys ask that too? Did you know readers always ask questions *before* they start to read?"

Heads nod.

"Now, I'm a really good reader, so I'm going to show you what readers do. I'm going to cut off the top of my head so you can see what I'm thinking." (Okay, that last line is graphic, but I use it—with every age group I work with—because it catches the kids' attention and they'll remember what I'm saying. Of course there are the students that immediately say "Cool!" and can't wait for the blood. But it's also a great way to demonstrate the difference between literal and figurative speech.) "No, not really cut off the top of my head—yuck! That would be *literal*, plus it would make a mess in the classroom—and hurt! I mean that as an example. I'm going to pretend that the top of my head is missing and I'll think *out loud* as I read, so you can hear the thought processes of a good reader. I'm going to do this because I expect you to be able to tell me what you're thinking as you read and how it's helping you make meaning. If I do it first, you'll know what I'm talking about.

▶ THE NITTY-GRITTY

This is a key concept for literacy—good readers always think about the book. Especially for struggling readers, I need to be explicit about what *readers* do. I want students asking the question, "What is this book about?" before beginning to read. It sets the purpose for their reading.

▶ THE NITTY-GRITTY

Thinking aloud allows me to model my thinking, make it explicit for my students. This technique has many names, but it started in the mid-1980s as *mental modeling*, a term used in the work of Pearson et al. (1992). It has since been referenced and discussed in many professional resource books. I have found it to be one of the most powerful ways to model what I want the students to do independently.

"You also have a really important job. Your job is to think about *why* I chose this book and *how* it fits with our discussion. How does it fit with the words *literate, literacy,* and *literature*? How does it fit with our study of living literate lives? How does it fit with both the reading and the writing? That's your job."

▶ THE NITTY-GRITTY

Although I will be doing much of the work as I'm modeling my thinking, I want to hold the students accountable. By setting a purpose—to listen and answer these questions—I'm modeling that even in group work there is an expectation to interact with the text.

I know I have to be explicit with my students. It's always the times I *assume* they understand that trip me up and I end up going back to reexplain. By being explicit and showing students exactly what I want them to do, I *scaffold* their learning. Just as a scaffold supports the building, modeling supports all the future learning that will occur. If the structure isn't there, there's no foundation on which to build.

I turn to the first page and read:

> The grandpa held the jar of honey so that all the family could see, then dipped a ladle into it and drizzled honey on the cover of a small book.
>
> The little girl had just turned five.
>
> "Stand up, little one," he cooed. "I did this for your mother, your uncles, your older brother, and now you!"
>
> Then he handed the book to her. "Taste!"
>
> She dipped her finger into the honey and put it into her mouth.
>
> "What is that taste?" the grandma asked.
>
> The little girl answered, "Sweet!"
>
> Then all of the family said in a single voice, "Yes, and so is knowledge, but knowledge is like the bee that made that sweet honey, you have to chase it through the pages of a book!"
>
> The little girl knew that the promise to read was at last hers. Soon she was going to learn to read.

After I finish, I put the book down and tell the students that I remember my own children going to kindergarten expecting to learn to read on the first day and coming home disappointed when they didn't. Then I say how struck I am by the image of honey. "I love the way Polacco writes this. So I'm not only noticing this as a *reader*, I'm noticing what Polacco does as a *writer*."

Then I turn to the next page. "Whoa! Something just happened here with the text—with the font. What's *font*?"

Blank looks.

"Think word processing on your computer."

"Oh, yeah, it's like the types of writing or the way the letters are," says Maddie.

"Yep. Look at this. Look how there's one type of font on the first page and then it changes on the second page. That's important. If the author or publisher does that, they want the reader to notice and there has to be a reason. Let's look at this first page, what's this font called? Does anyone know?"

A couple students call it "that squiggly writing" and then Maddie remembers it's italics. (If no one knows the term, I give it to them. I want my students to notice all text clues.)

"Okay, the next page goes to a regular text font. I wonder why. I'm going to read this page and then we'll figure it out together. But as a good reader, I know the author is giving me a signal to pay attention!"

I read the second page and ask again, *why?* Hays says the first page is in the past, then when it switches to regular font it's a story. He has it absolutely right!

This is an example of "weaving in the writing." My goal is to demonstrate what good writers do for the reader, and changing fonts is a technique to differentiate time, character, and so on. I have learned never to assume that my students already know a concept.

I'm doing a lot of the work, but students are adding their thinking to mine and creating depth and a sense of success for themselves. During the first week of school I'm demonstrating to my students that I'm curious about their thinking and I value their input. This in turn leads to success, trust, and most importantly, risk taking.

I continue to read the book, stopping at opportune times to put the book down (signaling that I am "cutting off the top of my head" and demonstrating my thinking). As the main character in the book, Trisha, continues to struggle with reading, I share that in my experience as a teacher this happens to many children—that we all learn and grow at different rates. For many of my students, this is incredible to hear from a teacher.

When we get to the page where Polacco writes, "Trisha began to feel 'different.' She began to feel dumb," I talk about how angry I am with the teacher in the book, that a teacher's job is to help every child learn, no matter where she is when she enters the classroom. This is a perfect segue into acknowledging and sharing the academic differences within our classroom, that we all have strengths and weaknesses. It's easier to focus on what we're good at, but sometimes we have to work extra hard on the areas that don't come as easily.

When Mr. Falker finally celebrates Trisha's talent in art and then diagnoses and remediates her reading disability, I again put the book down. "Finally! Imagine going all the way through fifth grade and not being able to read. Mr. Falker was finally honest with Trisha, and her teachers were able to find ways to help her learn to read. She was a smart little girl. There was just something getting in the way of her learning. Sometimes that happens. But just as Mr. Falker was honest with Trisha, I will be honest with you this year. Anytime you ask me how you are doing academically, I will tell you the truth—*and* we'll talk about how you can improve."

The last page of the book returns to italics. When I hold it up, the students pick up on this.

▶ THE NITTY-GRITTY

As the lesson ends, I ask the kids to explain their thinking regarding the initial question I posed. The more students can *connect* their thinking and new learning, the stronger the retention and the deeper the thinking.

"It went back to the past—or to the author talking," observes Hays.

This leads us to a discussion of *author's purpose*. Why did Polacco do that for the reader? When the kids discover that this story is semiautobiographical, the message becomes more powerful. They have enjoyed Polacco's writing and know that she is a famous author. They love her illustrations. Now to realize that she didn't learn how to read until she was in fifth grade lets even my reluctant and struggling readers know that there is time and hope—if they work hard and have a teacher who believes in them and will teach hard.

"I did a lot of thinking out loud for you guys so you could see what good readers do. I also asked you to do something as we read this book. I asked you to think about *why* I chose it and *how it connects*. That word *connects* is going to be important in this room, because good learners and thinkers connect new learning. So what do you think?"

Maddie raises her hand. "I don't know if Trisha was illiterate in the story, but she didn't know how to read. Mr. Falker taught her how to be literate. So this book is about learning how to be literate."

▶ THE NITTY-GRITTY

My primary intent in this minilesson is to present "living literate lives" as a theme to frame our initial work together, but we also work on community, trust, feedback, and creating an environment in which it is safe to take risks. And I get some insight into my students' background knowledge. My students also have come to realize that their thinking counts and that I'm not the kind of teacher looking for correct answers. Skills and ideas embedded in the lesson include:

- Developing vocabulary at the word level: root words and prefixes and how knowing one word helps us understand others
- Modeling what good readers do
- Setting a purpose for reading
- Thinking about the text *before* reading
- Picking up on font cues
- Discerning an author's basic reason for writing a text
- Benefiting from knowing about an author's life
- Benefiting from knowing the teacher's thinking as a reader
- Noticing beautiful language (strong writing) and beginning to imagine how to import it into one's own writing
- Learning about plot/problem
- Paying attention to character development and theme

Jonny observes that it isn't always easy to be literate, and Hays concurs. Sometimes reading and writing are really hard. My students are already on their way to becoming a safe community of learners. They are beginning to realize that I trust them, and in turn they are learning to trust me—and one another.

OWNING THE LESSON

Perhaps you're thinking, *My kids couldn't sit still that long*, or, *How do I possibly teach all those pieces included in this lesson?* Kids can sit this long when they're engaged, but it all boils down to knowing your kids and knowing yourself. What things seem easy to try? When you rehearse a lesson in your head, how do you name its purpose? Just as we need to be explicit with our students about the purpose for reading or writing (or learning any other content), we need to have a distinct purpose for each lesson we teach. Perhaps you want to start with only one facet of this lesson. That's fine. Keep it simple at first. Try one thing, then build on that. If you're afraid the students won't stay with you through this lesson, split it into two days! That's the joy of teaching and the power of this approach. There is no one way. Each time I present this lesson, it looks and sounds a bit different. Sometimes I do a lot of prompting and leading and even telling, other years the kids run with it. But the basic elements remain the same, and my main goal is to model what good readers do when they interact with text.

Do you have to do this minilesson with the same book I used? Absolutely not! Your job is to create a thirst for knowledge in your students, and you may discover another picture book that you like even more. Whatever story you use, the essential theme to convey to kids is that knowledge is sweet!

TO LEARN MORE

Harvey, Stephanie, and Anne Goudvis. 2007. *Strategies That Work*, 2d ed. Portland, ME: Stenhouse.

Wilhelm, Jeffrey D. 2001. *Improving Comprehension with Think-Aloud Strategies.* New York: Scholastic.

In Kids' Words

I've changed as a writer from the beginning of August to now by making my pieces longer, bigger, more detailed and interesting. Writing now is what I look forward to in school, it's my inspiration. I went from never writing to a writing hog! I've always had a passion for writing, I just didn't know my passion was this deep. Mrs. B. always tells us "Go deep, share your thinking." I've asked myself, "How can I make my writing better?" What helps me are the monthly pieces, because they give new vocabulary and give me ideas and topics to put into my pieces."

—Sydney, fourth grade

Rules and Rituals (and Routines)

PURPOSE

As odd as this might sound, I don't have a lot of rules in my classroom. Instead I have high expectations. During the first week of school, I invite students to help create the norms that we will live by. I use the word *norms* because I want my students to internalize that I am teaching them the way I would want to be taught; that I will use the terms and practices that they would hear in faculty meetings, colleges, and workplaces, for example. Whenever adults have meetings, we generally have agreed (either implicitly or explicitly) on rules, or norms. However, by the time we're adults, we drop the term *rules*. The connotation behind the word *norm* is that we're creating our expectations in a collaborative manner. Collaboration and expectations bring structure to the classroom, which fosters community and independence. As Katie Wood Ray (2001) observes, "A teacher telling everyone what to do every moment of the day is actually a very low-structured classroom—the only structure in place is the teacher giving directions!" (14). That is definitely not the case in my students' and my room.

However, I do run a tight ship; there are strict parameters for how we behave in and use our classroom. (This structure is essential if the workshop is going to run smoothly. Otherwise it's chaotic and little gets done—and at that point teachers often abandon the workshop approach.) Students who cannot follow expectations are corrected immediately—but in a gentle way. One parent of one of my students once described me as having an iron fist in a kid glove. I like that analogy. My kids know I'm strict, but they also know I'm fair (and I never yell).

HERE'S HOW IT GOES

"Usually on the first day of school your teachers spend a lot of time going over rules, right? Today, we're not going to spend a lot of time on them, because I don't have a lot of rules. I have *expectations* for you, for both your learning and your behavior, because we are going to be working way too hard this year for you to mess around. Plus, learning is going to be too much fun for you even to *want* to mess around! Bottom line, I *trust* you to behave. And my consequences may look different from those you've experienced in previous years. What would happen if you got in trouble in some of your other classes?"

"You'd have to put your name and a check on the board," explains Reed.

"Did that work?"

"Not so much," he concedes.

"If we're going to be in a safe learning environment, we all have to trust one another, and I'm going to trust that you'll make good decisions. You're probably saying to yourself, what happens if I make poor decisions? Here's my answer: you'll probably be asked to leave the room and come back when you're ready to participate appropriately. I've found that kids don't like leaving because they feel they're missing too much. Or I might ask you to come in at recess. The consequences will reflect the behavior. How's that sound?"

"I like that."

"But here are my nonnegotiables. I have four letters that we will live by this year. The first is the big *K*. What could *K* stand for?"

"*Kids*?" asks Jack.

"Good thinking, and yes, it's all about you kids, but I'm thinking of another *K* word."

"*Knowledge*. Gotta be *knowledge*, because you want us to learn this year," offers Naomi.

"Another great one. Yep, knowledge is important, but not the *K* I'm looking for. Here's a hint—it's the way we treat each other."

Isaiah's hand shoots into the air. "*Kindness*!"

"On the nose! We live by *kindness* in this room. You may not be best friends or even good friends with a classmate, but you treat everyone in this room with kindness. That's a huge part of us feeling safe. Then I have the three *R*s. Who wants to try those?"

"Well, it can't be *rules* since you already said that you don't have rules—could *responsibility* be one?" Emma says.

"Absolutely." I write *responsibility* on the board. "What does it mean to be responsible?"

The students offer lots of examples—for their behavior, for their work, and so on. I jot these down.

"How about another *R*?"

"Could it be *respect*?" asks Reed.

"Correct again. What do you think *respect* means in our classroom?"

Again, students offer suggestions, which I write down, adding points of my own: *respecting yourself*; *respecting others*; *respecting property*.

"Our last *R* is *rights*. We all have rights in this classroom. What might we have the right to do?"

"To learn."

With this *R*, I often have to do some nudging or leading: *We have the right to be heard, to be listened to, and to share. We have a right to do class work without being interrupted or distracted by those around us. We have the right to feel safe.*

"And to make those rights work, there are a few expectations." I add these components to the list as I share them with the students.

- If someone else is talking, you don't interrupt.
- You raise your hand to speak.
- If someone else is talking, you don't have your hand in the air. If your hand is in the air, your brain is thinking about what you want to say or ask and you completely tune out what is being said. I'll remind you to lower your hands by signaling you with a downward motion of my hands.
- I never call on the "ooh ooh" person—the one who besides having her hand in the air is also attempting to get my attention by making noise.
- We use the classroom appropriately.

This last expectation leads directly into minilesson 4, which follows.

OWNING THE LESSON

I have a sign on my desk that states, "Keep It Simple." Sometimes less *is* more, and that is applicable when it comes to rules. The above lesson reflects *my* expectations and what I need to have in place for my classroom to run smoothly. Here are some

▶ QUESTIONS TO THINK ABOUT

- What do I need to set in place?
- What are my expectations for behavior in my classroom?
- What consequences can I use to motivate students to toe the line rather than shame them into it?
- How do I make my expectations and consequences explicit?

We have an anchor chart in our room listing the three *R*s that the students sign. I've seen so many twists on this. Some teachers have students help write their "charter" and sign it to signify buy-in. In previous years, I've allowed groups to write additional norms to live by for our classroom, but this isn't as necessary anymore. Whatever you decide, the students have to understand your expectations and be able to practice them.

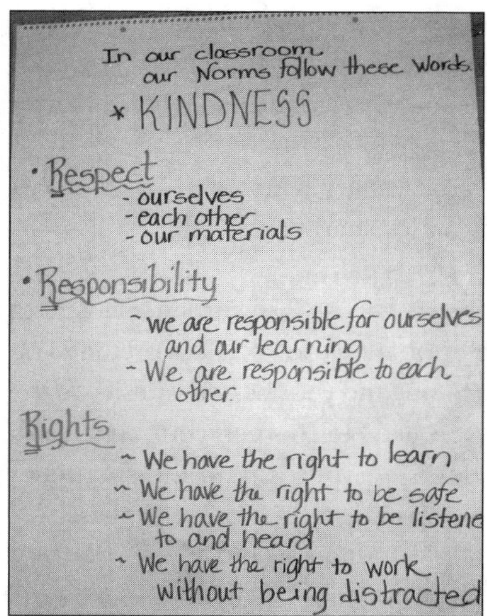

Touring the Room/Managing Movement

PURPOSE

Managing the environment and managing movement figure prominently in my planning and thinking about how I will arrange the physical layout of the room. Before the students walk through the door on that first day, I try to think through the *logistics* of setting up my classroom efficiently. To create independence, materials must be easily accessible, and I need to train students how to use supplies. I need to have a large-group area (meeting area), a small-group area (for direct small-group instruction), table groups, and lots of room to move around freely. Almost every professional book on reading or writing instruction discusses classroom environment. It really is that important.

To Learn More

To read more about defining your own beliefs *and* organizing your room, see Debbie Miller's *Teaching with Intention* (Portland, ME: Stenhouse, 2008).

HERE'S HOW IT GOES

Picking up where we left off in our discussion on classroom norms, I say, "So if we're going to use our classroom correctly, you need to see what's available, where it is, and how I expect you to use it. I want you to stay put while I give a tour of the room."

I stand up and, one section of the room at a time, show the class where supplies and materials (see the list in Figure 2.3) are kept. As I introduce each category, I tell students why we have the quantities we do and when and how they may be used.

Here's what I might say about the pencil sharpeners.

"Why do you think I have so many pencil sharpeners?"

"So we won't have to wait in line?" says Isaiah.

"That's part of it. Another part is so that you use the sharpener closest to your desk. Let me give you an example of what I won't see. Let's pretend you sit here [I'm standing on one side of the room] and your best friend sits on the other side of the room. So you decide you need to sharpen your pencil and you saunter right by several friends' desks on your way to the sharpener across the room. Of course you have to stop and say hi." As I'm explaining, I wander across the room, stopping at desks, pretending to say hi. "Are you using time well if you do that? Are you respecting others' rights?"

By this time the class is laughing with me and my point is made. The more I demonstrate that I understand behavior, the more they will buy into the way our classroom will operate. Humor does wonders. As does front-loading.

"So basically, use the one closest to you. And please sharpen your pencils at the beginning of the day. Don't wait until group time or independent reading. Be respectful."

The tour of the rest of the room follows, and as I finish I ask, "Am I missing anything? Can you think of anything you might need in here?"

If there are suggestions, I jot them down on a piece of chart paper hanging on the wall by the door; the sheet is headed *We need these supplies.* "If it

Figure 2.3 Supplies and Materials

- Passes and checkout form
- Pencil sharpeners (preferably four; I have them on all sides of the room)
- Staplers
- Tape dispensers
- Paper clips
- Sticky notes (in various sizes)
- Totes (for turning in homework, notes from home, etc.)
- Paper (lined, blank, colored, newsprint, etc.)
- Pencils, pens, highlighters
- Rubber bands
- Dictionaries, thesauruses, reference materials
- Classroom library

looks like we're running out of something, or if you discover that our class needs something that I don't have, would you jot it down for me here? That would really help me out."

A quick tour of the room won't solidify students' awareness of where everything is. To reinforce this lesson I hold a classroom scavenger hunt during the first week of school. Amazingly, students often suggest that their parents be sent on this same scavenger hunt on Back to School Night.

> ▶ **THE NITTY-GRITTY**
>
> Invite students in on the decision making for the classroom. Whether it's assigning "supplies" as a job or just posting lists, let the kids do the work! And always be explicit! The years I haven't been explicit or haven't spent time explaining correct use of supplies have been the years the kids have misused them and I've had to back up and start over.

OWNING THE LESSON

Regie Routman offers this advice in *Reading Essentials* (2003): "Look at your classroom through the eyes of your students. Would you feel comfortable and welcome spending six or eight hours a day in this room?" (17).

▶ QUESTIONS TO THINK ABOUT

- What supplies are essential to have available to my students? (Office Max, Staples, teacher websites, and organizing websites are full of ideas for classroom materials and storage systems.)
- In the past, what supplies have students interrupted me to ask for? How can I make everything accessible to the kids?
- What do I need to set up a reading–writing workshop?

Independent Silent Reading Expectations

PURPOSE

Richard Allington writes, "The amount of reading that students do in and out of school [is] positively related to their reading achievement, yet most students report relatively little reading in or out of school" (2001, 27). I believe students need class time in which to read. I also know that I have to hold the students accountable for this time—that while they are reading independently, I need to provide direct instruction in individual conferences, group work, or book clubs. For me to trust the students to make wise choices and use their time well—and thus free me up to instruct versus monitor behavior—I have to set ground rules. This is one of the few minilessons in which I do the "telling" and use the word *rules*. Students need to hear explicit explanations. Then we practice.

I introduce independent reading (basically, time during which students read books of their own choosing independently) during the first week of school. The letter I send before school starts asks students to bring a favorite book and a book they are currently reading, so each child has self-selected reading material available. I help students who have forgotten books to select one after the others have settled in to read.

HERE'S HOW IT GOES

I always start off by asking students what the time they spent reading silently was like in previous years. (I do this as both an assessment and to set the norms or expectations for our classroom.) After the students have responded, I explain that we will be spending a lot of time this year reading, but that we'll still be working. I explain how Nancie Atwell (2007) describes being totally engrossed in a book as *being in the zone*, and that although it's great when that happens, there are other times when I'll expect them to use the comprehension strategies we're focusing on.

Here are my expectations for independent/silent reading (as I go over them, I write them down on chart paper for everyone to see and refer back to—see the example in Figure 2.4).

1. As you settle in, you need to have everything with you that you'll need. That means your book right now. (As we progress through the year, this expands to include back-up books—especially if they are close to finishing the current one—as well as their book lover's book, pencils, sticky notes, etc.)
2. If you need to use the restroom, get a drink, and so on, do it as we settle in. Once we start, *you may not move*. The reason is that movement can disturb others. I will give you about three minutes to get materials and make decisions; then you need to stay put.
3. You may read anywhere in the classroom. This is where trust comes in, because I expect you to make really great choices. I know you have buddies in the classroom, but you might think twice about sitting with them if you could be distracted. Because you don't want me to make you move....
4. There is no talking. Even if you're at an amazing part in your book or it's hilarious or for any other reason, *no talking*. We will be practicing

respect for each other. The only people talking will be me and whomever I'm working or conferring with. And, of course, since you can't get up, you won't interrupt. I will give you plenty of other opportunities to talk or share your reading this year.

5. We are going to start off slowly at first and practice, practice, practice. As we get better at this, we will read for longer periods of time. That's building stamina.

6. I'll be talking with you about your reading and thinking and watching to see how you're using our lessons in your own reading.

▶ THE NITTY-GRITTY

Stamina is a word I want them to hear but will explain to them later. Stamina is a key element of working independently for extended periods of time—in both reading and writing. I also want my students to know up front what their job is during independent reading and that I will be talking with them about their reading and thinking while they read. I'm right next to them teaching—either individually or in a group—the entire time they're reading.

After going over these rules, I ask the students to take a minute and recall the title of the book they're reading. Yes, I have the students sit quietly for a *full minute.* After that minute, I quickly read each child's name and ask the title of the book, jotting it down on a "status of the class" record-keeping sheet. (I discuss this form in depth in Chapter 6; a copy is included on the CD.)

"When I call your name, just quickly tell me the title, then you may get up without talking, get your book, and find a spot in the room to read. I'll be writing down the title and the class will be watching to see how quietly everyone flows into independent reading."

Because I call the students one at a time, the transition is accomplished smoothly. If a student heads off noisily, I gently ask her to return to our meeting area and try again. Anyone who didn't bring a book may choose one from a tub I have in the meeting area (generally picture books or books I've been using as mentor texts in other lessons). Then I quickly "flow" through the

1. Take everything you need with you before you settle in to read (or work).
2. Once we start reading, you may not move. That means get settled (supplies, drinks, etc.) ahead of time.
3. You may read anywhere in the room.
4. Make really great choices about where you work.
5. No talking!
6. Read, read, read!

Figure 2.4 Independent Reading Expectations

room to make sure everyone is settled. If I notice a potential problem with certain students sitting together, I first ask them if they're making a good choice and then offer them the chance to make a better choice. I want the students to take control of their environment and learning, but it is essential that I firmly set the parameters and structure and immediately nip unacceptable behavior in the bud.

About two minutes before I'm going to call a halt, I quietly announce there are two more minutes to read and they should find a good stopping place. Then I gather the class together and we reflect on how independent reading went. We take a minute at the end of a lesson to articulate what went great and what we might want to work on. These "work on" items turn into future minilessons.

REINFORCING THE MINILESSON ONE-ON-ONE

When everyone is settled, I sit down beside one student and confer with him (conferences are covered in depth in Chapter 7). Usually on the first day of independent reading, I get through no more than one or two conferences, because I stop before the students get "wiggly"; if I interrupt them while they're still engrossed, they'll return to their reading with relish the next day.

Here's an example of one of my conferences. We've been in school nearly a week, and I'm finally sitting on the floor close to Felix. He is new to the school, so I don't have a lot of information about him. I've been observing him. Felix is quiet and watchful, soaking in what's happening around him. I'm also beginning to see that school might be tough for him. He barely participates, and his writing thus far has been limited. He hadn't brought a favorite book by the third day of school, so I helped him find one from our classroom library. He ended up with a Diary of a Wimpy Kid book.

"How's it going?" I begin.

"Okay," he replies.

"So, tell me a little more about how you decided to choose this book as your favorite. Then I'd love for you to pick a part in here and read to me so I can just kind of listen."

Felix tenses and a look of terror passes over his face. I have my arm around him and I can feel his body stiffen.

"Is this kind of scary, Felix? Maybe you haven't had a teacher do this with you before? Sit and talk to you about your reading?"

He nods.

"Remember, no secrets. As your reading teacher, I need to see how you are as a reader. That way I can help you find the right books. And remember how we did the lesson on how do teachers know how you're reading? That's what I'm doing here. Plus I'm really curious about what you think about this book."

"I didn't read it," Felix mumbles. He looks away but doesn't pull away.

"Okay, that's being honest. Can you tell me how you chose it to share?"

Felix looks at me, then looks away again. "A lot of the other guys brought it, and I listened to what they said, and I thought I could do that, too."

"Okay, that's actually pretty smart. You figured out how to participate and do what I had asked. The only thing is, you didn't read the book. Is it a book you'd like to read?"

"Yes, but I don't like reading. It's really hard for me. I don't get it," Felix admits.

"You know, Felix, you are being both brave and honest—and this helps me a lot. My job this year is to teach you, and even if it's really hard, we're both going to work at it together. You'll be doing some testing later this week, so that will help me get some information, but what I need right now is for you to tell me what you have read—what books did you read last year?"

"I don't know, I don't remember."

I can tell he is embarrassed. The last thing I want to do is embarrass him more. However, we need to find the right books for him so that he can be reading and learning—right away.

"You know what, Felix? I do a lot of research about how readers get better. And the main thing is that they read a lot of books at their appropriate level. The more they read, the better they get. So let's go get some books that I think might work and find an appropriate book for you. Remember honesty? These are going to be short books, but we're going to work really hard so that you'll be reading *Diary of a Wimpy Kid* soon. Is that a deal?"

Felix nods and we head to the section of the classroom library with easier books. I know this isn't going to be a five-minute conference, but I need to get the right book in Felix's hands. I pull a couple books at the first- and second-grade levels and have him look them over. When he chooses one at a second-grade level, we sit back down and talk about the minilesson on how we choose appropriate books. I have him look at the anchor chart the class co-constructed; he remembers the five-finger test, and I ask him to do that. He finishes a page and only has two fingers down for words he doesn't know.

We discuss those words, then I ask him to tell me about what he's read, and he can retell it.

"What do you think? Want to read this one?"

Felix seems a bit more relaxed and nods.

"Here's the deal, though—I'm going to be checking in with you tomorrow to see if it's still a great fit. Anything else you need before I go?"

I leave Felix with his book. And I will check in with Felix—a lot—during the year.

OWNING THE LESSON

The lesson focuses on these concepts:

- Front-loading the structure and procedures of independent reading at the beginning of the year (This leads to more freedom and independence as the year progresses.)
- Establishing expectations
- Envisioning silent reading
- Starting with small increments—success right from the start
- Practicing following procedures and meeting expectations
- Finding teachable moments—immediately catching when something isn't working and teaching the correct way

How do you envision silent reading in your classroom? I allow students to choose where and what to read, but I expect them to be quiet and stay put. That's another reason for starting in small increments. Sitting in one place (even if it's on a pillow or the couch) can be tough if you're not used to it. Here are some questions to ponder as you design your own lesson for sharing your expectations regarding independent reading.

▶ QUESTIONS TO THINK ABOUT

- What rules do I want to set for my kids?
- What rules can we negotiate together?
- What do I worry about when it comes to students reading on their own?
- What do I want to accomplish in the first weeks of school? In a month? How do I see my students in April?

Your Own First Weeks of School

What do you want to accomplish during the first weeks of school? How can your lessons launch you and your students into deeper learning and thinking in literacy? Once students have discovered the power of literacy, know how their room functions, and understand how independent reading is structured, it's time to create an environment in which rich, deep conversations are valued—where they are the norm, where students know how to access books and make wise choices over their own learning, where the workshop runs seamlessly. The lessons in the next chapter will help you make that happen.

CHAPTER 3

Cultivating Students' Identities as Readers and Writers

Your kids have the rules of engagement down—the *who, what, where* of your classroom. Now it's time to teach them explicitly how they are going to live and grow as readers and writers. The lessons in this chapter help students develop a mind-set for deeper thinking. They include:

- How Teachers Come to Know Their Students as Readers
- How Teachers Assess Their Students as Writers
- Tracks in the Snow: How Readers and Writers Hold Their Thinking
- Holding Class Thinking with Anchor Charts
- Saying Good-Bye to Fake Reading
- Choosing Appropriate Books
- Why We Drop Books and When That's Okay

- Great Listening
- Phenomenal Talk
- What Wise Readers/Engaging Writers Do
- Understanding What We Read—or Not
- Noticing Beautiful Language
- Debuting the Book Lover's Book: A Segue

How Teachers Come to Know Their Students as Readers

PURPOSE

One of my bedrock beliefs is that students deserve honest, constructive feedback all the time. They need it to grow. A big part of how I carry off this continuous feedback is by being transparent about how I evaluate my students day by day and about the standards to which they are being held, either informally or via grades and report cards.

We need to repair the disconnect between students and the assessments that define them academically. State standards, for example, often use terms like *nonproficient*, *proficient*, and *advanced*. All fine and good, but students aren't aware of these terms until they see them in print! How can they *work toward* these standards when they're in the dark about them? What about graded report cards? Same deal. Too often students are unaware of how teachers view them academically until report cards come out. Even then kids are not sure why they received certain marks.

When we are explicit with students from the outset, we can move students from saying, "The teacher *gave* me an A," to the far better response to learning and grading, "I *earned* an A because. . . ." When students know the qualities of a good performance, they can repeat it.

HERE'S HOW IT GOES

"Remember how I told you the first day of school that there are no secrets in this room? That you are able to ask me any question—except my weight—and I'll give you an honest answer? Well, today I have a question for you. How do teachers evaluate or assess how you're doing as a reader? How do we know how you're doing?"

My students seem taken aback. They've always assumed teachers just "knew" how they were doing.

"Tests?" Trinity offers.

"Yes, testing gives me a lot of information. And I can look at the numbers and the data and get a good glimpse of you as a reader. But is that all? Is that fair? Are you just a number? Sometimes we don't always do great on tests. How else?"

"You watch us?" asks Jack.

"What do you mean?" I really want to know.

"Like, you see if we're reading."

"So, teachers have ESP and we know you're reading and understanding?"

This elicits laughs, but I continue. "You know you're on to something there. I do watch how you read and how you use your time. But reading is quiet, isn't it—so I can't really just watch you and know what's going on in your head."

I tell them that I use many assessments to gauge where my students are and guide my instruction. Test data are abundant; I can observe students reading; but I can also use writing as an assessment tool. I want as much authentic assessment driving my instruction as possible.

"How many of you are better readers than writers?" Most students agree with this statement. "So if I only used writing to assess your reading, that wouldn't be fair either, would it? However, you need to be able to explain your thinking through writing, so that's something we'll practice a lot this year. You'll especially be doing a lot of writing to me about your reading through your lit log letters in your book lover's book [see Chapters 4 and 5].

"The other way I can assess your progress is by listening to you. I will be doing a lot of conferring with you and asking you questions. Every time I have a conference with you, I will tell you what you're doing well as a reader. I will also teach you one thing during that conference. That's my job as your reading teacher. Every time I meet with you, I need to leave you with one new piece of learning.

"I can also eavesdrop in on your conversations. I'll be listening and taking notes on what you're saying about your reading as you're talking with your classmates.

"And there's one other way I can follow your progress—and that's through the way you mark or hold your thinking. How you leave the tracks of your thinking."

▶ LESSON LINK

The minilesson Tracks in the Snow: How Readers and Writers Hold Their Thinking begins on page 45.

OWNING THE LESSON

Standards and measurement differ between districts and states. Teachers around the country operate under different expectations and mandates. While assessment should drive instruction, it needs to be authentic, meaningful assessment. Here are some things to consider as you adapt this lesson.

▶ QUESTIONS TO THINK ABOUT

- How do I report student progress? In relation to standards? By assigning grades?
- Do I use informal assessments?
- What are the state's requirements? The district's? The school's? My own?
- For each of the above, how might I be more transparent with my students about the criteria I'm using? How might I guide my lessons and my teaching with this concept of transparency in mind?

While this lesson and the next are foundational and are presented to the whole class, they can be beautifully retaught in one-to-one conferences. As I confer with students, I ask them how they view themselves as both readers and writers and then discuss progress with them. I also revisit these lessons at the end of each trimester, when I have students reflect on their literacy progress in their book lover's book.

How Teachers Assess Their Students as Writers

PURPOSE

Just as students need to know how they are being evaluated as readers, they need to know how they're being evaluated as writers. Percentages and letter grades do not provide meaningful feedback. However, rubrics and/or lists of criteria do.

HERE'S HOW IT GOES

Before presenting this minilesson, I ask students to write a paragraph in their notebooks about what makes good writing. *How does a teacher let you know how you're doing in writing? How are you assessed or evaluated in writing?* By this time, the class understands that I'm genuinely curious and that their responses will guide my instruction.

Often I get responses such as, "Handwriting," "Spelling," "You can spell really good," "You use good punctuation." The focus seems to be on editing and appearance. Not all teachers use rubrics, so some students might comment that they get grades or comments, mostly having to do with spelling and conventions. After I read all the responses, I bring the class together for a minilesson.

"I read your thoughts about what makes good writing yesterday after school. Lots of you said handwriting and spelling. But I want you to think about something. When you brought in your favorite books on the first day, did any of you say it was the appearance and the spelling that made it your favorite?"

"No!" the kids respond, almost as one.

"So, I'm really curious why you think that makes good writing."

"Because that's what we worked on last year."

"Okay, I get that. And those things are important. But I want you to think about the books you love and why you love them. What always brings you back to them?"

The kids think for a minute. Then Lucie raises her hand. "Well, the characters pull me in. I remember characters."

"Or the action," adds Scott.

"That would be the plot. So you're saying that writers have to have something to write about—and there has to be some sort of organization. And the characters need to be memorable. I'm betting the author provided a lot of details about them." I'm trying to lead them into the traits of writing that will be included in our rubrics.

"I like the books that make me laugh, like *Diary of a Wimpy Kid*," adds Reed.

"Okay, you guys are starting to get it. What you're beginning to talk about are the traits of writing—organization, ideas and content, voice, word choice, sentence fluency, and conventions. If you look around the room you'll see posters listing these traits. I know they might be new to you this year, but they're how I'm going to assess you. Have you ever heard of a rubric?

▶ THE NITTY-GRITTY

I decide whether I want to spend a lot of time explaining and showing what a rubric is or tell them we'll look at rubrics in more depth later. Generally, at the beginning of the year I save the rubric for another day and another lesson. It all depends on the class and their background knowledge.

"We're going to use rubrics this year and I'm going to explain them to you a little later. But I want you to write the way real writers write. And I want you writing for the same reasons that adults and writers write. Do you remember how we said that I could listen to you to assess how you're doing as a reader? Do you think I'll be doing the same thing with your writing?"

"Do you mean that you'll be sitting with us talking about our writing, too?" asks Kylie.

"What do you think? Do you think that would help?" I throw back at her.

After a little thinking, Kylie nods and says, "I think so."

They're beginning to get it!

OWNING THE LESSON

Assessing writing and using rubrics can't be discussed and explained in one lesson, or two, or three. Rubrics take time. Conveying the traits of writing takes time. In fact, I spend at least half the year introducing the traits (see the yearlong chart in Chapter 1). The traits are an assessment tool, and just as I want my students to internalize their progress as readers, I want them to internalize their progress as writers. Well-written rubrics are explicit and students know exactly how they will be evaluated if rubrics are used consistently and properly.

▶ QUESTIONS TO THINK ABOUT

- How do I assess student writing?
- How do I communicate to the kids how they're doing?

Tracks in the Snow: How Readers and Writers Hold Their Thinking

PURPOSE

Writing and talking are two important ways I assess my students, but this lesson introduces the idea that whether I'm reflecting on their reading progress or their writing progress, I'm looking at their thinking. I let them know that I'll give them as many opportunities to demonstrate their thinking as possible, and I'll give them short, manageable tools to hold their thinking. One way I teach students to hold their thinking is by leaving "tracks in the snow," a

TO LEARN MORE

Spandel, Vickie, and Ruth Culham. 2010. *Traits of Writing*. Portsmouth, NH: Heinemann.

great metaphor for ink on paper used by Stephanie Harvey and Anne Goudvis in *Strategies That Work* (2000). These tracks may be left by jotting notes on stickies, on bookmarks, or in a book lover's book (see Chapters 4 and 5). Teachers in the south may want to use the analogy "tracks in the sand," and as one teacher in a New Orleans workshop recently observed, it could be "tracks in the mud"! Make the metaphor work for you and your students.

The picture book *Tracks in the Snow*, by Wong Herbert Yee (2003), in which a little girl follows tracks she finds in the snow, trying to figure out who made them, illustrates how someone's tracks can tell a story. Before I read the book (the cover is reproduced in Figure 3.1), I introduce the concept.

HERE'S HOW IT GOES

"When it snows at night, I can go out the next morning and sometimes there is a story there. It's not a written story, but I can follow the tracks in the snow to figure out who's been in the yard. For example, I can see if rabbits have come through or if any cats have wandered in. And in my backyard I can see exactly where the dogs have walked. If they only leave footprints on the deck,

Figure 3.1 Cover of *Tracks in the Snow*

I can be pretty sure the snow is deep down on the lawn. Have you guys ever noticed this?" Of course there are numerous connections, because in Denver we get a lot of snow. My students can relate!

"Now I'm going to read you a story called *Tracks in the Snow* to show you how leaving tracks leaves a message."

After I read the book and we've discussed it, I tell the kids that this year I want them to leave tracks in the snow for me, and that this means leaving evidence of their thinking. I hold up a piece of paper with a paragraph of text on it and explain that the white space around the words is the "snow." "Your tracks are the comments you write in that white space. The writing doesn't have to be long, but it does need to help me understand your thinking. Merely highlighting isn't enough; I'm always going to push you to explain why you highlighted or why it's important, so if I walk by your desk and comment, 'Tracks in the snow,' you'll know I want you to record your thinking. That way if I can't confer with you, I can still collect the paper and get a glimpse into your thoughts about what you read that day.

"Sometimes I'll ask you to leave me tracks in the snow on sticky notes or in your book lover's book or in some other way, but it's always because I want to see and understand your thinking. That way you're teaching me, and I know how to instruct you even better."

Figures 3.2 and 3.3 are examples of tracks students have left me of their thinking.

OWNING THE LESSON

No matter at what grade level, kindergarten through high school, this metaphor truly makes a difference in the way students interact with text. The more examples you can bring into the classroom to make the analogy understandable, the better. In Colorado, our fourth-grade social studies curriculum includes a unit on Colorado plants and animals, which gives me an opportunity to integrate books focusing on animal tracks. I also connect my bulletin boards with footprints. After we do this minilesson, students often say, "Oh! That's why there are footprints on the boards!"

Figure 3.4 is an example of an anchor chart on listening and talking.

▶ QUESTIONS TO THINK ABOUT

- Will my students understand the *tracks in the snow* metaphor or would a different metaphor make more sense?
- How do I want my students to record their thinking?

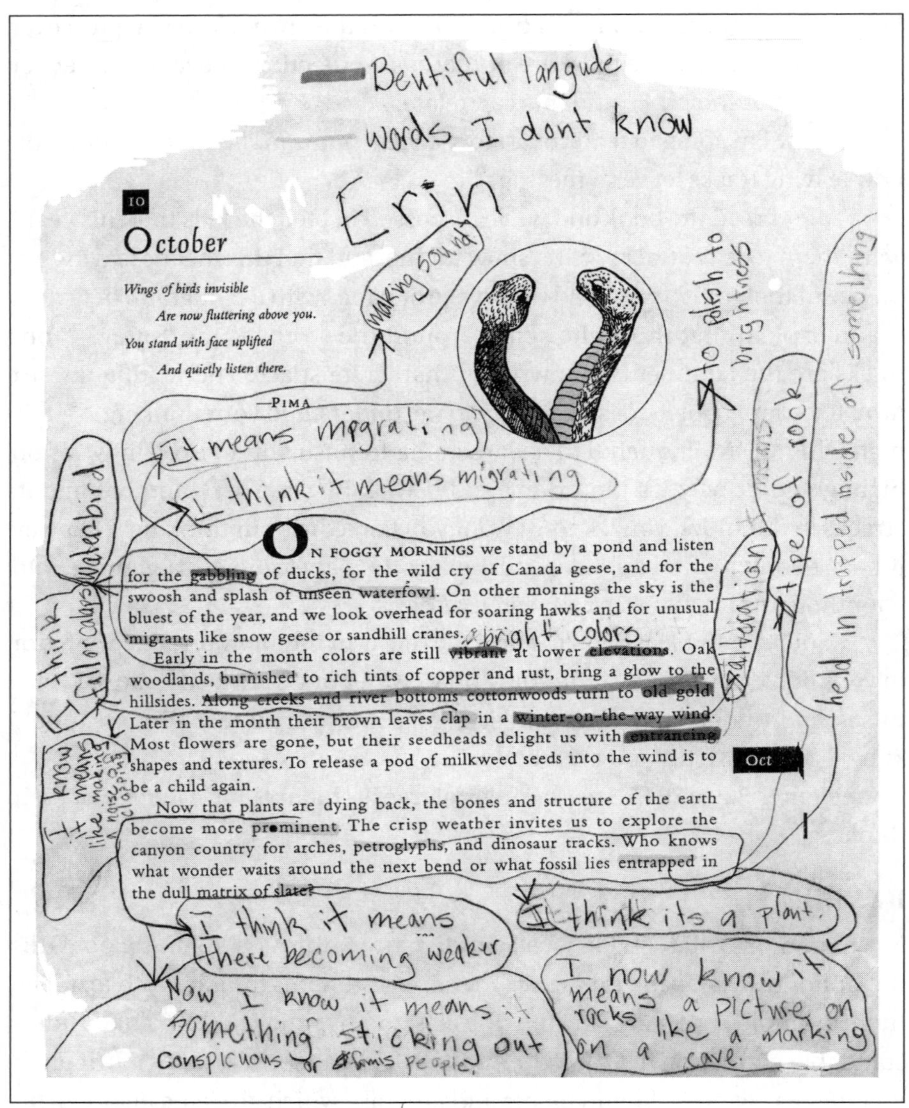

10

October

Wings of birds invisible
Are now fluttering above you.
You stand with face uplifted
And quietly listen there.

—PIMA

ON FOGGY MORNINGS we stand by a pond and listen for the gabbling of ducks, for the wild cry of Canada geese, and for the swoosh and splash of unseen waterfowl. On other mornings the sky is the bluest of the year, and we look overhead for soaring hawks and for unusual migrants like snow geese or sandhill cranes.

Early in the month colors are still vibrant at lower elevations. Oak woodlands, burnished to rich tints of copper and rust, bring a glow to the hillsides. Along creeks and river bottoms cottonwoods turn to old gold. Later in the month their brown leaves clap in a winter-on-the-way wind. Most flowers are gone, but their seedheads delight us with entrancing shapes and textures. To release a pod of milkweed seeds into the wind is to be a child again.

Now that plants are dying back, the bones and structure of the earth become more prominent. The crisp weather invites us to explore the canyon country for arches, petroglyphs, and dinosaur tracks. Who knows what wonder waits around the next bend or what fossil lies entrapped in the dull matrix of slate?

Oct

Figure 3.2 Student Work with Tracks in the Snow

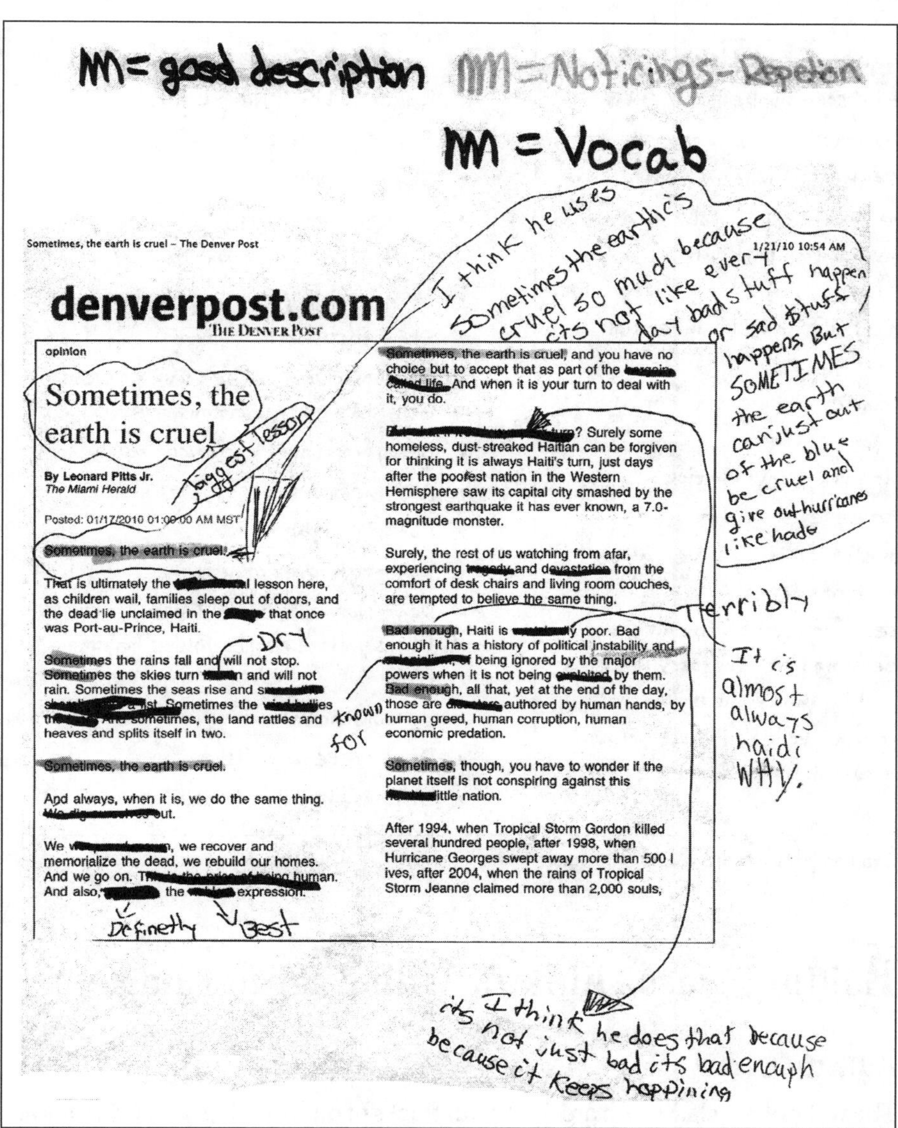

Sometimes, the earth is cruel – The Denver Post

1/21/10 10:54 AM

denverpost.com
THE DENVER POST

opinion

Sometimes, the earth is cruel

By Leonard Pitts Jr.
The Miami Herald

Posted: 01/17/2010 01:00:00 AM MST

Sometimes, the earth is cruel.

That is ultimately the [illegible] lesson here, as children wail, families sleep out of doors, and the dead lie unclaimed in the [illegible] that once was Port-au-Prince, Haiti.

Sometimes the rains fall and will not stop. Sometimes the skies turn [illegible] and will not rain. Sometimes the seas rise and [illegible] Sometimes the [illegible] And sometimes, the land rattles and heaves and splits itself in two.

Sometimes, the earth is cruel.

And always, when it is, we do the same thing. [illegible] out.

We [illegible], we recover and memorialize the dead, we rebuild our homes. And we go on. [illegible] human. And also, [illegible] the [illegible] expression.

Sometimes, the earth is cruel, and you have no choice but to accept that as part of the [illegible] life. And when it is your turn to deal with it, you do.

[illegible] turn? Surely some homeless, dust-streaked Haitian can be forgiven for thinking it is always Haiti's turn, just days after the poorest nation in the Western Hemisphere saw its capital city smashed by the strongest earthquake it has ever known, a 7.0-magnitude monster.

Surely, the rest of us watching from afar, experiencing tragedy and devastation from the comfort of desk chairs and living room couches, are tempted to believe the same thing.

Bad enough, Haiti is [illegible]y poor. Bad enough it has a history of political instability and [illegible], of being ignored by the major powers when it is not being exploited by them. Bad enough, all that, yet at the end of the day, those are [illegible] authored by human hands, by human greed, human corruption, human economic predation.

Sometimes, though, you have to wonder if the planet itself is not conspiring against this [illegible] little nation.

After 1994, when Tropical Storm Gordon killed several hundred people, after 1998, when Hurricane Georges swept away more than 500 l ives, after 2004, when the rains of Tropical Storm Jeanne claimed more than 2,000 souls,

Figure 3.3 Student Work Showing Tracks in the Snow

What Makes Great Listening?

- Look at person—make EYE CONTACT
- Ask questions
- Pay attention—don't zone out
- Don't be shy—keep up your side of the conversation without monopolizing
- Let others finish—don't interrupt them
- Don't wander off, mentally or physically
- Stay with the conversation
- Sit at same level
- You can change the conversation, but not at random
- Apologize, if you're not listening, and say something like, "I'm sorry I missed that. Could you repeat it?"
- Don't pretend to listen while you are thinking about something else

Great Conversations

- Refer to LISTENING CHART
- Share your ideas
- Stay on topic
- Let everyone talk
- Don't be a "conversation hog"
- Be honest
- Stay focused
- Stay involved in the main conversation; side conversations are NOT OK
- Be appropriate; know your audience
- Ask questions
- Don't interrupt
- Don't talk over others
- Don't play with stuff/distractions; focus on the people you're talking with
- Be considerate
- Don't pretend to listen
- Give insightful responses

Figure 3.4 Anchor Chart on Listening and Talking with Others

Holding Class Thinking with Anchor Charts

PURPOSE

The walls of my classroom are thick with tracks of our thinking. By April, they are covered with charts on which I've captured my students' words and thoughts. These charts, labeled and dated, are a visual record of our group work. New students can see where we've already been. The charts are more meaningful to my students than any commercial bulletin board displays I've ever purchased.

A caution, though: They don't work as well when transplanted from one year to the next. They need to be co-constructed with the class at hand: you have to capture *these* students' words and thinking. Even though my beginning lessons are the same every year, the class thinking I capture each year is not. This in and of itself is an assessment tool to determine where my students are and where I need to take them.

HERE'S HOW IT GOES

"You know how I've been recording your thinking on chart paper since the start of school? And sometimes I even write your name by your exact words so that we can all remember them? Well those charts are called *anchor charts,* and as you can see, I've already started to hang them up in the room. Let's talk for a minute about *why* they're important. What does an anchor do?"

Erin offers, "It holds down a boat?"

"That's right. It holds a boat in one place so that it can't float away. Why do you think we call these anchor charts?"

"Because they hold our thinking?" Geoffrey asks rather dubiously.

"Again, right! They hold our class thinking so that we can go back to it throughout the year. That way we can all see where we've been and we can notice how our thinking changes and grows and how we connect new learning to the old. Plus if anyone comes to visit our room—kids or adults—we can easily catch them up on what we've done. And there might also be times we forget something that we've worked on, and we can just point to the anchor chart to refresh our memory."

Figure 3.5 is an example of an anchor chart.

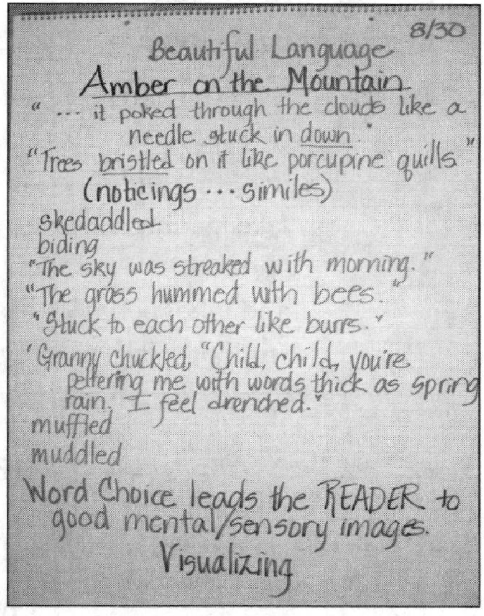

Figure 3.5 Anchor Chart: Beautiful Language

OWNING THE LESSON

This

Anchor Charts

- They are co-constructed with students, capturing *their* thinking; they are more meaningful references.
- Students' words count as much or more than the teacher's.
- They are created for the specific classroom of learners.
- They are a record of classroom learning.

Versus That

Typical Commercial Posters

- Reading Is Life!
- Writers at Work!
- We Are Superstars!
- Classroom Rules
- Skills Good Readers Use
- Proofreading Skills

And the list goes on . . .

▶ QUESTIONS TO THINK ABOUT

- How can I record my class' thinking?
- What is important for me to have on my classroom walls?
- What are some easy daily rituals I can use to keep these references fresh?
- Could I revisit yesterday's thinking at the beginning of today's lesson?
- Is there a Friday reflection practice that will help my students anchor the week's learning?

Saying Good-Bye to Fake Reading

PURPOSE

We've all had students who avoid reading like the plague—or who pretend to read. It's often these students who keep us up at night. How about approaching the problem head-on? Kids often think their teachers *don't* know they're fake reading. If you are creating an honest classroom, you need to be up-front about this. It's particularly beneficial if the students themselves acknowledge and label behavior associated with fake reading. Then when you discover a student is fake reading, you can name the behavior and explain your expectations for changing it without surprise or embarrassment.

THE LANGUAGE OF LEARNING

This lesson has the potential to embarrass students who fake read. The discussion needs to be empathetic, not flippant. My approach is direct–deliberately demystifying something often hidden and shameful and letting the entire class know I'm here to help. But there has to be trust in place in the classroom community before this group lesson is presented. Until then, I bend over backward to identify fake readers early and give them support privately and individually.

HERE'S HOW IT GOES

"Remember when we talked about how teachers assess kids and their reading? Do any of you know when someone is fake reading?" The students look at me in amazement. "Come on! You think I don't know when a student is pretend reading? You guys know, I know you do. What are some things that are giveaways? Besides this one?" I hold a book upside down and pretend to be engrossed in it. Of course the kids giggle, then hands shoot up.

"They keep changing books every day."

"They turn the pages really fast."

"They try to talk or to mess around."

"If you're talking about the book in a group they don't talk."

"Or if they have to talk, they say stuff like, 'Yeah, I'm thinking what so-and-so just said.'"

"Or they say, 'All of my ideas have already been discussed.'"

The list continues. Kids are smart and when we give them opportunities to demonstrate it, they shine. I usually have to stop the discussion given the wealth of responses, but some years, I have to add to the list (always being explicit).

"Great, so as your reading teacher, what do you think I'm going to do when I notice someone fake reading?"

Kids offer a few suggestions, but I don't let it stretch on too long. Instead I explain exactly what I'll do. "You know, probably all of us have pretended to read at some point. I bet I did as a kid. A friend of mine said when she was six, she used to pretend to read this big fat encyclopedia to try to keep up with her big brother!" The kids chuckle. I'm turning fake reading into a fact of life, not a crime.

"Sometimes kids fake read because they just can't find the right book," I continue. "Or else the book isn't at the right level. So my job as your reading teacher is to first of all ask *you* why you're doing it. Then I'm going to find some books at your level that you might be interested in and give you a couple of choices. That's why it's so important for me to know you as a reader and also to know your interests. After that, I'm going to expect you to read the book, *and* I'll probably be coming around a bit more to confer with you to hold you accountable and make sure that it's a good fit. What do you think of that?" What can they do but agree?

On the basis of this short lesson, the entire class knows I'm going to hold each and every one of them accountable in a respectful manner. They also know that I truly know them as learners and as people.

OWNING THE LESSON

This is a great place to think about the problems that seem to crop up in your classroom every year. It might be little things that begin to snowball. Ask yourself these

▶ QUESTIONS TO THINK ABOUT

- What drives me nuts because I can't "solve" it soon enough in the school year?
- Could I do a brief minilesson at the beginning of the year that throws the problem out there for the class to solve, thus allowing my students to help me "head it off at the pass"?
- How do I help my struggling readers and writers?

Choosing Appropriate Books

PURPOSE

Many students do not have the scaffolding necessary to be able to choose appropriate books on their own. These are often the same students who fake read or abandon book after book. Chryse Hutchins calls it the "snag and grab" method—a student needs a book to read, quickly goes to the bookshelf, pulls out a book without any intention or thought, pretends to read for the period, returns the book to the shelf, and repeats the process the next day! Whenever I've assumed that my class knows how to make wise decisions when choosing books, I've always had to go back and present this minilesson. I am then reminded that if I'd done it at the beginning of the year, I would have avoided a lot of problems. Another reason this is such an instrumental minilesson is that it continues to build a community of readers. I like to do this lesson before my class makes a field trip to our library. That way I know they are prepared.

HERE'S HOW IT GOES

"This year you will have lots of class time to read books that *you* choose. You will also be reading books of your own choosing at home. It's important that you read books that are appropriate for your reading level and that hold your attention. There are so many books available, why not choose the ones you really want to read?

"You brought in your favorite books at the beginning of the year, and I also shared some of my reading. I talked about the books that are *easy* for me, the ones I call my 'beach reads,' the books I take along on trips that I can read and not really have to think about. I enjoy them when I'm reading them, but I don't usually remember them. I understand the content, the vocabulary is easy, and I can just zip through them. Do you guys have some easy books you remember?"

Students invariably mention a few books they've read in previous years. Some of them admit that they like to return to those books periodically.

"You know we all need easy books once in awhile, so I can understand why you return to favorites. That's okay once in awhile, but I want you to push yourselves.

"Then there are the *just-right* books, the ones that you understand and can read right through but that may have a few new words, and you sometimes have to stop and think about what you're reading. Sometimes teachers call these the books *at your independent reading level.* These are the ones I want you reading a lot.

"Finally there are the *challenging* books, the ones that stretch you. It could be because of the vocabulary. Or it could be because of the content, what it's about. For example, *The World Is Flat* is a challenge for me, because I don't have a lot of background knowledge on that subject, but for someone who knows a lot about economics, it would probably be just right. As your reading teacher, I will be giving you a lot of challenging texts this year, but I will be there to support and help you through them. Did you know that if you try to read challenging books all the time, your reading won't improve? Once in awhile is okay to stretch yourself, but I want you reading just-right books most of the time.

"So let's start an anchor chart. I want to capture your thinking at the beginning of our year together, and then we can keep adding to it throughout the year. How do good readers choose appropriate or just-right books?"

▶ THE NITTY-GRITTY

We return to our chart the next day and go over the ideas and add more. I like giving that extra day so that students can continue to reflect on the topic.

Students start sharing ideas, and I chart their preliminary thoughts. If they're missing certain key concepts, I bring them up. One is the readability level often included on the backs of books, which is often a mystery to kids. There are no mysteries in my classroom. Another important concept I want my entire class to internalize is the "five-finger rule." When applying this rule, you choose a book, pick any page, and read it. When you come to a word you don't know, you fold down a finger. If you have a closed fist by the end of the page, the book is too hard—the vocabulary is most likely going to get in the way of comprehension.

Figures 3.6 and 3.7 are examples of anchor charts from two different years. The similarities and differences between them show why it's imperative to capture students' thinking anew every year. When students know the charts reflect their thinking, they will pay attention. The beauty of anchor charts is that you can revisit them throughout the year, adding and deleting as thinking changes.

Figure 3.6 How Do Readers *Choose* the Right Books?

HOW DO READERS *CHOOSE* THE RIGHT BOOKS?

- Their brother, sister, family member recommends it.
- They read a page to see if it's well-written/interesting.
- They can understand it.
- They notice the vocabulary (five-finger rule).
- They get recommendations from friends.
- They don't "snag and grab."
- They read the back cover or the inside jacket flaps.
- They like the genre.
- The book has a catchy title.
- They like the pictures/illustrations.
- They recognize the author.
- It's part of a series they like.
- It's the right readability level.
- It's not too long or too short.
- The type size isn't too small.
- It's gotten good reviews.

HOW DO WE CHOOSE AN *APPROPRIATE* BOOK?

- Friends give or recommend it to us.
- Family members recommend it.
- We read the "blurb" on the back or on the "fly" and decide if we'll like it or not.
- We read the first paragraph/page and see whether it's a good fit.
- It's part of a series we know and like.
- It's about something that interests us.
- We like the genre.
- It's at the right readability/age level.
- It has a great cover.
- We like the title.
- We're familiar with the author
- The book has generated a lot of excitement in the world.
- The vocabulary isn't too hard.
- It's easy, just right, or hard/challenging.

Figure 3.7 How Do We Choose an *Appropriate* Book?

OWNING THE LESSON

Many schools use Accelerated Reader or guided reading. While I don't recommend using only these leveling methods, I'm happy to weave them into the anchor chart. In my school, students are welcome to take Accelerated Reader tests in our library, receive points, and get rewards. That's fine with me. But I want students to choose books that interest them and to learn how adults choose the books they read. When my students grow up they won't be able to go to the bookstore and find colored dots on book spines that tell them which books they can read. I want them to internalize and understand their reading level. That's part of honest feedback.

▶ QUESTIONS TO THINK ABOUT

- How do I communicate a child's reading level to him?
- How do I ensure that every child in my classroom knows what an appropriate book is for her?
- Do I have leveled libraries or leveled books?
- How do I want to guide my students to books suitable to their level and interests?
- If I use leveled libraries and programs like Accelerated Reader, how can I make sure my students retain an element of choice?

Why We Drop Books and When That's Okay

PURPOSE

No matter how many lessons on choosing appropriate books I present, there are always a few students who can't seem to find the right book. Every day it's a new one: read, drop; read, drop; read, drop. At some point I have to put a stop to it, and I've found from experience it's easier to label and root out this behavior early in the year, before it becomes a problem. Every reader drops books—that's what a critical reader does—but when it's habitual, I need to step in. (Chapter 4 addresses how I keep track of what the students are reading and watch for patterns.) This quick minilesson is a nice follow-up to choosing appropriate books.

HERE'S HOW IT GOES

"Have you kids noticed how I write down the books you're reading every time you head off to read? I do that so that I know what you're reading. It keeps me accountable, plus it's another way for me to assess you and your progress. You also know that I write down notes from our conferences. That way I remember what we talk about and what I've taught.

> ▶ **CHAPTER LINK**
>
> "Status of the class" record keeping is discussed in Chapter 7.

"Sometimes I notice that students start books and stick with them for a bit, then they drop or abandon them. Sometimes this becomes a habit. Now I know we sometimes start books and they get boring or they're not what we expected, and we stop reading them, but what about students who never finish a book?"

"Maybe they just haven't found the right book," says Jonny.

"I think that may be part of it, and I also think maybe they're not choosing the right books. So my job as the reading teacher is to ask what's up, choose a couple of books, have them pick one, and actually finish it. What do you think of that?"

Maddie offers that it sounds fair, especially if the students still get to make a choice. (By this time, the students also trust that I will be offering them good books.)

"So, when is it okay to drop or abandon books? I'm going to be honest with you. When I've read two or three chapters of a book and I'm not sure whether I want to continue, I'll read the end. Then I'll decide whether or not to finish it. I don't do that very often, because I've usually read reviews or talked to friends before I start a book, so I'm pretty sure it's going to be a good fit. I'm curious about what you think. When or why do you guys drop books?" As they answer, I chart their thoughts (see Figure 3.8).

> **THE LANGUAGE OF LEARNING**
>
> There are readers who consider skipping to the end of a book a sacrilege. But there are so many books from which to choose and only a finite amount of time, so I need to be choosey. That's why I make this point with my students. I'm not advocating the strategy, but I'm allowing them to see me as a reader.

OWNING THE LESSON

Great learning can occur when students reflect on exactly why they dropped a book, learning that can be tucked away for future reference and result in better book choices later on. Here are some questions to consider as you adapt this lesson for yourself.

▶ QUESTIONS TO THINK ABOUT

- How far into a book do I expect students to go before abandoning it?
- Who chooses the books my students read—me, my students, or a mixture of both?

To make this lesson more meaningful to my students, I often give examples of when I drop books or which books I have an aversion to. "You know there were times in college when I'd be required to read a book for a class, and I couldn't drop it. That was pure torture. For example, one book that stays with me is *Zen and the Art of Motorcycle Maintenance* (Pirsig 1974). I still couldn't tell you what the book was about. I read it because I had to, but I remember I hated it. I think it had something to do with the title—I couldn't figure out how Zen and motorcycle maintenance connected, plus I had no interest in motorcycles."

Figure 3.9 lists some reasons kids say they don't like book, along with things I might do to try to get them over their distaste.

Figure 3.8 When (or Why) Do We Drop Books?

When (or why) do we drop books?	When is it okay to drop a book?
• Boring • Gets old • Your mind starts to wander • Repetition • Vocabulary too hard • Can't understand	• Can't relate to the characters • Can't visualize (picture in your imagination) • Don't like the author's style

Reasons Kids Don't Like Books	Ways I'd Try to "Fix It"
Long, detailed beginning	Choose a read-aloud book that takes a while to work into the story and model it. OR During a conference, discuss how sticking with the book for a bit longer may be worth the payoff. OR Present a quick class minilesson on how books written long ago have much longer intros, but are worth the wait!
Too many characters	Present a minilesson on characters and how to keep track of characters. This is also a terrific opportunity to discuss monitoring meaning and comprehension—if the reader can't name the main characters, then the reader isn't interacting with the text.
It's about war	Read aloud a beautiful short story or picture book like Pink and Say or a scene from a longer book, then have the class read it as a choral reading.
It's a "girlie book"	If the student (usually a boy!) selected it, talk about being choosey from the beginning. If it truly is a girlie book, let the student abandon it!
Dialogue goes on and on	Model how reading and writing connect, and look at punctuation. OR Read a great book with lots of dialogue, using a different voice for each character or present it as reader's theatre.
I just don't like it	Accept the reason once or twice, but if it's a recurring theme, select three titles about things I know (from conferences and observations) he's interested in that are at his reading level and tell him to choose one and finish it. Then confer with him regularly to make sure he is reading the book—and finishes it!

Figure 3.9 Reasons Kids Don't Like Books

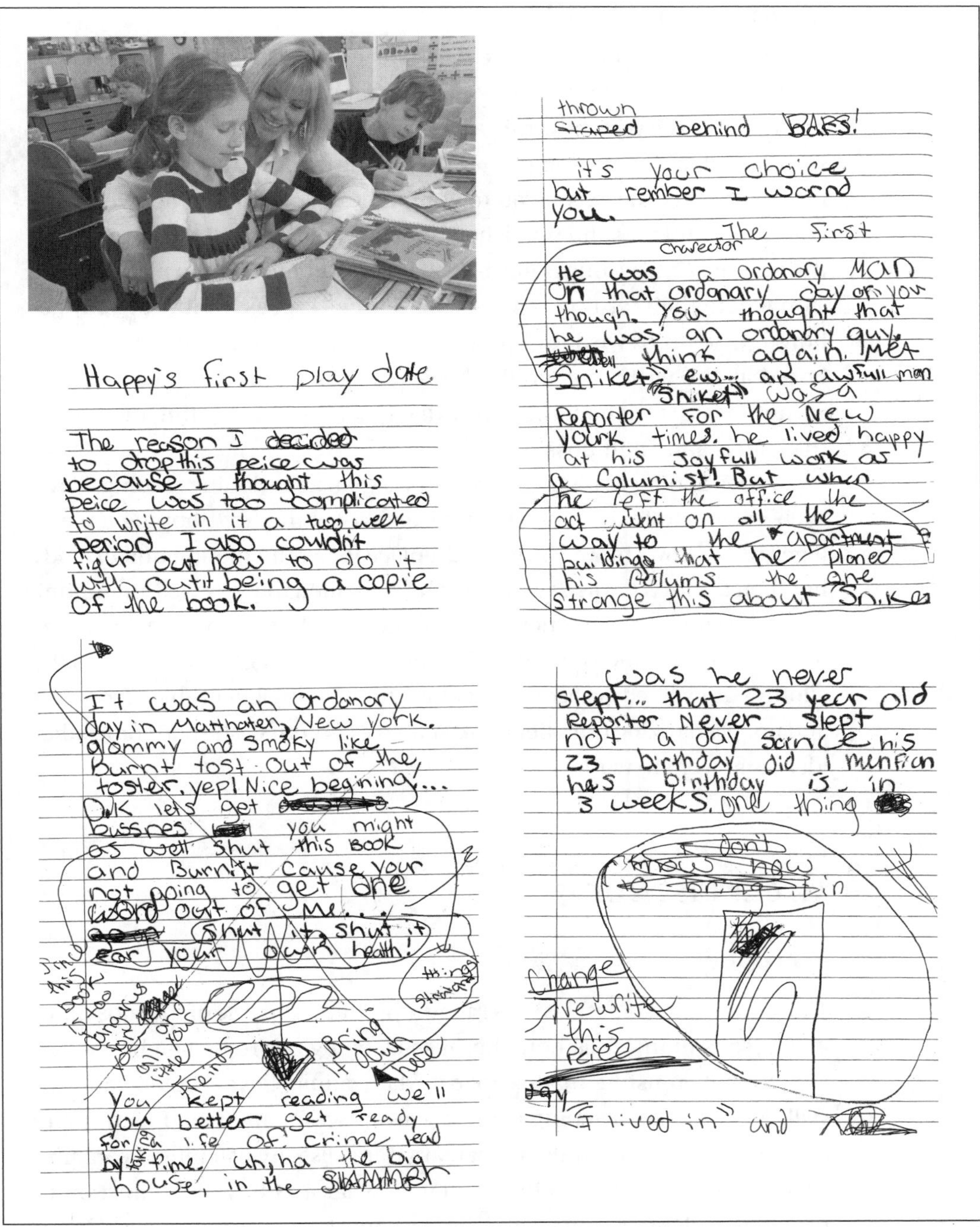

Happy's first play date

The reason I decided to drop this peice was because I thought this peice was too complicated to write in it a two week period I also couldn't figur out how to do it with out it being a copie of the book.

It was an ordanory day in Matthaten, New york. glommy and Smoky like Burnt tost out of the toster. yep! Nice begining... OK lets get bussnes you might as well shut this book and Burn it cause your not going to get one word out of Me... Shut it, shut it for your own health!

Since this book is too dangrous for all you little ... freinds

things strange

Bring it down here

You kept reading we'll you better get ready for a life of crime lead by taking time. uh, ha the big house, in the SLAMMER

thrown behind BARS!

it's your choice but rember I warnd you.

The first charector

He was a ordanory MAN on that ordanary day or you though. You thought that he was an ordanbry guy. Well think again. Mef Sniket" ew... an awfull man "Sniket" was a Reporter for the New york times. he lived happy at his Joyfull work as a Columist! But when he left the office the act went on all the way to the apartment buildings that he planed his colums the one strange this about Sniker

was he never slept... that 23 year old Reporter Never slept not a day since his 23 birthday did I mention has birthday is in 3 weeks. one thing

I don't know how to bring in

Change rewrite this peice

"I lived in" and

Figure 3.10 Leslie and Kylie conferring about a fiction piece that isn't progressing the way Kylie envisioned

BRINGING IN WRITING

When do we abandon or drop a piece we are working on? This version of the when-do-we-drop lesson would probably not be appropriate at the beginning of the year; however, as students begin to write pieces and start, stop, and abandon the things they're working on, it's a natural.

Not every piece is taken to completion. Unlike reading, which involves a completed and published book or text, the students are creating the writing. And writing is hard. Even when students have a plan or envision where their writing is going, sometimes it goes adrift—or they get bored. One bit of wisdom I pass on to my students is that when you're bored as the writer, generally the reader got bored two pages earlier. Sometimes a student comes up with a great idea but writing more than the lead is almost impossible.

Abandoning writing is more natural than abandoning reading. However, I want students to be able to explain why they're dropping a piece. Figure 3.10 shows how Kylie started a piece for a punctuation unit of study but then decided it wasn't working. She explained that she was attempting to write a story using her novel as a mentor text, but discovered that it was too complicated and she wouldn't be able to create a good story line in the allotted time. She was also struggling with creating believable characters and not plagiarizing from her book. After we conferred, she had some other ideas and went to work.

Great Listening

PURPOSE

This is one of the oldest lessons in my repertoire, and one of the most integral lessons in my classroom, because listening has to be taught and the components must be made explicit. Many adults have trouble with this skill. As a teacher, listening is my biggest assessment asset. I learn more from listening to my students than anything else. By listening, I can offer honest feedback. By listening, I know how far and in which direction to push my students. When I listen, my students know I care. Because I listen and pay attention, my students trust me. Creating an anchor chart labeling good listening behavior creates an entire classroom of great listeners.

HERE'S HOW IT GOES

"Do you have friends who are great listeners? Have you been around people that just seem to be able to listen to you and remember what you've said? Have you ever noticed how people kind of gravitate to great listeners? Why is that?"

"Because it gets kind of old just being around someone who talks and talks and talks," comments Geoffrey.

Heads nod, agreeing.

"Well, sometimes it's really fun to be around people who can talk and tell great stories and jokes," adds Jonny.

"But sometimes you just want people to listen to you," says Trinity.

"I think you're all right. Have you noticed that we do a lot of talking in this room? That talking is huge—and we learn so much from one another. But in order to do that, we also have to listen. Have you noticed how I listen to you when we're in group or I'm conferring with you? I really want to hear what you say; I want to find out what you think. What do you notice when I'm listening to you? What are some specific things I do?"

"You look at us and you sit at the same level," Hays says.

"You get close to us so we can talk softly. And you ask a lot of questions," Annie adds.

I write his comment down on the chart paper to start our anchor chart. Then I ask for other ideas. If the class gets stuck, I nudge gently, asking how students know when someone isn't paying attention or listening; then we turn that behavior around into what students should be doing. The class anchor chart (see Figure 3.11) reflects students' knowledge about listening and how they want their classroom to operate. As always, the chart is the kids' words!

THE LANGUAGE OF LEARNING

I always sit at the same level as my students when I confer. If they're at a desk, either I'm on my knees or I have a stool I drag around the room to sit on. I also sit close to my students—so I can put an arm around them. If they're on the floor, I'm on the floor right next to them so I can look over their shoulder at the book they're reading (or at their writing if it's a writing conference) and they can also look at my chart to see the notes I'm jotting down—there are no secrets. See Chapter 7 for more on conferring.

OWNING THE LESSON

Here are some questions to get you thinking about the place that talk and listening have in your current teaching.

WHAT MAKES GOOD LISTENING?

- Be on the same level.
- Make eye contact—look at the speaker.
- Pay attention.
- Stay put!
- Don't interrupt (no side conversations).
- Respond—ask questions, make comments.
- Take turns.
- Make good choices.
- Cooperate.
- Let others finish their thoughts.
- Stay on topic.
- Don't talk when the other person is talking.
- Be honest.
- Don't raise your hand when someone else is talking.
- Focus your attention (your brain) on the speaker.
- Don't fiddle; it's distracting. (Nodding is okay!)
- Show your attention with your body.

Figure 3.11 Anchor Chart: Good Listening

▶ QUESTIONS TO THINK ABOUT

- Where and when do I want my students talking? Are any "but what will the neighbors think?" inhibitions holding me back? (Some teachers worry that the "noise" of students' engaged voices will be perceived as a class off-task by other teachers or administrators. Or they are concerned about losing control during small-group work and conversations.)
- Do I have different expectations for effective conversing depending on the activity? If so, how can I adapt this lesson to articulate these expectations?
- How are my students seated or grouped in the room? Is this conducive to talk?

BRINGING IN WRITING

Listening is a key component to effective peer revision conferences or to sharing writing from the author's chair. Present a companion lesson and create a companion anchor chart about how to listen to another person share their writing. How do you hold your thinking about the piece while listening well? How is listening to a peer read her piece aloud to the class different from listening during a peer writing conference? (Lessons on writing conferences are in Chapter 7.)

Phenomenal Talk

PURPOSE

After students create norms for great listening, speaking norms are the natural continuation. We all have students who monopolize conversations or whose voices we can hear from the opposite side of the room—those with built-in megaphones! If students are unaware of expectations, then anything goes. Again, as teachers we must be explicit about why talk is helping them think at a deeper level, about how great talk encourages great thinking. Just creating an anchor chart is not enough. As with the skill of listening, talking must be practiced and the norms revisited throughout the year. Teachers are the best models for this, too.

By the time I conduct this minilesson with my class, they have had many opportunities to watch me having great conversations with individuals, groups, and the entire class. Our classroom talk is purposeful and safe, and students know their words and thoughts are valued. This leads to incredible risk taking.

HERE'S HOW IT GOES

"We've done a lot of talking already in this class, so it's time to chart our norms for great conversation. This way we'll have an anchor chart to refer to, and if anyone enters or joins our classroom, they'll know our guidelines and expectations. Shall we have a go?"

As the students offer suggestions, I guide their responses, nudging them to add ideas. I also create an anchor chart like the one in Figure 3.12.

OWNING THE LESSON

Meaningful talk and conferring is the topic of Chapter 7.

THE LANGUAGE OF LEARNING

"Three-inch voices" comes from work we've already done in class. When students are working in their table groups they use three-inch voices—voices that can only be heard by those three inches away. This keeps students who tend to project their voices across the room in check. A simple "three inches, please" is a great reminder to hit the mute button.

▶ QUESTIONS TO THINK ABOUT

- How do I set up talk about writing and reading in my classroom?
- How do I group kids to facilitate talk? Do they sit in table groups? Do they talk with partners?
- Who does most of the talking in my classroom?

PHENOMENAL TALK

- Listen while others are talking (see listening chart).
- Be appropriate.
- Stay on topic.
- Help each other talk—make it safe to talk.
- Get everyone on the "same page" about the topic.
- Don't interrupt.
- Ask questions.
- Use appropriate voice level (three-inch voices; don't mumble).
- It's okay to disagree.
- It's okay to "piggyback"—takes the conversation deeper.
- Let others finish their thoughts.
- Don't fiddle—it's distracting.
- Don't leave the conversation.
- Stay put!
- Face each other.
- Get on the same level.
- Don't talk over each other.
- Don't look around/"space out."
- If you're going to disagree with someone, let him finish.
- Ask for clarifications.
- Don't switch topics midway through a conversation.
- Cooperate.
- Be aware of body language.
- Think about the people who are talking and what they're saying.
- Don't go though every detail (boring!).

Figure 3.12 Anchor Chart: Phenomenal Talk

What Wise Readers/Engaging Writers Do

PURPOSE

If I am going to push all my students to the highest level, I need to provide instruction on what is happening in the minds of good readers. Struggling readers watch the other readers in the room and have no clue about what's happening in their brains to engender the magic of reading and comprehension.

Strong readers use skills automatically and I want to bring these to my students' attention. Although I don't always use the word *metacognition* (thinking about your thinking), I want my students to be aware of how many strategies they are using independently to deepen their understanding of text. By asking the kids about these skills, I'm assessing their background on reading strategically while also making the skills explicit.

HERE'S HOW IT GOES

"By now you guys know I'm a pretty good reader; I've had a lot of practice. I've also been showing you what I do as a reader. I've been modeling my thinking as we've been reading our books on literacy. I will continue to do that throughout the year as we work on different comprehension strategies. What I'm curious about today, though, is what you think a good reader does. Take a couple minutes and just think quietly about what you know. It might be from your own experience or from watching or talking to people you know who are good readers.

"Okay, now that you've had a couple minutes to think, let's hear your thoughts." I take out chart paper so I can capture their responses. Figure 3.13 is a chart resulting from one class' ideas.

▶ THE NITTY-GRITTY

Wait time is huge. I know it's hard to give students two minutes to think (two minutes is a long time), but if I don't give them time in which to reflect, I lose my students who take time to process—and they're usually the deeper thinkers. When I first assign "think time" I hold my watch in front of my face and track the time. That way the students who think they have an answer can't catch my eye and interrupt. I'm also very adept at gently signaling kids to put their hands down. After a couple of times, students realize I'm serious about waiting the entire time and they need to continue to think.

OWNING THE LESSON

As the year progresses, I revisit this chart every couple of months—it's a work in progress. As students become more sophisticated readers, they add more sophisticated characteristics to the chart.

▶ QUESTIONS TO THINK ABOUT

- How can I use this lesson in my classroom?
- Do I have practices I return to every couple of months?
- What practices should I revisit?

BRINGING IN GO-TO WRITERS

I often repeat the previous lesson in relation to writing. The main concept I want the students to grasp is that you must be a reader to be a good writer.

WHAT DO GOOD READERS DO?

- They think about reading strategies.
- They stay with a book until it gets interesting.
- Before starting a book, they make sure they like it (read the back).
- They stop and ask questions and notice important parts.
- Before and while reading, they ask questions and guess what's going to happen.
- They visualize what they're reading.
- They substitute a name for a character's name they can't pronounce.
- They make connections, compare what they read to other things they've read.
- They don't read really fast. They take their time.
- If they have trouble understanding, they get help from someone who does understand.

Figure 3.13 Class Thoughts About the Traits of Good Readers

Good writers start as readers. However, you can be a reader without being a writer. I want my students to see the connection between the two and understand the importance to our study of literacy.

I also encourage you to find your favorite authors. Collect them and learn about them and think how you could weave them into your literacy classroom. Here are some that I wouldn't be without: Eve Bunting, Nicola Davies, Ralph Fletcher, Douglas Florian, Thomas Locker, Jonathan London, Patricia MacLachlan, Patricia Polacco, Cynthia Rylant, Chris VanAllsburg, and Jane Yolen.

The appendix lists a number of mentor texts, along with suggestions for using them in reading and writing minilessons.

Understanding What We Read—or Not

PURPOSE

In their groundbreaking book on comprehension, *Mosaic of Thought* (1997, 2007), Ellin Oliver Keene and Susan Zimmermann list the strategies that proficient readers use to solve comprehension problems.

- *Monitoring for meaning*: knowing when you know, knowing when you don't know

- *Using and creating schema*: making connections between the new and the known, building and activating background knowledge
- *Asking questions*: generating questions before, during, and after reading that lead you deeper into the text
- *Determining importance*: deciding what matters most, what is worth remembering
- *Inferring*: combining background knowledge with information from the text to predict, conclude, make judgments, interpret
- *Using sensory and emotional images*: creating mental images to deepen and stretch meaning
- *Synthesizing*: creating an evolution of meaning by combining understanding with knowledge from other texts/sources (2007, 14)

Although at the beginning of the school year my focus is launching the literacy study, I want my students to be aware whether or not they understand the text they're reading. I use this short minilesson more as an *assessment* to help me guide my instruction and identify students who don't know when they don't know.

The resulting anchor chart (see Figure 3.14) articulates what good readers do as they're reading—another opportunity for my struggling readers to hear (and learn about) strategic reading from their classmates.

HERE'S HOW IT GOES

▶ THE NITTY-GRITTY

Some years I create a T-chart with two columns, one for understanding and one for not understanding.

"How many of you have ever been reading and all of a sudden you kind of shake your head and say to yourself, *what did I just read?* Sometimes that happens to me." Kids say that yes, this happens to them too; some offer examples. "Then I have to figure out where I zoned out and go back to that place and reread. Or else I have to decide what was preventing me from interacting with the text—why I wasn't comprehending what I was reading.

"Good readers know when they're getting it—in other words, comprehending—and when they're not. I really want to know what you guys think—will you help me with this chart? Let's start with how you know *when* you're understanding."

After we finish that, we move on to how you know when do you know you're not understanding.

I know I'm understanding the text when...	I know I'm not understanding the text when...
• The author describes or tells. • I use background knowledge (or prior knowledge). • I see the book from a different point of view. • I'm wondering what the characters in the book are wondering. • I can predict what's going to happen. • I can't put it down, except to think about what's going to happen. • I can picture the characters. • I can make connections outside of the book.	• It's odd or confusing. • The subject changes. • The book is boring. • I can't explain it to someone else. • I have to go back and read tons of times. • I'm thinking about what I did that day. • It just doesn't make sense. • After I read a word it's like I never read it. • I can't see the main characters. • I don't have a picture in my head. • I can't make any predictions.

Figure 3.14 Class Anchor Charts About Understanding or Not Understanding

The second part of the lesson is how to repair meaning using "fix-up" strategies. I generally do this lesson the following day.

"Yesterday, you gave me terrific input on how you know you're getting it and how you know when you're not. Those charts are now hanging up in the room. Today, I want to go a little further. I want to know what strategies you have to 'fix up' your understanding. What do you do when you get stuck? This will really help me as your reading teacher, because I can see what you already know, and I'll be able to teach you some new strategies."

I invite the students to share and I write their responses on a chart (see Figure 3.15).

To Learn More

Harvey, Stephanie, and Anne Goudvis. 2000/2007. *Strategies That Work.* Portland, ME: Stenhouse.

Keene, Ellin Oliver, and Susan Zimmermann. 1997/2007. *Mosaic of Thought.* Portsmouth, NH: Heinemann.

Zimmermann, Susan, and Chryse Hutchins. 2003. *7 Keys to Comprehension.* New York: Three Rivers Press.

- I slow down and make the thing I don't understand into everything it could be. Then I narrow it down to two things. Later in the book if I am wrong about one, the other could be right.
- I go back to the last place I understood what I was reading and try to get back on track.
- I reread the beginning of the book.
- I think about what's going on in a character's mind.
- I ask my parents.
- I think about it.

Figure 3.15 Fix-Up Strategies

OWNING THE LESSON

I also use these lessons to identify students who need immediate intervention. I give them direct instruction in specific strategies in a small guided reading group.

▶ QUESTIONS TO THINK ABOUT

- How do I correctly identify kids in need?
- Do my students know when they're understanding and when they're not?
- Do they have strategies to help them get "unstuck" or do they depend on me or another adult?

Noticing Beautiful Language

I can think of no better way to develop students' appreciation of beautiful language and word choice than reading aloud and discussing picture books.

PURPOSE

To emphasize how reading and writing are interconnected, I often use the same text for the reading lesson (generally on comprehension strategies) and then again for the writing lesson. My students need to be reading like writers when it's time for them to write. And writers read with a different set of eyes. *Amber on the Mountain*, by Tony Johnston (1994), is a beautiful picture book about friendship and learning how to read and, finally, how to write. This book is another "must read" for me when I launch my literacy study at the beginning of the year. As in the lesson in which I model thinking aloud, I tell students that as they listen, I want them to think about how this book connects to our studies on being literate. However, in this lesson I chart my thinking about the beautiful language Johnston uses.

▶ THE NITTY-GRITTY

Although my class focus is on building literacy—hence my emphasis on *connections*—I am also providing a lead-in to our next study on background knowledge (or prior knowledge, or *schema*).

HERE'S HOW IT GOES

"I have another favorite book to read today. This one is *Amber on the Mountain*, by Tony Johnston. Besides enjoying the book, your job as you listen is to think about how this book *connects* to our thinking about literacy.

"I'm going to do something a little different today as I model my thinking for you. Instead of cutting off the top of my head and letting you hear my thoughts about the content, I'm going to share what I notice about Johnston's writing. I'm going to lift some of my favorite lines and words and jot them down on this chart. I'm always struck by beautiful writing and I want to capture some of it here for you."

The rest of the lesson follows the same pattern as the think-aloud lesson. We talk about our thinking *before* we start reading, asking questions, and making predictions. Then I read aloud, this time sharing my thoughts on the writing. Following is an example.

"Wow, look at this lead. I am struck by how Johnston's first sentence is so descriptive. I can imagine those mountains, and it helps that I've seen some pretty high peaks. I also love her line about the needle stuck in down. I can picture that. She's doing something specific as a writer right there. Does anyone know what 'like a needle stuck in down' is called?"

THE LANGUAGE OF LEARNING

Teaching figurative language at the beginning of the year, along with studying vocabulary and word choice, is a way to get students reading like writers and noticing words.

Reed's hand shoots up, "It's a simile! I remember that from last year!"

Reed is right, that's what I am looking for. After I write the line down, I continue through the remainder of

▶ THE NITTY-GRITTY

If no one in the class had responded, I would have said that Johnston has written a simile—a comparison using either the words *like* or *as*—using this teachable moment to expose my class to figurative language. We'll study it in depth later.

NOTICING BEAUTIFUL LANGUAGE IN *AMBER ON THE MOUNTAIN* BY TONY JOHNSTON

- Mountain so high, it poked through the clouds like a needle stuck in down
- Trees bristled on it like porcupine quills
- Soaring
- Skedaddled
- The sky was streaked with morning
- Stuck to each other like burrs
- Melted into the blue mountain mist
- Jibbering
- "you're peltering me with words, thick as rain. I feel drenched."
- Muffled in white
- Huddled

Word choice leads the reader to good mental images, sensory images, visualizing.

Figure 3.16 Noticing Beautiful Language in *Amber on the Mountain*

the book the same way. Figure 3.16 is my chart of "noticings" and Figure 3.17 shows a student's version. Of course, when we finish reading, we discuss how noticing beautiful language connects to our reading studies.

▶ THE NITTY-GRITTY

I want to underscore that there is no magic sequence to these lessons and you can teach them and reteach them at any juncture of the year. Also, it's okay to "jump ahead" in these lessons to introduce concepts you won't get to in earnest till later in the month or year. When I taught this lesson, the kids and I weren't yet focused on the comprehension strategy of visualizing/creating sensory images, but I knew they were ready to start becoming aware that beautiful language allows the reader to create mind pictures.

OWNING THE LESSON

Having favorite authors—and learning about them—is a great place to begin. As you read, pay attention to how you read both as a *reader* and as a *writer*, so that you can be explicit with your students.

▶ QUESTIONS TO THINK ABOUT

- Do I use the same book more than once?
- Are there books I can use that lend themselves to both reading and writing instruction?
- How can I used well-written text so that kids do the "noticing" rather than my "telling" them?
- Do I have favorite authors that I return to again and again? That I know about?

Like butter on pankakes

what we notice	how it helps us as readers	how it helps as writers
Sun ticks bird talks A clould drifts by draging a shadow cat prrs raling in the light a puddle of sun moon spils milk for the cat to drink Slipper whisper across the floor a helping verbs in the entire books Strong verbs present	don't need to look at pictures in the book I can just see the pictures in my mind than I look at the book the pictures are totaly different ▽△▽△▽△▽△ e.g. p.o.k.	the athor helps us see more what simmiles are verbs whisper, spils, drink, ticks, talks, use more stong verbs not week verbs
bright sun outside feeling I could do in my writing		puddle feeling I could do in my writing

Figure 3.17 A Student's Noticing of Beautiful Language in *Like Butter on Pancakes*

If I always "work" a text—read it only to notice the writing—my students lose the beauty of the story, so sometimes I read a short picture book aloud just for the enjoyment of the story. My students deserve the chance just to listen and enjoy. We call this "letting the book wash over us." I always chuckle when my students stop me at the beginning of a minilesson and ask, "May we let this wash over us before we work it?" After we read through the first time, we go back and "work" the text as part of our writing instruction.

An option for this lesson would be to use the book first as a model for reading, then return to it during writing workshop (possibly on another day or even later in the year) to focus on the beautiful language in the writing.

Debuting the Book Lover's Book: A Segue

"Today? Do we get them today?" There's a hint of urgency in Isaiah's question. Is one of my most reluctant readers really asking the question the rest of the class wants the answer to as well?

The second Monday of the school year, and my students are anticipating getting this year's "reading book." I know they've seen my "rollie cart" filled to the brim with brightly colored books, and I know some of them recognize the cover they created a week earlier, laminated onto one of those books. Then, too, I had promised I'd bind the books during a Sunday football game, and the Broncos played the day before.

"Absolutely," I answer, holding back a smile. "After all, I promised. Do you want them before or after group?"

That's a no-brainer; the children say in unison, "Our book lover's books!"

As I hold each book up and read the name on the front, I can feel their excitement and admiration. They're not only entranced by their own book, they're also congratulating their peers on the creativeness of the cover designs. Twenty-five different covers, but on this very first day, the insides are all the same. However, by the end of the day, even the insides will begin to reflect its owner.

I look forward to this day every year, because my class may change, my grade level may change, the students' abilities and needs may change, but what doesn't change is their excitement and love of their book lover's books. And how many of us get to experience the thrill of watching children *want* (even yearn) to get their hands on a book that will authentically capture almost all their reading for an entire year? How many children look forward to the day that they get their reading workbook? But this is not a workbook, it's a *thinking book*, and my students already know that. From Heather and Patrick, who are more than three years below grade level in reading, to Geoffrey and Nicole, who are already comprehending at the high school level, these books are something to be cherished.

When I gave these students the assignment of creating their covers during the first week of school, I introduced the concept of the book lover's book, showing them examples of books from previous years. I explained that students had *loaned* me their books so I could use them to help me with a book I was writing, but I had had to promise to return the books to the kids when I was done. I also told them about a student from many years ago who immediately found his book lover's book when Stephanie Harvey asked him if he still had it so that she could put a copy of his literature log letter in her book *Nonfiction Matters*.

Now I tell the kids that these books will become a kind of record of their lives in fourth grade, that it will be fun to go back to them when they're adults. They can't wait to dive into them.

And that's where we'll go in the next chapter. We're going to dive into the book lover's book, a new way to hold all your students' reading (and a lot of writing) in one place—without going crazy!

CHAPTER 4

The Book Lover's Book

A Year of Thinking and Learning

How can oak tag and a hundred sheets of notebook paper stuck together amount to so much in a child's reading life? What is it about this particular response journal? As I hope you'll see, its power as the ultimate reader's notebook is clear and replicable. I use the book lover's book (BLB) to differentiate my reading instruction for each child. It is an organizational tool that also gives me insight into my students' thinking and their lives in the classroom.

The books evolved over the years through trial and error and implement the ideas of other educators. The nitty-gritty is that they capture the thinking your class does about reading and writing, especially writing in response to text. To reuse the "tracks in the snow" image, you can flip through these books and trace every step of your reading workshop—from minilessons, to guided practice, to independent work and reflection. They harbor the vocabulary of literacy. They hold the history of your reading instruction.

I've split my discussion of the BLB and the teaching it holds into two chapters. In this chapter are the basics—the standard version to get you started. Feel free to incorporate just a few parts of it and see what works. Tweak it, try it, then add or subtract. Make it reflect your goals and your students' needs. Chapter 5 gives you the deluxe model—I go deeper into the book's potential, addressing the more complex thinking and writing it's capable of capturing. These chapters are both menus and recipes. Select items you want to try from the menu, and I'll give you the recipe to blend them all together.

The BLB is a tangible artifact I can wave in the air, my secret weapon. It ties learning together and holds my students' and my thinking. So here it is: the stuff it holds, the rationales, and the thinking behind the BLB!

What's in the Book Lover's Book?

- Table of contents
- Comprehension strategies
- Class thoughts
- Minilessons
- Lit log
- Anchor texts
- Directed instruction
- Constructed responses
- Book clubs
- Reflections
- Glossary
- Vocabulary
- Books I've read
- "Someday" list

Perusing the BLB

I present this lesson on Monday of the second week of school.

CLASSROOM EXAMPLE

As I finish passing out the BLBs, the students are already looking through them. I give the kids a few minutes to do this on their own, then invite them to bring their BLBs up to the group area.

"What do you think?" I ask.

"They're awesome," says Erin.

"But, man, they have a lot of paper in them. Are we *really* going to be doing this much writing in these?" asks Dexter, as he dubiously flips through the pages and pages of lined paper.

"What do you think?"

"Yeah, probably," he admits.

"Yes, you'll be doing a ton of writing in them, but so will I. In fact, in your lit log section you and I will be writing letters back and forth. How about that? And these books will be our record of all our learning and thinking together about reading this year."

The class has their BLBs in hand; it's time to open them up and see what's inside.

"I know a lot of you have already looked through these, but I'd like you to take a few minutes right now and see what you notice about the organization and the sections I've included. Would you do that quietly? Then we'll talk about what you've noticed."

▶ THE NITTY-GRITTY

The day I bring in the completed BLBs is magical, because the students are so proud of them. Amazingly, in fifteen years, I've never had a student lose one or had one destroyed—the kids take too much pride in them. The most telling feedback I've received is that students tend to hold on to them—even as adults. They have become a way to remember their childhood.

The kids now have a purpose, and the pages start turning. The covers are created on colored oak tag and laminated. Students decorate their covers however they want. My only requirement is that they include their name and *Book Lover's Book*. Individuality is apparent. Some covers have just the student's name and the title; others have intricately drawn and colored pictures—of books, rainbows, puppies, flowers. The names of sports teams emblazon others. Some students have created comic strips, and others have glued on favorite photographs or images downloaded from the Internet. (See the examples in Figure 4.1.) Inside the books are sections delineated by different-colored sheets of oak tag. Much of the book is simply lined paper, although the glossary, vocabulary, and books I've read sections contain photocopied forms. (See Figure 4.2.)

Figure 4.1 Covers of the BLBs

After a couple of minutes, the students start sharing.

"It looks kind of like a real book," observes Maddie.

"What do you mean?" I ask.

"Well, it has a table of contents at the front and all the sections are in the order of that table of contents," she explains.

"There's a glossary, and a lot of nonfiction books have a glossary," adds Jonny.

"Do you think I did that on purpose?" I ask.

"Yes!" they all answer. By week 2, students know I'm big on purpose.

"You're right, I did, because I want these to resemble authentic published books—

In Kids' Words

I grew over the year. What I mean is that my brain grew. I learned a ton. My brain was like a sponge, at first it was empty, but a teacher squeezed out information and I absorbed it. Now my brain is full. My goal is to become a bigger sponge.

—Gina

Figure 4.2 Different Sections of the BLB

more like nonfiction, though. Sometimes you might see some of these glossary terms on a test, and I'd rather have you practicing by seeing and using them in your BLB.

"I like the poem you have at the very beginning," adds Emma.

"Why do you think I put that in?"

"Because it's about books, and this is our book about books," Nicole says.

In Kids' Words

Dear Mrs. B,

I think you have taught me so much about writing, I would have never gotten this far if it wasn't for you. What has helped me the most was The Tiger Rising. When we stopped and we all shared our feelings and asked words we didn't know it helped because you were right there with us. You were asking the same questions too. Reading has also taught me a lot too because of book clubs. I think it's really cool how the kids run it, I get so many questions from friends. Lastly I think BLBs teach me tons. When we write to you and ask q's you are super speedy about giving feedback. It's almost like you're a reporter interviewing us. I think rubrics help and when we have to pick our own scores and then you write the real ones. Sincerely,

—Micha

▶ CD-ROM LINK

You'll have your own ideas about which sections you'll want to use and how you'll assemble the books—it truly needs to reflect you, your classroom, and your school's standards and curriculum. On the accompanying CD-ROM, you'll find a downloadable, editable version of a BLB to give you a running start. This beautiful rendition was created by Becky Hansen and Lori Hasselquist, teachers at Covington Elementary, in South Sioux City, Nebraska, with Amy Hill and Sue Galvin's guidance.

Since the books are thick, it's easy for students to carry them and write directly in them—we don't need clipboards. Most of the work in the BLBs is done at school, so they don't get lost in backpacks or left on the bus. And they are an invaluable assessment tool when I prepare for student conferences, fill out report cards, or share progress with parents.

FIRST STEPS

- Before the school year begins, I reflect on what needs to be included *and why*.
- The contents reflect my beliefs, curricular requirements, and accountability.
- I add or delete sections depending on the grade level I'm teaching and the sophistication of the students.
- I finalize my decisions about what to include.
- During the first week of school, I copy everything I want to include and make sure I have enough blank lined paper. (I use lined 8½-by-11-inch paper without margins or holes.)
- I lay out the section dividers and the lined paper and assemble the insides. (Some years I lay it all out and collate it myself, other years I have the kids do the collating in an assembly line.)
- Using 1½-inch spiral combs and a binding machine, I spend an afternoon binding the books. (Yes, it's time-consuming, but I can usually get them done during one Broncos football game!)
- I can add paper during the year if I need too, by removing the spiral comb, adding paper, and rebinding.

Opening Pages

The opening pages include an initial poem, the table of contents, and comprehension strategies. These sections are copies of prepared material, not sections for capturing student work.

PURPOSE

I want the first thing my students see to be a beautiful piece of text on the power of reading and books, so the first page is a poem. After the initial poem is the table of contents, which changes each year to reflect changes I make in the sections I include.

The next section is comprehension strategies (which I also label *Thinking Strategies*); I want students to have a list of strategies at their fingertips. When I am differentiating my instruction for each reader, I have the student refer to these strategies. Here is an example of the sheet I include:

COMPREHENSION STRATEGIES (THINKING STRATEGIES): HOW READERS MAKE MEANING

- Use background knowledge (prior knowledge, schema).
- Draw inferences.
- Ask questions.
- Monitor comprehension and meaning.
- Visualize/create mental images.
- Determine what is important.
- Synthesize information.
- Use "fix-up" strategies.
- Be metacognitive!

Directly behind this page is another sheet listing fix-up strategies, a list created by Regie Routman in *Literacy at the Crossroads* (1996, 198). Some of my fluent readers use these interventions automatically, while I need to provide direct instruction to other students. Even intermediate students struggle and need direct instruction, continued support, and reinforcement on how to fix up their reading at a word level. Here's Regie's list:

REGIE ROUTMAN'S READING STRATEGIES FOR UNKNOWN WORDS

- Skip the difficult word.
  Read on to the end of sentence or paragraph.
  Go back to the beginning of sentence and try again.
- Read on.
  Reread, inserting the beginning sound of the unknown word.
- Substitute a word that makes sense.
- Look for a known chunk or small word.
  Use a finger to cover part of word.

- Read the word using only beginning and ending sounds.
  Read the word without the vowels.
- Look at the picture cues.
- Link to prior knowledge.
- Predict and anticipate what could come next.
- Cross-check.
  "Does it sound right?"
  "Does it make sense?"
  "Does it look right?"
- Self-correct and self-monitor.
- Write words you can't figure out and need to know on sticky notes.
- Read passage several times for fluency and meaning.

Use errors as an opportunity to problem solve.

Behind this chart are single sheets labeled at the top with individual strategies. When I introduce a strategy, students record their initial thinking on that page. As we continue to work on the strategy, they add to their thinking. When the majority of the class is using a strategy independently and I'm going to move on to another, I have students use that page to write their thoughts on *why* using that specific strategy helps them improve as a reader. In this way, students track how their thinking changes as we move through strategy instruction.

THE LESSON CONTINUES...

"Does this table of contents look like most of the ones you see in nonfiction books? I think there's something missing in this one."

Kids pore over the table of contents, then Jack's hand goes up. "It's missing page numbers!"

"That's it. Did you notice that the pages aren't numbered? That's because I bound these books individually and couldn't use numbered paper. You can number your pages now if you want, or you may want to mark your table of contents another way." Prompting, I add, "Look at the dividers I've put in to show the different sections."

"They're different colors," observes Erin. "Oh, we could record the color of the divider by the name in the table of contents."

"That's a great idea. So as we flip to each section and I describe it, you can jot down the color in your table of contents."

Together, we begin to learn about all the sections of the BLB, starting with comprehension strategies. "I've already started talking about these comprehension strategies—or thinking strategies—because they're strategies we use in all our school subjects. I know they're posted in the room, but I wanted them right here in your BLB so you'd be able to think about your thinking. I also have a list of fix-up strategies in this section. That's going to be a lesson on another day. What do you see on the pages after that?"

"More pages on the strategies. But it just has the strategy at the top and then it's blank," Geoffrey observes.

"I bet we're going to have to write on them," adds Annie.

"You guys are figuring things out quickly," I laugh. "That's exactly why I left it blank. Because I always want to know *your* thinking."

And then we move on.

MAKING IT YOUR OWN

As you look at the table of contents and read through the descriptions of the sections, think about which ones are manageable. Ask:

- How can I use a book like this in my class?
- Which sections will push my students to deeper thinking?
- Which ones will help me with instruction, assessment, and accountability?
- Could I substitute different sections?
- Are there activities I typically do in my reading class that I can add here and my students can complete authentically?

BRINGING IN WRITING

Dexter was right when he observed that there was a lot of lined paper included in these books and that *students would be doing a lot of writing.* Although this is a *reading* book, it also includes a lot of writing practice. I try to weave in different aspects of writing in each section. For example, by the time students have written a month's worth of lit log letters, they definitely understand correct letter format. Writing summary paragraphs becomes second nature after working in the constructed response section. And being able to write reactions and opinions and use persuasive arguments is practiced in the reflection section. As you think about tweaking the table of contents, also think about the writing in response to reading your students can accomplish.

Class Thoughts

PURPOSE

Remember the list of favorite books my students generated on the first day of school? That typed-up list is the first thing in this section of the BLB. Behind it are blank pages waiting to be filled with the collective thoughts of the class. Most of our co-constructed work ends up recorded on anchor charts hung in the room, but often there are more ideas than we can possibly record on one or two charts. These class thoughts ground our thinking and create our community.

Key lessons such as what makes a good reader or choosing an appropriate book are also included in the class thoughts section. That way, when students get "stuck," we can revisit class thinking. As we talk and piggyback on one another's thinking, the discussions and new thinking become richer and deeper. Having captured their own language, the kids also have a record of how brilliant they are. I always put a child's name next to his words, to credit the thoughts.

Below is an example of class thoughts at the beginning of a unit of study on making inferences.

INITIAL THOUGHTS ON MAKING INFERENCES

- When you visualize, you're inferring–Trinity
- When we're answering our questions–Reed
- When we come up with the nitty-gritty of the piece–Naomi
- When we notice a character's feelings and emotions–Maddie
- If you go back and reread and it's not right in the text you're reading between the lines–Geoffrey
- You have to understand to infer–Jinu
- Tie inferences to the text–Nicole
- Using clues in the text to guess what will happen–Jonny
- Using your own words to fill in the blanks–Cole

MAKING IT YOUR OWN

Besides being a tool to create community and record thinking, the class thoughts section is also a testimony to honoring and valuing the kids as the thinkers and learners. As you think about this section, ask:

- What would I include in it?
- Are there additional ways I can honor the contribution students make in class?

Some years I use this section extensively; other years I depend more on anchor charts to hold classroom thinking. But students are incredibly empowered when they can go back through this section and see exactly what they were thinking and saying on a specific date. I want to push each student as far as I can, and here I have a written record of how everyone's thinking evolves. When students reflect on their learning at the end of each trimester, this section is an invaluable tool to help ground their thinking about how far they've come!

Minilessons

PURPOSE

In this section, students record their thinking before, during, and after minilessons. At the beginning of a unit of study on a specific comprehension strategy, I do most of the modeling by thinking aloud. As I begin releasing responsibility to the students, I have them write their thinking directly in this section of the BLB. Since every student has to respond, accountability is ensured.

Students gather in the group area with their BLBs and co-construct learning while I'm presenting a minilesson. If I'm reading a picture book, I'll pause and ask kids to write what they're thinking, then move around taking quick glimpses of student work (see the example entry in Figure 4.3). When I collect the BLBs each week so that I can respond to lit log letters, I look through this section to see how students are progressing with strategies and where my instruction needs to go (so that my assessment drives my instruction). I can also determine who needs more direct instruction in a needs-based group.

Rather than using a lot of graphic organizers of the sort typically included in professional books on reading, I give my students other ways to organize

The Stranger

by: Chris Von Allsburg

Before: I wonder why the guy on the cover looks so scared. Who is the stranger. Why would they make the cover of a mom making soup for a boy. Is the stranger across table.

During: Is farmer baily boy on corer? What was the thamp? Is the man dead? Did he even run over him? Is that man the stranger? Does the guy have a home? What does hermet mean? How did he lose his memery. Is he old cause he lost his memory. What does Mercury mean. How does it work. The guy on the cover is the stranger. Why woulden't the rabits run away. Why would the rabbitt's think he'd go with them. How can he not sweat after working so much. Is he goid to go back out. Why since the strainger is here is it not changing to fall when before he came it was about to come to fall. I bet he's magic cause in his other book there was someone magic? Why is he so scared. How when he blew on the leaf it turned colors. He's the oposate of Jack Frost. Why is he learning just cause the leaf was green. He is father fall.

Figure 4.3 Example of a Student's BLB Entry About a Minilesson

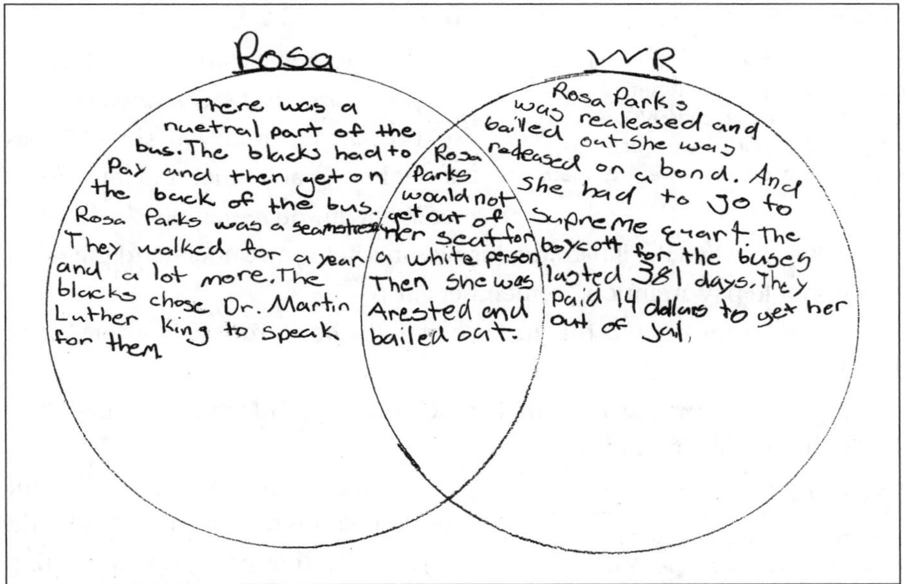

Figure 4.4 Graphic Organizer Inserted into a BLB

their thinking and responses. Sometimes, though, I copy an organizer and glue it directly into the minilesson section (see the example in Figure 4.4).

Chris Van Allsburg is one of my favorite authors to use for comprehension minilessons. He's not only the author of his books but also the illustrator, which means the pictures are guaranteed to enhance understanding. Van Allsburg's books also lend themselves to asking questions and inferential thinking. I use his book *The Stranger* (1986) every year without fail and take it along when I'm doing demonstration lessons in other schools. I can use it with first grade all the way through high school. (In the story, after a hermit is hit by Farmer Bailey, he comes to stay with the family and odd things happen when summer doesn't want to make way for fall to arrive. The reader is left hanging at the end.)

The material my students and I generate in the BLBs varies significantly from year to year, because the students are different every year. The BLBs are tangible evidence of this infinite variety and allow me to recognize my students' differences fully. Below I summarize two different lessons based on *The Stranger*.

CLASSROOM EXAMPLE 1

"Earlier we read Chris Van Allsburg's book *The Garden of Abdul Gasazi* (1979), so I've already told you some things about him as an author and an illustrator. What do you remember?"

> **▶ THE NITTY-GRITTY**
>
> The more you know about a book and its author, the more relevant you can make it to your minilesson and to your class. I love author studies. Van Allsburg's books always lead to rich, deep discussions, precisely for the reasons my students have named.

"Because he's the illustrator, his pictures help you understand the story, so we should pay attention," remembers Erin.

"And he always puts that funny dog in the book. You told us that," adds Isaiah.

"His ending was really weird in that book. It kind of left us hanging. Does he do that all the time?" asks Naomi.

"Great question, Naomi. I want you to hold on to that as we read. And I'm noticing that you guys are making text-to-author connections. You're using what you know about Van Allsburg to start asking questions and to really think about this book even before we start to read."

> **▶ THE NITTY-GRITTY**
>
> Even though the strategy is *questioning*, I'm still going to name comprehension strategies kids are using to deepen understanding.

"So let's take a look at the cover. The cover of *The Garden of Abdul Gasazi* was black and white, but this one is in color. I want you to turn to the minilesson section of your BLB and let's get the date written down and the title—remember, it's a title so it needs to sit on the shelf, you need to underline it—and then write the name of the author. Then I want you to write *Before*." As I'm giving directions, I'm writing on the chart paper on my easel.

"Then I want you to write down at least three questions you have before we start to read. And please make sure you end each of these with a question mark."

> **▶ THE NITTY-GRITTY**
>
> I'm reinforcing basic mechanics—the question mark. Also, a trick of the trade: If you ask for three, you always get at least one response. (Not sure why, but it works!) If you ask for one, often kids come up with none.

I read over shoulders, monitoring how the kids are doing. I stop by the students who appear stuck and prompt them to suggest questions, usually about the title or the picture on the cover. When everyone has jotted down some questions, I ask the kids to turn and talk. This way, *everyone* gets to share his thinking and I can eavesdrop and informally assess. After a minute or two I note *a few* of their questions on the chart.

"Now write down *During*. As I read, I want you to jot down your questions. I'll stop once in a while and ask you to write what you're thinking, but whenever questions pop into your mind, get them down even if I'm still reading. I really want to be able to go back and find out what you were wondering." As I'm talking I write *During* on the chart paper.

▶ THE NITTY-GRITTY

An hour! That's the entire workshop! But if my purpose is to develop *thinkers*, I need to linger and dig deep. The benefits of working through this book are enormous. The text anchors our thinking. I'm very mindful of the texts I use in my minilessons. Are they worth the time? What do the children gain from the lesson? I don't do long minilessons very often, and they're generally at the beginning of a study on a strategy.

We read the entire book this way: stopping periodically, jotting our questions, turning and talking, and recording a few questions on the class chart. Because *The Stranger* is a long picture book and the text is sophisticated, this lesson takes about an hour. When we finish the book, the students are left hanging—Naomi's initial observation proves to be correct.

"Van Allsburg did it again, didn't he? Sometimes authors leave us with more questions than answers. Would you please write *After* in your BLB, followed by what you're thinking. It could be more questions or just lingering thoughts."

After the students have responded, I have one more goal for this lesson. When readers ask questions they should also attempt to answer them. I'm explicit about this.

THE LANGUAGE OF LEARNING

I love the word *lingering*. To linger over something gives it value—it's worthy of our time and attention. To linger over our work and our thinking validates being metacognitive. It deepens understanding. Even though we have so much to "cover," shouldn't we linger over the really good stuff and make it stick? (And, yes, every year I need to discuss and define the word, because the kids don't know it. They sure know it when they leave my classroom at the end of the year, however!)

"Now we have this great list of questions. Were all of them answered?"

"No," the class choruses.

"We're going to go back through these questions and code which ones were answered and which weren't. We're also going to code the answered questions a step further. We'll write an *L* if the question was answered literally. Remember, *literally* is right there on the page, smack me upside the head, you can highlight the *actual words* to prove the answer. But we'll write an *I* if we think the question was answered *inferentially*—if we took clues Van Allsburg gave us and our own background knowledge and came up with

▶ THE NITTY-GRITTY

Again, although the focus strategy is questioning, the thinking strategies are inextricably woven together and cannot be taught in isolation.

the answer. Nevertheless, if I asked you to prove it to me, you could go back to the text and point out the clues; inferences are always tied to the text."

"Let's start with this first question, *If the mercury was stuck at the bottom, how could the doctor tell that the stranger had amnesia?* Was that answered?"

Reed has already been thinking about this and his hand is up. "No, I don't think it was answered. Van Allsburg doesn't really write about how the doctor knew. And I don't think the mercury being stuck helped him make that decision."

"Nice thinking. What do you guys think? Was it answered?"

The consensus is no, so I write *NA* by the question, for *not answered*. Then we move on to the next question: *What is his temperature?*

"How do we mark this one? Answered?"

"Kind of," Emma thinks. "Like we know it had to be really low because the thermometer's mercury was stuck at the bottom and the doctor thought it was broken. But Van Allsburg doesn't come right out and tell you."

"Yes . . . so how should we mark it?" I'm not going to do the work; I want the students to finish the thinking.

Jack answers and asks simultaneously: "That would have to be an *I* then, because we're inferring the answer, right?"

"Yes, to both."

We continue coding the chart (the coded version is shown in Figure 4.5), and then the students code the questions in their minilesson section. I've done the modeling, and I'm giving them the opportunity to practice independently. Coded questions from a student's BLB are shown in Figure 4.6.

CLASSROOM EXAMPLE 2

This group of students didn't understand who the stranger was when they finished the book. I could tell from the looks on their faces and their out-in-left-field "after" responses that they weren't getting what Van Allsburg was alluding to. As their reading teacher, I would have been remiss not to offer some additional instruction. This was a teachable moment, an opportunity to discuss monitoring comprehension and meaning and ways to fix up confusion.

"You're still really confused, aren't you? Van Allsburg gave us some clues,

▶ THE NITTY-GRITTY

Since *The Stranger* is a long book and the minilesson has already taken most of the period, asking the kids to sit and listen to it again would be futile. By taking a break, we'll come back to it the next day with fresh eyes. Flexibility and teaching to the needs of the class are key. Sometimes it takes two or three days to make it through a lesson and make it stick. Lingering is essential!

The Stranger

by Chris Van Allsburg

Before

Who is the stranger? I

During

- If the mercury was stuck at the bottom, how could the doctor tell that the stranger had amnesia? NA
- What is his temp? I (really low)
- Who is the man? I
- Why did he want to run? I
- Can he talk, or is he injured? I
- Is the stranger okay? I
- Why is it so weird/what is up with the stranger? I
- How could his breath turn the leaf red? I (picture clue)
- Is the stranger the guy who makes the wind blow? I?

After

What are you thinking?

Figure 4.5 A Coded Anchor Chart
(*NA* means *not answered*; *I* means the answer was *inferred*; L means answered *literally*)

but right now we're looking at the questions. How about if we revisit this book tomorrow? You bring up your questions in your BLBs and we'll use those questions to help us figure it out as we read it a second time."

On day 2, I begin, "Before I reread the book, I want you to look back through the questions you wrote down yesterday. I have a feeling that as I reread the book and you think about *why* you asked those questions, you might discover clues that Van Allsburg is leaving in the text and the pictures. You're going to use your questions to help you determine what's important in the text. That's why asking questions is such a huge strategy—it helps us with all the other strategies. So as I get the chart together, glance back through your notes from yesterday."

Before I can even get everything written on the chart, hands go up.

"You're already discovering some clues?" I ask.

Rebecca says, "Well, when I went back through my questions I saw that when he leaves at the end, the trees immediately changed from green

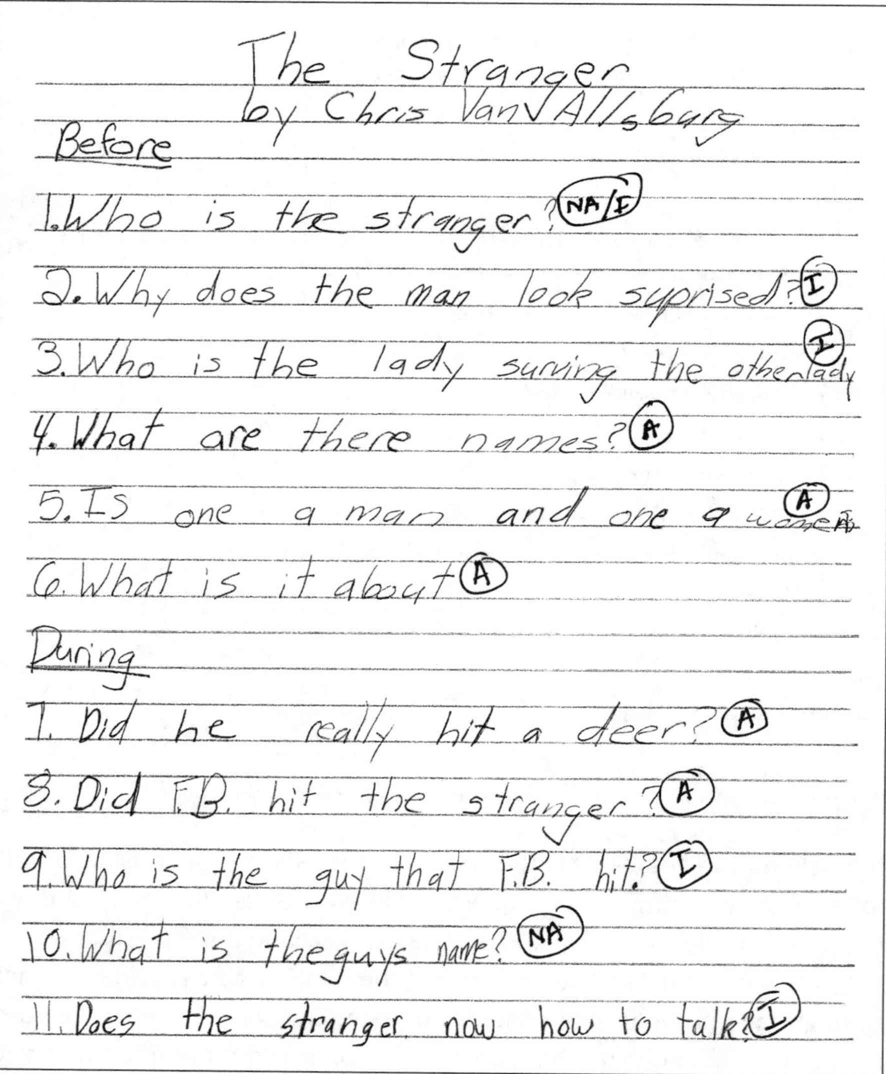

The Stranger
by Chris Van Allsburg

Before

1. Who is the stranger? (NA/I)

2. Why does the man look suprised? (I)

3. Who is the lady surving the other lady (I)

4. What are there names? (A)

5. Is one a man and one a women (A)

6. What is it about (A)

During

7. Did he really hit a deer? (A)

8. Did F.B. hit the stranger? (A)

9. Who is the guy that F.B. hit? (I)

10. What is the guys name? (NA)

11. Does the stranger now how to talk? (I)

Figure 4.6 Student's Minilesson Questions, with Coding Added

to red/orange/gold. I don't know why that happened, but I think it's important."

"I think you may be right. Let's write that down. Anything else you noticed that we should write down before I start to reread?"

Many students offer other examples that they remembered, and I write them on the anchor chart (see Figure 4.7). Then I begin to reread the book as

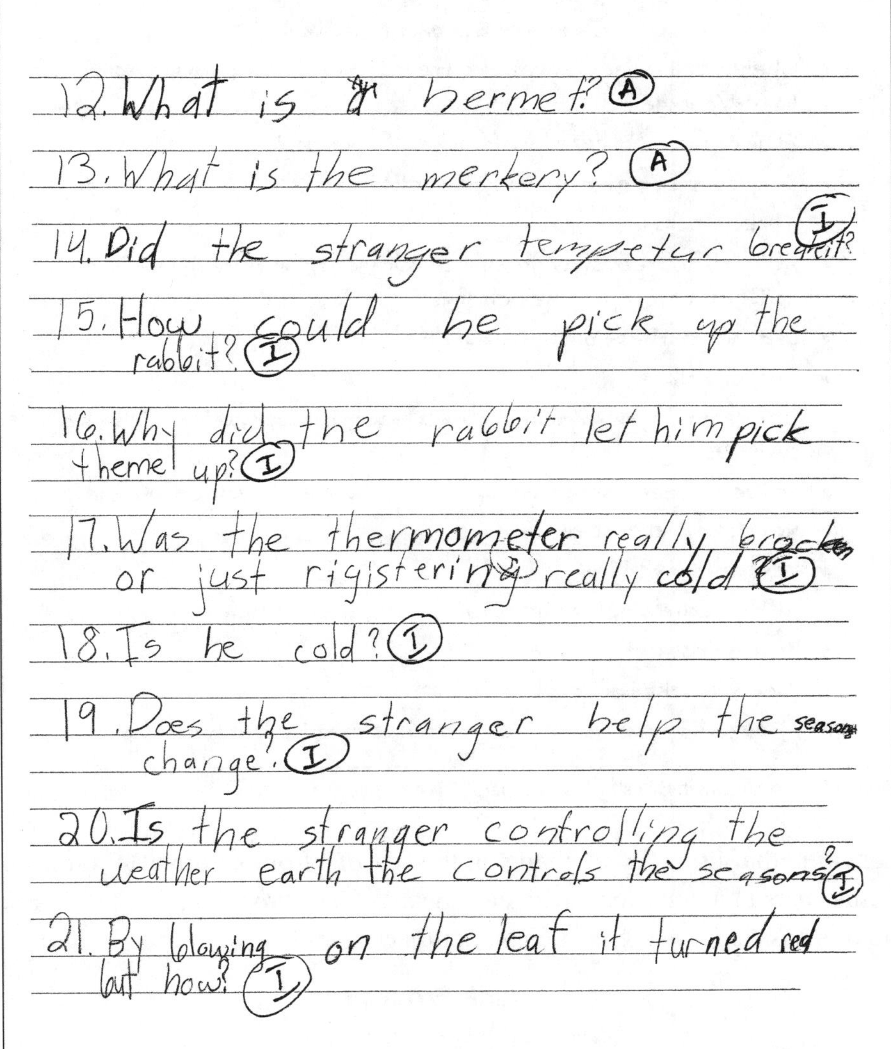

12. What is hermet? (A)
13. What is the merkery? (A)
14. Did the stranger tempetur break it? (I)
15. How could he pick up the rabbit? (I)
16. Why did the rabbit let him pick theme up? (I)
17. Was the thermometer really bracken or just rigistering really cold? (I)
18. Is he cold? (I)
19. Does the stranger help the seasons change? (I)
20. Is the stranger controlling the weather earth the controls the seasons? (I)
21. By blowing on the leaf it turned red but how? (I)

Figure 4.6 Continued

my students listen, their questions from the previous day in front of them. We periodically stop and add to the chart. This time my class is paying much closer attention to the text, and their initial questions are helping them frame new understanding.

After we finish the second reading, I ask the kids to write down who they think the stranger is now that they've revisited the text. Most are able to

Clues for Second Reading!

- When the stranger leaves, the trees immediately change from green to red/orange/gold
- Blew on soup—"Breeze/draft in here"—got cold
- Bunnies aren't afraid—they expect him to follow
- Three weeks
- After that, trees stay green weeks longer than they should in the north and overnight they change
- Leather clothes—buttons—didn't get it
- Doesn't talk
- Before hit "autumn around corner"—weather got weird—felt like summer
- Leaves—green—bothered/upset him—wanted them red/orange
- No one had ever seen him
- Mercury stayed low
- Just appeared before he got hit
- He didn't sweat
- "See you next fall" etched in frost
- At beginning the farmer felt a breeze right before he hit him

Figure 4.7 Anchor Chart: Clues to *The Stranger*

conclude that he is key to changing the seasons from summer to autumn. Some years I have students who have heard of Jack Frost. In this year's class, no one has. So I give them a poem about Jack Frost.

Jack Frost

Someone painted pictures on my
Window pane last night–
Willow trees with trailing boughs
And flowers, frosty white,
And lovely crystal butterflies;
But when the morning sun
Touched them with its golden beams,
They vanished one by one!

–Helen Bayley Davis

After they have read the poem, I ask them to write a brief explanation of how they think the poem and *The Stranger* connect. Andrew writes: "Both the stranger and Jack Frost painted pictures on someone's window pane. Maybe the stranger is Jack Frost. Jack Frost is winter and the stranger is autumn. They're both seasons." Clare writes: "My connection between the poem and Chris Van Allsburg's book *The Stranger* is the stranger controls the weather. But ...every year the stranger comes back and gentaly tutches [sic] their windowsill with the words 'see you next year.' But in this particular poem, "Jack Frost" by Helen Bayley Davis, the window was touched with snow by Jack Frost just like the stranger etches the window."

The minilesson sections of my students' BLBs clued me in to their lack of understanding and alerted me to adjust my instruction in order to improve their comprehension.

▶ BUILDING CONNECTIONS

The students are tying pieces of text together to enhance understanding.

▶ THE NITTY-GRITTY

I agree, a lot of time to spend on one text. However, look at all the skills and strategies that were covered:

- Questioning (the main focus of the lesson)
- Answering questions literally or inferentially
- Using background knowledge
- Monitoring meaning and comprehension
- Using fix-up strategies
- Rereading to fix up lack of understanding
- Paying attention to text clues
- Using questions to help with comprehension
- Making inferences
- Making text-to-author and text-to-text connections
- Writing as a way to reflect on and solidify understanding
- Bringing in other texts, including poetry, to help build and solidify background knowledge

OWNING THE LESSON

Each year my minilessons reflect my students. The joy of this approach is that it's not one size fits all; you teach the readers what they need. The minilesson section of the BLB gives me a quick glimpse into my students' thinking and ability to use a strategy. It also holds them accountable for interacting with the text and the class during whole-group instruction. No one is allowed to tune out.

▶ QUESTIONS TO THINK ABOUT

- How can I use this minilesson to inform my instruction?
- How can I use it to improve student accountability?
- How can I use it in connection with grading my students or reporting their progress in relation to standards?
- What instruction currently in my classroom could be replaced by or combined with this minilesson?
- How can I bring in other books and texts to enhance and solidify a strategy or continue to build background knowledge?
- How can I integrate other content areas with my literacy instruction?

BRINGING IN WRITING

As we use mentor texts for both reading and writing, students record in their writer's notebooks what they notice about the writing and the language. Writers notebooks and quick-writes are discussed in Chapter 7; however, the poem in Figure 4.8, taken from one of my fourth grader's notebooks, shows how the work in reading and writing connects. (I've included my comments about where he's gotten specific language.) This is another example of the power of mentor texts.

Henry starts with a question that's catchy, but his first verse isn't as powerful as the end of the second through the remaining verses. He begins using onomatopoeia and simile. His reference to the electric guitar is great, and comparing the sound of crunching leaves to a dinosaur's roar is a wonderful surprise. When he writes "the most important part," I know as his literacy teacher that he is piggybacking off Margaret Wise Brown's *The Important Book*. Good for him!

Figure 4.8 Henry's Finished Poem

Fall

What does Fall mean to me?
It means a lot
Not just when I go to school, Come home and go to bed.

It means,
I go to school, have a great day, and then
I get to come home to
The delectable smell of hot chocolate
That makes me zip towards it
Like a magnet.

It means Crunch! Crunch!
I'm not talking about Captain Crunch.
I'm talking about the leaves under my feet
Making noises not even an electric guitar could make
Because the noises echo in the air
Like a dinosaur's roar.

But the most important part is
The pumpkins.
They get picked out and carved and soon
Become more than a pumpkin but a
Jack-O-Lantern.

Anchor Texts

PURPOSE

The anchor texts in the BLB differ from the texts I share with the kids in minilessons in that BLB anchor texts are *novels*. Also, minilessons are just that—*mini*. We work on the novel anchor texts for two weeks or more. During those weeks, part of every reading workshop is spent reading the book together and marking and discussing our thinking. I want to stress *together*—as a class. Normally when you hear "whole-class novel," you think of everyone in the class reading the same novel independently and then answering questions at the end of chapters—one size fits all. That is *not* what this is!

Yes, everyone has the same novel in hand; however, instead of students reading in isolation, this is a shared experience—I read and the students follow along. Reading the novel becomes a think-aloud co-constructed with the entire class, a shared journey that provides the foundation for book clubs. As I model recording our thinking, students get guided practice marking and thinking about text.

▶ THE NITTY-GRITTY

Choose books that push the envelope, that challenge your students. Because I read the book aloud, I'm able to support even my struggling readers. I'm giving them the opportunity to interact with text they would not be able to read on their own and to make insightful discoveries as they do so. Asking them to read these texts independently would be setting them up for failure.

A lot goes into choosing these mentor texts. When I select whole-class novels, quality is a huge consideration. Another important factor is integration. How much can I teach the students *through* the book—and not necessarily just about literacy? The main instructional point for me is to *model* what good readers do and support the students' thinking. Reading the novel together, we all share the experience of the text and the richness of one another's talk and thinking.

I read only one or two anchor novels during the year, so I need to choose them wisely. Some favorites include:

- *Something Upstairs,* by Avi
- *Love That Dog,* by Sharon Creech (Connecting poetry to this novel is especially appropriate; Jen Bryant's *A River of Words: The Story of William Carlos Williams* and *William Carlos Williams,* edited by Christopher Macgown, are two suggestions.)
- *The Tiger Rising,* by Kate DiCamillo
- *Music of Dolphins,* by Karen Hesse
- *Bearstone,* by Will Hobbs
- *Number the Stars,* by Lois Lowry (A terrific picture book to use in connection with it is *The Yellow Star: The Legend of King Christian X of Denmark,* by Carmen Agra Deedy.)

In Kids' Words

Reading and writing slither together like snakes slither across the rough grassy floor. Giving kids packets is like giving a dog a banana instead of a monkey. When you throw out worksheets after books that you know the kids won't like, it makes them not want to read the book anymore. Questions in packets at the ends of books have to be questions that you can answer. I guess they don't get that when you ask questions that have no answer it brings deep rich conversations. We read the Tiger Rising. The author Kate Dicamillo followed you the whole way with the suitcase full of worries and [the main character] finally lets his deep and dark sad feeling RISE up and waft away. A month or two later we read as a book club, Esperanza Rising. The girl in the book had to go to her work camp and her grandma had to stay behind but the grandma said after many mountains and valleys (ups and downs) on the quilt we will be together. It is the same idea of rising.

—Claire

- *Peace, Locomotion*, by Jacqueline Woodson
- *Westing Game*, by Ellen Raskin (appropriate for upper grades)

My selections differ every year depending on the class. Since the books can be obtained in bulk at a discount, most students can afford to buy their own copy to write in and take home. Being able to write directly in the book boosts their investment in understanding it. (I also have extra copies students can borrow; they use sticky notes to record their thinking.)

If this is our first shared novel, talk is a major component of our study. Although we have practiced talking in conferences, pair shares, compass groups, and so on, talk is an essential part of launching and practicing our thinking *about* the text and then *being aware of how our thinking changes* when we listen to others and their perceptions. Another key aspect is *how* we hold our thinking so that we can share it with others. Learning these skills scaffolds our future work in book clubs.

In the interests of integrating curriculum, I often choose novels that dovetail with social studies. In sixth grade, I choose novels that reflect the countries we are studying. In fifth grade, I tend to choose historical fiction that corresponds with important events in American history (there is a wealth of choices). My third-grade choices are more open ended, as I push literary techniques more than integration. And in fourth grade, I often tie the novel to Colorado history. A fantastic book is *Bearstone*, by Will Hobbs. In the novel, an orphaned Ute boy, Cloyd, goes to work for a widowed rancher, Walter, outside Durango, Colorado. At the beginning of the novel, Cloyd is not a very likeable character and is filled with a lot of conflict. As the book progresses, the two form a father-son bond, but not without problems and conflict. Hobbs incorporates many aspects of Colorado history in the plot, as well as specific places, especially in the Weminuche wilderness outside of Durango. Ultimately Cloyd discovers that revenge is not worth the pain it causes. Both boys and girls love this book, which is another reason I continually return to it. The integrated learning I introduce and teach using *Bearstone* is itemized in Figure 4.9.

CLASSROOM EXAMPLE

After passing out student copies of the anchor text, I have the students join me in the group area with their book, a pencil, and a highlighter (and, for those borrowing a book, sticky notes).

"Before we start to read, I'd like you to read the blurb on the back, and then look through the entire book and see if you notice anything."

Literary	Science/Social Studies
• The obvious—setting, plot, problems, resolution • Character development • Conflict—within characters, between characters, and with the environment • Mood • Foreshadowing • Theme • Climax • Vocabulary	• Colorado history • Anasazi Indians • Ute Indians • Colorado life zones and geography • Colorado ranching • Colorado mining

Figure 4.9 Integrated Learning Chart

As the students are skimming the novel, I begin a T-chart on the easel.

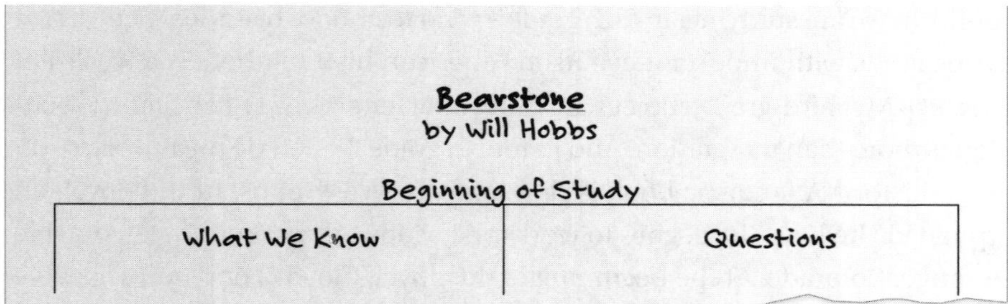

Then I say: "Now that you've had a chance to look everything over, let's capture your thinking right here. I want you to tell me what you already know—in other words, your background knowledge—and then questions that you have before we even start. I'm betting you know a lot just by reading the back."

With that invitation, kids start throwing out ideas for one side of the chart or the other. They tend to start with what they know, but that often leads directly to questions. I draw arrows back and forth between the columns to

▶ THE NITTY-GRITTY

I always have kids do this in our book clubs as well (book clubs are discussed in detail in Chapter 9). It sets a purpose for reading the book. Teachable moments often pop up during these initial perusals—maps, prologues, font changes. I want kids to notice these kinds of things; then we'll figure them out together.

demonstrate the connections. A completed chart a class created before starting *Bearstone* is shown in Figure 4.10 (on the next page).

> **▶ THE NITTY-GRITTY**
>
> See how much background knowledge and how many questions can be generated by simply reading the blurbs on the cover? The questions help set a purpose, and as we read the book, we will attempt to answer them.

Now that the students have tapped into their background knowledge and have a purpose for reading the book, it's time to start. I have my own copy of the text and a pencil and highlighter close by. Although I use the same novel over the years, I always start with a clean copy. It never ceases to amaze me how different facets of learning are revealed in different classes. It's truly never the same!

> **▶ THE NITTY-GRITTY**
>
> I model the process at the beginning but then gradually release responsibility to the kids as we proceed.

The first chapter is short. In it, the main character, Cloyd, who has never met his father but has searched for him his entire life, finds his father in a coma (a "vegetable") in the hospital. His dreams of what finding his father would mean are destroyed. I put my book down and ask the students to write what they're thinking right there in the white space where the chapter ends ("tracks in the snow")—questions, predictions, and so on. (You could ask students to write these thoughts on a Post-it note instead if you teach in a district where writing in books is a no-no.)

After all the students have had time to jot down their thoughts, I have them turn and talk with a neighbor or two as I eavesdrop on their conversations.

"Are you hooked?"

Many heads nod in agreement, but a few students haven't made up their mind yet—we're not far enough into the text.

"We'll read chapter 2 tomorrow [some kids are already begging to read more right now] but here's the deal. You need to leave your books here at school and you must promise not to read ahead. I'm serious about this—if you do, you might spoil it for the rest of the class."

We return to the book the next day. Again, I model thinking about and marking the text and writing down my "wonderings" or questions, asking the students to mark their text as I mark mine. Every couple of pages, I stop and ask the students to write down what they're thinking in the margin. I always have them write down their thinking at the end of each chapter. And I give them lots of opportunities to turn and talk with their neighbors and discuss important points as a group. A major goal is getting my students to internalize how group

Bearstone
by Will Hobbs

Beginning of Study

What We Know	Questions
• Main character—Cloyd Atcitty—Ute—fourteen years old, skipping school for years	• What does it mean to be skipping school for years?
	• Why doesn't Cloyd go to his tribe?
• Ran away from a "home"	• What's the home like?
• Works for Walter Landis	• Why is Cloyd working for Walter?
• Colorado	• Does Cloyd get into contact with Indians?
• Abandoned gold mine—Walter's	
• Trying to reopen it	
• Cloyd finds a turquoise stone (bear shaped) in a cave above the ranch	• How did Cloyd get the turquoise bearstone?
	• Where is the cave?
	• Will the bearstone help Cloyd?
• "Last grizzly" is important	• What does "the last grizzly in Colorado" mean?
• Something bad happens	• What happened to all the other bears?
	• What is the "terrible blow-up"?
	• What disaster happened that ruined it with Walter?
	• Is Cloyd going to mess up his last chance?
	• How is the stone going to help Cloyd?
	• What is the deal with Cloyd and the grizzly?
	• Does the grizzly come with the stone?
	• Did he mess them up?
	• Will he see the tribe again?

Figure 4.10 T-Chart Completed by Class

talk deepens and enriches understanding—that while not everyone has the same viewpoint or opinion, listening and sharing result in great conversations.

Because I know the text well, I stop at key points—new vocabulary, instances of foreshadowing, connections to Colorado history. I'm explicit about these.

In addition to the notes they jot directly in the text, I periodically ask students to use the anchor text section of their BLB to write and reflect about key aspects/teaching points. For example, if we're focusing on characters, I may have them record what they know about the main characters. The chart in Figure 4.11 shows Reed's understanding of Cloyd and Walter after we've read a couple chapters.

Figure 4.11 Reed's Understanding of Two Characters

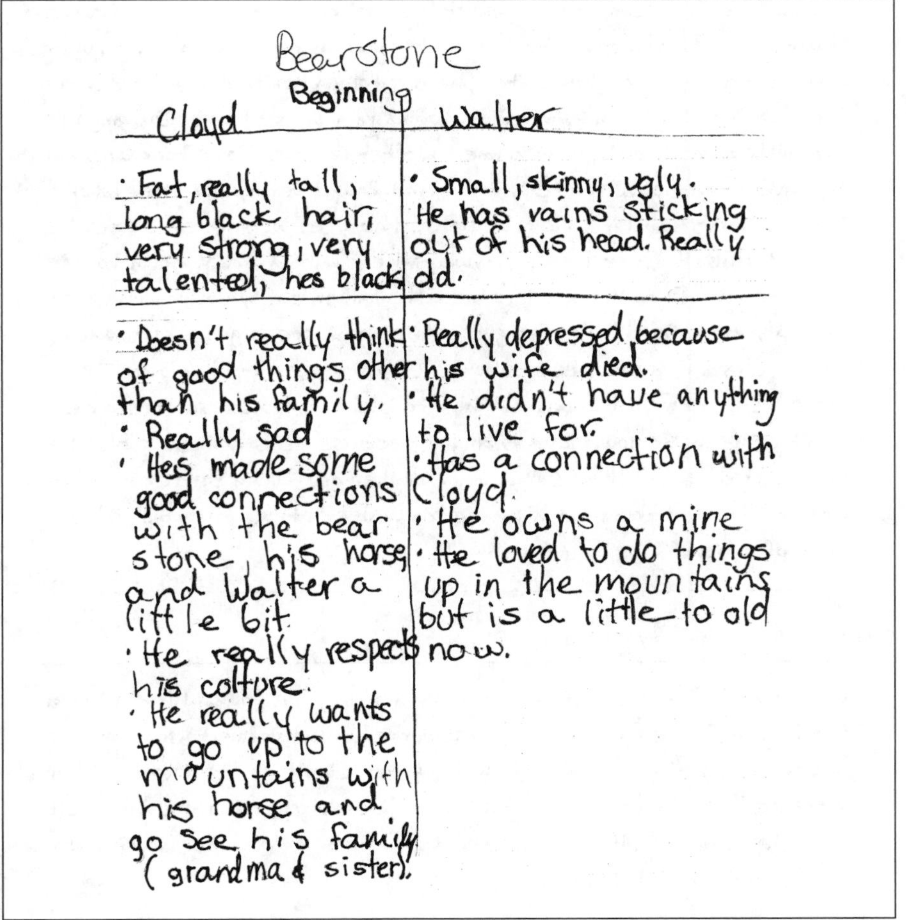
Bearstone

Beginning

Cloyd	Walter
· Fat, really tall, long black hair, very strong, very talented, hes black	· Small, skinny, ugly. He has vains sticking out of his head. Really old.
· Doesn't really think of good things other than his family. · Really sad · Hes made some good connections with the bear stone, his horse, and Walter a little bit · He really respects his colture. · He really wants to go up to the mountains with his horse and go see his family (grandma & sister).	· Really depressed because his wife died. · He didn't have anything to live for. · Has a connection with Cloyd. · He owns a mine · He loved to do things up in the mountains but is a little to old now.

When we finish the novel (or a major section of it), I always hold the students accountable with a culminating activity. I may give an open-book test, ask them to write a summary, or just have them reflect on the things the novel has led them to think about. Figure 4.12 is Emma's summary of Chapters 1–6. Compare hers with Reed's hit-the-high-spots approach in Figure 4.13. Both students demonstrate that they understand the plot and the characters. The difference between these responses is typical of the way girls and boys tend to write (see Ralph Fletcher's *Boy Writers* or Thomas Newkirk's *Misreading Masculinity* for more on this). Another factor in my choice of anchor texts is that I

Figure 4.12 Emma's Summary of Chapters 1–6

Cloyd, a fourteen-year-old Ute boy, searched for his dad for four years. Then he searched a quiet hospital and he found his dad... brain dead. So that was his dream to find his dad, but now was over and he was alone. A while after the boy found his dad, the housemom from where Cloyd ran away from found him, drove him to Durango to live with a short, bald man named Walter Landis. Cloyd took a climb to caves high above Walter's farm and found a tiny blue bearstone. That bearstone Cloyd kept, because the Utes worshipped bears. He named himself "Lone Bear." Anyways, he climbed back down to the farm/ranch. He didn't want to be with Walter, but Walter was a nice, friendly man. So they're living together and life is good, but Walter asked Cloyd if he wanted a horse. Cloyd named it Blue-boy. Things were well, then Walter asked him to build a fence, so trespassers don't come in. So now Cloyd is angry because he is homesick and he has to work. Now I hope Cloyd and Walter get along better now because Cloyd is taking out his anger on Walter. I think they will. It's too good of a book!

Figure 4.13 Reed's Summary of Chapters 1–6

When we first met Cloyd he was very unhappy. He found his dad in a hospital brain dead. Then his caseworker brought him to someone he never met before—Walter Landis. After Cloyd got to know Walter more he liked him. When he found the bearstone he named himself Lone Bear. Now he has a horse and is working on a fence so this guy can't come on Walter's property.

want to read a book that will appeal to *both* girls and boys. Too often the literature in classrooms tends to focus on girls' interests.

Finally, here's a reflection by Addison.

> What I learned about reading and comprehension is that the author makes you surprised by doing something you didn't think he would do, but then turns it into a good thing. The authors also get you hooked so you can't stop reading. For instance I was mad when the bear died and sad when Walter was hurt but then I realized why Hobbs had the bear killed.
>
> I was glad when Hobbs made Cloyd nicer but I didn't like him in the beginning. I also learned that everything in a book happens for a reason. It was such a good book I could read it again and again. I learned that there are ups and downs in books, that there's always a problem—whether it's small or large, there's a problem. And the problem probably clears up. The book always has a main character. I also learned about idioms, or as my teacher calls them "tongue in cheek." In this book there are a lot of idioms.

Addison has internalized so much of what Hobbs has done as a writer that when I respond, I nudge her to do that in her *own* writing: "Great observations about what the author does—how can you do that in your *own* writing? Let's talk about that when we confer next."

OWNING THE LESSON

Favorite read-aloud books that you think will lend themselves to digging into are perfect choices for anchor texts.

▶ QUESTIONS TO THINK ABOUT

- Do I use whole-class novels?
- What is my purpose in choosing these novels?
- Do I have the unsettling feeling that the one-size-fits-all novel isn't working so well for some students?
- Are these books my students will remember and use to build on, or are they simply books to get through?
- Are there novels I can use in my literacy lessons that will enhance my students' understanding of another content area?

I use no more than two anchor novels during the year. I like to do one early on—usually by the second month of school—so I can introduce book clubs right afterward. Even my students, in their end-of-the-year reflections, encourage me to start early. As Rachael so wisely suggested, "I enjoyed book clubs a lot. I think you maybe should start book clubs even earlier so the kids can read more books." If I do another anchor novel, I save it for the second half of the year or when I can integrate it into another aspect of my curriculum.

This	Versus That
• Teacher reads, students follow along in their own text.	• All kids read the same book independently.
• Teacher and students co-construct meaning.	• They answer questions at the end of each chapter.
• Everyone can access the text.	• Questions don't lead anywhere.
• Students, guided by the teacher, capture their thinking and ask their own questions–they interact with text.	• There is no discussion.
• Students have rich, deep, meaningful conversations, which carry over to their book club discussions.	• Teacher does the thinking.
• Students are engaged and learn from their peers.	• Students aren't engaged.
• Teacher and students are the audience for the thinking–this shared experience builds community.	• There is no peer learning.
	• Work is done in isolation–no sense of community.
	• Doesn't lead to future learning.

Directed Instruction/Guided Reading

PURPOSE

When I pull together a needs-based group or any other small group for instruction (these groups are meant to be flexible), we record our work together in this section of the BLB. (It's generally the other sections of the BLB or individual conferences that help me determine who needs additional support or who needs extensions.)

CLASSROOM EXAMPLE

Sometimes I notice from a student's lit log letters that she is struggling with a strategy or specific skill, and I'll meet with her in a conference and teach/ reinforce the strategy or skill. However, if several students need direct instruction in a specific area, I pull together a group.

For example, Gina wrote me about her struggles with choosing appropriate books.

> Dear Mrs. Blauman,
>
> I'm reading Midnight Magic by Avi. I don't get the story, though. It is a long chapter book. Obviously it is also about magic at midnight. Please give me advice.

Gina was new to our class in January and I didn't know her as a reader yet. (Often when students arrive midyear, their records don't accompany them.) I wrote back:

> Dear Gina,
>
> I want you to think a little about *why* you're not getting it—is it that the vocabulary (words) are tough, or do you not get the story itself? As a reader, what are you doing to make sense of it? I'll confer with you, so that I can see what's going on!

When I conferred with her, I found that vocabulary was interfering with her comprehension. She was a fluent reader, pronouncing all the words, but she was often unaware of what they meant (English was her second language—she was fluent in it, but spoke Korean at home). We decided she would write down words she didn't know on a bookmark and I would confer with her at least every other day to discuss vocabulary.

But that wasn't enough. A day or two later Gina wrote:

> Dear Mrs. Blauman,
>
> I need more help on vocabulary. No matter what I do, I can't help it. Please tell me what to do.

Since I knew a few other students who would benefit from a "refresher" on this topic as well, and because sometimes other students are the best "teachers," I formed a group "by invitation" to review how to choose the right book.

Dear Gina,

Keep writing down the words on the bookmark and I'll help you with those. I'm also going to have some of the kids help catch you up on our discussions from the beginning of the year about choosing the right books. I think that will help.

After the group lesson Gina found a book that she could understand.

Dear Mrs. Blauman,

I'm reading a book called The Dollhouse Murders. It feels like I'm solving a puzzle. It's the first time I'm feeling that feeling. It feels great!

I wrote back:

Dear Gina,

HOORAY! Will you tell me about the puzzle and how you're trying to solve it?

P.S. You still have to do the vocabulary—we've got to keep learning new words!

Text/Page number	WORD	What I think it means	Actual Meaning (Dictionary)	Ways to Remember
September piece	waftedl	fly, drift	to float lightly	hippogriff in Harry Potter wafts over the lake
"	anthrapomorphic	an impossible question too answer	giving human form or atributes to a non human thing	morph = change eg. The trees are dancing
"	bountiful	plentiful	plentiful abundant a-lot	bounty paper towels have a lot more paper in them than other paper towels
princess Academy	tethered	Something to do with teeth	to tie up something	You can bite through a rope your tied to with your teeth
"	Shorn	short	just cut grass or mowed freshly	sound like short grass gets shorter when you mow
"	quarry	barn or place were stuff is stored	a big hole they get rocks from	quarry reminds me of shaky the earth could have shook to make that hole
"	solitude	work	to be alone and lonley	it sounds like a sad lonley word
"	wager	guess/asume	something risked or staked on a uncertain event	I wasn't sure what it ment which is what it means
"	luster	[illegible]	state of quality of shining by reflecting light	I guessed what it meant
"	caverous	huge	a large cave that is mostly underground	Lilly's story
"	confine	reavel	to enclose or to keep within bounds	caution tape to keep you within bounds but it says confine
"	adjacent	huge	nearby	

wow! great words & effort!

An example of a student's BLB vocabulary work

OWNING THE LESSON

▶ QUESTIONS TO THINK ABOUT

- Do direct-instruction groups have to be static and keep a regimented schedule?
- What are my goals for group work?
- How do my students record their work when they meet in small groups?
- Which of my students would benefit from small-group instruction?
- Which students require remediation?
- As the majority of the students in my class begin to use a strategy independently, which students need more time and practice?
- Which of my students would benefit from extension activities?
- Which students would benefit from sharing their thinking in a small group?

Vocabulary

PURPOSE

Vocabulary is one of the first language skills I teach. Words give us power. A rich, wide vocabulary gives us incredible power. In Chapter 3, I explain how I introduce vocabulary and "noticing beautiful language" at the beginning of the year. Vocabulary is woven throughout everything we do in our classroom.

While I draw students' attention to vocabulary at every opportunity, I also want them to find new words independently. If students are choosing just-right books, they should be encountering some new vocabulary words. After a month of modeling vocabulary and creating anchor charts, my students must find, and record in their BLB, a *minimum* of three words a week from their reading. And I emphasize *from their reading*. Dictionaries don't count. If they can't find three words, either the books they're reading are too easy or they're not paying attention. Even more importantly, this is differentiated instruction at its most basic and effective: I can push my gifted students and develop the vocabulary of students who have been exposed to very little writing. Students are finding words *they* don't know and adding them to their repertoire. Vocabulary development and dictionary skills are being taught authentically. (After a year of looking up three vocabulary words a week, my students become very familiar with a dictionary!)

SAMPLE ENTRY

Instead of a classroom example, below is the vocabulary chart I use in the BLB, along with an explanation of the headings. I model using the chart and have students practice (with my support) before it becomes an independent activity.

Text/Page Number	Word	What I Think It Means	Actual Meaning (Dictionary)	Ways to Remember
Students should be able to refer back to the text and page number if necessary.	The word itself. We also discuss what part of speech it is and how to look it up in the dictionary.	From the context of the passage. "What would make sense?" "Take a stab at it." Weaving in grammar, "Take a guess at what part of speech this word is."	Students look up the word and find the meaning appropriate to the context. (Step you can add: have them record the part of speech.)	This is based on the research of William Nagy (1996): how to make the word part of your long-term memory. "What is the hook you're going to hang it on?" "Draw a picture or write a connection to hold your thinking."

OWNING THE LESSON

Ways to highlight vocabulary are endless. New vocabulary words are perfect additions to individualized spelling lists and can also be added to classroom word walls. My students write down sentences that include phenomenal words and post them on the "wondrous words" board. The most important thing is for the vocabulary to become part of *long-term* memory and for the students to *use these words in their own work.*

▶ QUESTIONS TO THINK ABOUT

- How do I want to teach vocabulary in my classroom?
- How can I differentiate vocabulary for the different reading levels in my room?
- How can my students internalize new vocabulary *from their own reading* and then begin to use these words in their writing?
- How can I make sure that new vocabulary enters my students' long-term memory?

Closing Sections

The opening sections of the BLB are overviews of the content followed by a place to hold class thinking. These concluding sections are copies of forms on which students can record their work. They are a record of what students have accomplished over the year.

GLOSSARY

I want my students to be familiar with a glossary and how to use it. Our curriculum guide delineates "literacy" vocabulary by the grade level at which the words should be mastered. But since the bedrock principle of my teaching is to push students as far as they can go, I include all the lists, K–12. The words are in alphabetical order, but the definitions are missing. I leave space for the students to write their own definitions as we learn (or review) the words. Here's the first page:

LITERACY GLOSSARY	
act	author's perspective
alliteration	author's purpose
analyze	bias
antagonist	cause/effect
assessment	character
audience	classify

BOOKS I'VE READ

This is exactly what it says, a list of all the books the student has read during the year (see Figure 4.14). When I began using BLBs, I didn't require my students to keep this list, but my thinking has changed. It goes back to accountability; the information is instrumental in helping me assess where the students are in relation to the standards. Are they consistently reading books (independently) at grade level? Are they reading a variety of genres? By referring to this section, I'm able to notice reading patterns quickly and easily.

"SOMEDAY" LIST

Since I've added the "someday" list to the BLB (see the Shopping for Books lesson in Chapter 6), I've watched my students make more informed decisions regarding their independent reading. It's a place where they can note books their friends or family members recommend, or books they may want to read in the future (see Figure 4.15). This is what Nicole said about her list:

> Dear Mrs. Blauman,
>
> Shopping for books in the classroom was the most fun ever! I got a lot of books written down. All About Sam is like Ramona Age 8 because they are both about themselves in first person. Flush is getting really exciting. There are kind of a lot of bad words in it, though. I think I'm going to read Where the Red Fern Grows after I read Flush.
>
> Your reader,
> Nicole

And here's Ben:

> Dear Mrs. Blauman,
>
> I am going to read The Boy Who Saved Baseball because it sounds SO!!! good. I wonder what John H. Ritter will do to make it exciting. What do you want to read when you are done with your book? Do you want it to be an adult book or a kid book as in a book we would read? I've got so many books I want to read as of now. Thank god books wait. They sure have a ton of patience because if they didn't have, all the books I want to read wouldn't let me read them!
>
> Sincerely,
> Ben

Book's I've Read

Date Completed	Title	Author	Genre
7/28	Peter and the secret of rudoon	Dave Barry and Ridley Pearson	fantasy-fiction
8/27	dragon rider	Corniella Funke	fiction-fantasy
10/6	Henry and ribsby	Beverly Cleary	fantasy
9/29	Fire within	Chris O'Lacey	fiction-fantasy
9/13	Diory of a wimpy kid #3	Jeff Kinney	fantasy
9/16	Diary of a wimpy kid #4	Jeff Kinney	fantasy
10/29	Eragon	Christpher Paloni	fantasy

Figure 4.14 Books I've Read

Someday List

Title	Author	Genre	Location/Notes
100 cupboards	N.D wilson	Fiction	Favorite Basket
smokey the cow horse	will James	Fiction	Animal Fiction
when Zackery Beaver came to town	Kimberly Willis Holt	Fition	
The winged colt of Casa Mia	Betsy Byars	Fiction	Fiction
Doe Sa	Tomasina	HF	HF
Kavik	Morey	Fiction	Anmals
Gentle Ben	Morey	Fiction	Ben

Figure 4.15 "Someday" List

Ben is right—books have patience and will wait for him—and he knows he will return to them when his hockey tournaments and busy life allow him to.

Tweaking the BLB So It's Your Own

▶ QUESTIONS TO THINK ABOUT

- What kinds of records are important to me?
- What kind of information will help me demonstrate my accountability?
- How can I incorporate curricular requirements in an authentic, manageable way?
- What components do I think are missing?
- What components would I add?
- What components would I replace?

Next Steps

This chapter has presented the basic steps in my students' dance with their BLBs. You've seen how the BLB helps me move through a lesson and check kids' comprehension, stepping back and reteaching what they aren't getting or pushing them forward. The BLB helps bring order and organization to a classroom of twenty-five diverse students! I use the information in the BLB to scaffold kids' learning *while I'm teaching*. In the next chapter, which discusses lit logs, constructed responses, book clubs, and reflections, I show you how to use the BLB to push kids' thinking.

CHAPTER 5

Raising the Bar

Strategies for Heightening Students' Writing About Reading

Ever since I was a kid, I've loved playing pinball. Give me a bucket of quarters and I'm good to go. I love the lights, the sound of bells, and that silver ball careening around at great speed, the satisfaction of whacking the ball with those paddle thingies so it sails up again and racks up more points. But it's awful when the ball plummets downward and I press those whackers at the bottom frantically to no avail—all the bells and victory and thrill and engagement are gone—the ball vanishes, game over.

This is not unlike what happens when my students' book lover's book (BLB) entries dim from the dazzling light of a halogen bulb to the faint rays of a flashlight whose battery is dying fast. If I get too busy, my students can coast for weeks and months like a dormant pinball machine, their writing the wan red LED above the

coin slot. There's too much at stake to let rich practices such as this tank, whether from the business of the year or other demands pulling at you.

This chapter shows you how to keep the lights of students' thinking on—keep those silver bullets of thought firing—in the sections of the BLB in which kids do the most thinking, writing, and reflecting and go most deeply into their learning. Those sections are:

- Lit log
- Constructed responses
- Book clubs
- Reflections

Lit Log

PURPOSE

In 1987, Nancie Atwell's *In the Middle* was released, and my reading workshop forever changed. Atwell's ideas about responding to student readers in dialogue journals captured a level of real, honest talk about books that toppled my assumptions about the "limits" of what children and early adolescents can do. Although she worked with eighth graders, students worlds apart from my fourth and fifth graders, the teaching and learning she described were so powerful I wanted to re-create them in my classroom. And I did, discovering that her approach to the reading response journal was applicable across grade levels. I came to call it a *lit log*, and in time imported it into the BLB.

Hokey as it sounds, the pen pal dynamic of the lit log lets me relate personally with and spin my instruction so it points at each student in my room. Each week, the students write me a letter about their reading and their *thinking*, and I respond, monitoring their progress and nudging them further. They may write about whatever they want and ask questions. I find out tons about my students and what's happening in and out of the classroom. Our exchange is a safe haven.

Here's how lit logs help me:

- When I read an entry, I pick up signals about book choice strengths and weaknesses, the extent to which the student has really connected with the book and is able to use comprehension strategies, the depth of his understanding.
- Interpreting these signals, I write a response pitched to the most important next step or concept for the student to practice or for the student and me to continue conversing about.
- I also use the responses (individually and collectively) to decide what I need to teach in upcoming minilessons and what needs-based instruction I need to provide.
- The entries help me uphold three of my core beliefs: I provide honest feedback, cultivate students' independence as readers, and push them as far as possible intellectually, analytically, and creatively.
- They hold students accountable for their in-class *and* outside-class reading. No more lists to fill out of what they read at home, no formulaic response sheets about that reading, no book reports, just an honest letter about what they've read that week. Hard to fake, and the letters include a lot more information.

The lit log section of the BLB is a powerhouse. You're there on the other end of the correspondence, a patient, wise blend of teacher, pen pal, book-loving cousin, paying attention to what the student says and then writing back in ways that make her feel understood as a person, appreciated for her quicksilver mind, celebrated as a learner.

Here's a typical exchange:

> Dear Mrs. Blauman,
>
> Right now I'm reading Lord of the Rings and Sky Horse for the second time. I'm really excited about reading The Tiger Rising. I really like book clubs. Are we going to do the packets after each chapter? I hope not. They're so boring. I mean, come on, I bet the class can think up 100 times as good questions, especially you! Anyway about Lord of the Rings, how many Black Riders are there? Frodo has seen them 4 times and I still don't know if it's one or two, etc. I have this feeling that the book told me the answer but I still don't get it. Do you know that feeling? Can you recommend any books for me to read at school? Since Christopher Paolini hasn't written the 4th book, I'm kind of stuck. By the way, do you have Among the Imposters? Oh, I forgot to tell you, thank you SO much for lending me Swindle. It's really, really good. Is it okay for me to check it out?
>
> Sincerely,
> Anna

> Dear Anna,
>
> You may check out any of my books—that's what they're there for. I'm not sure if I have *Among the Imposters*, but I'm almost done with *Found* by Haddix and it is TERRIFIC, plus I bought the book that follows it. Great mystery—not fantasy, but I think you'd enjoy it. And I'll buy the next book after *Swindle* so you can read that one too.
>
> I've forgotten how many Black Riders there were, but I think Tolkien does say. However, is that something super important to remember? Yes—I do that too—I don't always pay attention to every detail. I get wrapped up in the story.
>
> Sincerely,
> Mrs. Blauman
>
> P.S. Nope, no packets at the end of chapters.

Is Anna an advanced reader? Absolutely. Does she devour books? Yes—and sometimes she reads too quickly and misses things. However, as her reading teacher I know how she's doing. I know she is reading Tolkien at home. She and I both know it's a challenging book, so if she misses some details, that's okay. She is monitoring her own comprehension and checking with me! We are discussing books and authors, and she sees me as a reader. Anna is an avid fantasy reader and I am trying to nudge her into a few other genres. I also know what to work on with her when we confer—I'll discuss slowing down and savoring the book, point out that speed isn't always best. She didn't get the packets idea from me—that was what she was used to before coming to our class.

INTRODUCING THE LIT LOG

Reading response journals of any kind run the risk of becoming dullsville for you and the students if they are not introduced and sustained as places where students are to think—really think—about their reading and can feel trusted and safe enough to wonder, venture eclectic connections, and reveal ways in which something in a book echoes something in their life. A student better understands the bond between Daniel and his cat in *Smoky Night*, by Eve Bunting when the student has a cat too. A connection of bigger import—when a character's problem or loss matches the student's problem or loss—makes a deeper impression.

The day after I give my students their BLBs, I ask them to take them out again and open them to the lit log section.

"I'll bet you noticed how much paper is included in this section, didn't you? That's because we're going to be doing a lot of writing back and forth. If you turn the page, you're going to see a letter from me. I want you to read that right now." (See Figure 5.1.)

I read the letter out loud and then ask, "Do I ask you to summarize or retell the book?"

"No, you asked us to write about our thinking," Maddie says.

"That's because I want you to go deep into your mind. And if all you do is retell what you read, you're just giving me literal comprehension. Plus, I've read a lot of books, and if I'm just reading retellings, it's going to be really boring for me. When you write about your thinking and your questions, then I have more to write back to you about.

"I know this is something new for you, so I'm going to show you some great letters from kids I've had before and I'm going to be explicit in telling you what they're doing in the letters that makes them so great."

At this point, I share great examples and models from previous years. Technology is advancing so quickly I no longer have to make transparencies

September 00, 2010

Dear _________,

This section is your lit log, where you and I write letters back and forth about your reading. When you write me a letter, I want you to write down the title of the book you're reading and then tell me about *your thinking*. What I mean by *your thinking* is I want to know if you're enjoying the book and *why or why not.* I want to read about your questions, connections, predictions, and thoughts. I want to know how it's going—are you understanding? And of course, I'll write back!

Basically, this is a place for the two of us to talk about books, reading, and sometimes life! You can ask me questions, too. I'm looking forward to reading about your reading and also getting to know you as a student!

Please remember to use correct letter format. I'm including this letter at the front, so you can always refer to it!

Happy reading!

Sincerely,
Mrs. Blauman

Figure 5.1 My Lit Log Letter for Student BLBs

▶ THE NITTY-GRITTY

If you don't have models, write a letter yourself showing what you expect!

but can put pieces on the document camera or the SMART Board. I point out how the students always include the title and some form of thinking.

"Did you also notice that these examples are in correct letter format? I'm going to hold you to that. I need to see the date, the correct greeting, and *Sincerely* spelled correctly.

"Your letters are due on Fridays, but you can write them any time during the week. In fact, some of you may choose to write your lit log letter during independent reading, which is absolutely fine. If that's something you want to do, just take your BLB and a pencil along with the book you're reading when you settle in. I'd prefer that you do your letters in class, that way you're not hauling your BLB back and forth between school and home. It's really important that you have your BLB here every day, because we'll use it almost every day.

This also helps prevent BLBs from getting lost or damaged.

"Today, though, we're going to practice together. I'm going to have all of you write your first letter right now, so that I can take the letters home tonight and write back. You're going to write me about what you've been reading these last couple of weeks and how it's going. I know there's always one question that comes up, so I'm going to answer it right now. Someone always asks how long the letter needs to be. And you've probably already noticed that when you ask me questions like that I tend to answer, 'How long do you think?' And you know I expect you to do your best. But I'm going to set a minimum length for these letters. I expect you to write at least two-thirds of a page. Let's open to your first blank page and you can put a little mark two-thirds of the way down. That's the *minimum*. You can always write more.

"And finally, one more thing that always comes up when I hand these back. Sometimes kids ask why they have to write two-thirds of a page but my return letter isn't as long. Let me answer that by asking two other questions. How many letters do you have to write?"

"One."

"And how many do I have to write?"

"Twenty-five."

"Yep, so I think you can see why sometimes mine might be shorter. But if you write great questions and thoughts, then you'll probably get a longer letter from me. It all depends."

With that, the students start writing. This first go-round, I move through the room, double-checking letter form and content and whether students understand my expectations. Those who finish early begin reading independently.

BEST BOOKS

Here are some great picture books that introduce both literacy and the letter format:

Ada, Alma Flor. 1994. *Dear Peter Rabbit*. Fullerton, CA: Aladdin.

---. 1998. *Yours Truly, Goldilocks*. New York: Atheneum.

Christelow, Eileen. 2006. *Letters from a Desperate Dog*. New York: Clarion.

Cronin, Doreen. 2000. *Click, Clack, Moo. Cows That Type*. New York: Simon & Schuster.

---. 2002. *Giggle, Giggle, Quack*. New York: Simon & Schuster.

Danneberg, Julie. 2003. *First Year Letters*. Watertown, MA: Charlesbridge.

Teague, Mark. 2002. *Dear Mrs. LaRue: Letters from Obedience School*. New York: Scholastic.

---. 2004. *Detective LaRue: Letters from the Investigation*. New York: Scholastic.

James, Simon. 1996. *Dear Mr. Blueberry*. Fullerton, CA: Aladdin.

These books are also terrific for teaching the trait of voice in writing.

▶ THE NITTY-GRITTY

In Chapter 6, I discuss what the kids do when they walk in the door in the morning. On their desks are worksheets reviewing grammar and mechanics and geography that "warm up" their brains. We knock out basic skills in a short amount of time, no time wasted during the day. While the kids are warming up, I'm taking attendance, among other things. Returned BLBs always take precedence over warm-up worksheets!

GIVING FEEDBACK: RAISING THE LEVEL OF THINKING AND WRITING

I read and respond by the next day. The BLBs are waiting on students' desks the next morning when the kids walk in the door. Of course, my students read my letter *before* they do their warm-ups—which is exactly what I want.

Often these first entries tend to be literal. Even though I've showed them examples of higher-level thinking, most students still focus on *retelling or summarizing* their independent reading, because that's what they are used to. I use my return letters to nudge each child to go deeper.

When students' entries begin to move beyond the literal, I ask permission to share them with the class as "mentor letters." The more examples students see of what I expect, the more their own work improves. I'm explicit about *why* I'm sharing a particular piece and *exactly what* the student is doing in the writing that takes the entry to a deeper level. After sharing a few mentor letters, I invite students to help analyze why the examples are positive. And I'm very careful to use only *positive* examples of student work. This goes back to *trust*. If I'm asking the students to take incredible risks, they must *always* trust that I won't embarrass them.

I remove the names from papers even though they're being used as positive examples. I don't want to set up any child to be teased. In addition, I try to find examples of great work from *every* student throughout the year. A child feels special when her thinking is honored—a flush crosses her face when she sees her piece being used as a teaching tool.

ALIE AND ME

Let's track the letters in Alie's lit log through the year. Notice how text-based her first entry is (at this point in the year I'm not sure if she is really "making pictures in her head" or just repeating the comprehension verbiage).

> Dear Mrs. Blauman,
>
> I am reading The Curse of Ravenscourt, it's a Samantha mystery. This book is kind of scary because the author makes some sounds in the background. Samantha, Nellie, Jennie, and Bridget had to stay at Ravenscourt. While they were there weird things happen!

I've been reading this book for a while I'm almost done. I read a ton! I love to read! But I don't like to write very much. I love this year's class. I think reading is easy. When I read I get pictures in my head, if it is a good book. When I choose a book I read the first page. If I don't like the book I usually put the book down. I am also reading a kit mystery. I don't like it very much but I'm still reading it. It's about a writing report. I will be reading something different soon.

Sincerely,
Alie

Dear Alie,

If you're not enjoying the Kit book, why are you still sticking with it? I'm thrilled that you make pictures in your head when you read—that's a really important part of being a great reader! And you know—good readers are very often good writers! Maybe you just haven't realized what can happen when you write.

Sincerely,
Mrs. Blauman

It's obvious from Alie's letter that she's a writer—she just doesn't know it yet! I will build her up as a writer as we progress.

I really want to know why she's staying with a book she doesn't like. If I just tell her to drop it, she won't be thinking about or owning her independent reading. This is an opportunity for me to learn about her as a reader and nudge her to internalize herself as a reader. It's also an "aha" moment for me as a teacher—after reading Alie's letter and a few others, I know we need a whole-class minilesson on *why* we drop books and when it's okay to do so (there's a sample lesson in Chapter 3).

Compare Alie's first entry with what she's thinking in November (and see whether you can identify the comprehension strategy being focused on in class).

November 17

Dear Mrs. B,

In A Dog's Life I got so mad when George threw Bone and Squirrel out of the car! It makes me so sad when any animal gets hurt! The book keeps getting better and better. My questions are

Will Squirrel find Bone?

What happened to their mother?

My prediction is that their mom either got shot or she just left the puppies. Now that Squirrel is all alone, what's going to happen to her? How will she survive her life alone? I love this book but not how "Mine" [the name of the dog] died.

Write back soon.

Sincerely,
Alie

November 19

Dear Alie,

I love this book, too—I couldn't put it down the first time I read it—made me totally empathize with what it's like to be a stray—as I read I wondered *how* Ann M. Martin figured out or researched this book!

Sincerely,
Mrs. Blauman

It's obvious Alie is becoming more metacognitive and strategic in her reading and her thinking. A short response from me, but we're dialoguing about reading and our books. Notice that I use the word *empathize*—I never restrict my vocabulary in these letters. In fact, I use as many adult words as possible. I want to push my students as far as they can go every chance I get. Children who don't know a word I've written always ask what it means in the next letter.

Oh, the comprehension strategy was asking questions. Alie is asking questions and predicting the answers, and I can tell she is monitoring her comprehension. I also can tell she is interacting with the text. Although her letter is short, she demonstrates a lot of comprehension. Alie also knows that I know the story well, so she's not summarizing, she's writing about her *thinking*. Fabulous!

Now on to February. Notice the depth of Alie's response now.

February 10

Dear Mrs. B.,

I finished The Secret Garden! I absolutely loved it! I like how Mary and Colin both learned how to be kind and how to behave to each other and everyone else. Also, now I know what genre my book is from my book review. At first I thought it was fantasy but now I realize it's historical fiction. I wonder if Mary and her friends Colin, Martha, and Kickon ever fight after the story ends. I'll never know because Frances Hodgson Burnett no longer lives to write a second. Why was Colin so depressed all the time, he acts like every other person in the world is a servant to him. Mary was so nice to help him by reading to him every single day. I liked Mary's character better as the book went on because she learned to be more caring. I am so glad I read this book for my book review. It is awesome even though the characters are not very kind but it gets better!

Write back soon!

Sincerely,
Alie

February 12

Dear Alie,

Do you think some of your characters from your book were spoiled or entitled? That they didn't know how to be kind or even think of others? I love how you've identified the changes in character(s). That's what tends to make a book memorable!

Sincerely,
Mrs. B.

Alie is writing about what she wonders *after* the book ends. She also knows what genre it is (and mentions how her thinking changed as she read—fantasy to historical fiction) and facts about the author. She has synthesized in this letter, as her views about the characters demonstrate.

BOYS WRITE TOO

Eight of my male students were reading Gary Paulsen's *Hatchet* in their book club. Discussions were lively and in depth. Despite our book club norms, some of the boys talked over one another and not everyone got to share all his thinking.

Brett shares his thinking in the lit log letter below. He has noticed aspects of the book different from those the other boys have noticed. He has taken the questioning strategy to heart and interacts with everything Brian experiences in the story.

Dear Mrs. B,

<u>Hatchet</u> was amazing! Brian is really smart. And it's cool how you have to aim under the fish and what I thought was really weird was when Brian was getting the survival pack when he saw the pilot. It's weird how the fish were eating him and you could see his skull. And what is an Emergency Transmitter? Is it like a walky talky or something? And how can Brian hold his breath for so long? I have tons of questions. What book are we going to read next for book clubs? Are we going to have the same groups or different ones?

Sincerely,
Brett

Also notice the sensory image—he's used Paulsen's writing to picture the pilot in the lake.

Many of Brett's questions were answered in the book club meeting held after he wrote this, and the boys had quite a discussion about the pilot. Some of the group decided to stay together and read Paulsen's *Brian's Winter*; others, like Brett, decided to read something different.

PUSHING STUDENTS AS FAR AS THEY CAN GO

The lit log is also an important tool for my advanced students. The young lady who wrote the following entry is thinking way beyond grade level.

January 19

Dear Mrs. Blauman,

I enjoy <u>Esperanza Rising</u> so dearly. My favorite part of this book is when Esperanza's dad dies. I mean I'm not happy about her dad dying. (If I was [it would be someone] like Sudan Husane [sic] who's dead.) I mean I love the language: Esperanza's heart dropped. And then she started sobbing. I loved how the book didn't say her papa was dead until the next page. (Inferential.) I just could see Esperanza's face as Esperanza's heart "dropped." It's just so beautiful—the vineyard and how Esperanza and Miguel have their own flowers and how Miguel and Esperanza are on different sides of the river. It's just so beautiful.

Now that I've told you about what I think about <u>Esperanza Rising</u> I need to talk to you about my non-fiction project. I don't think there are any books out there about figure skating conflicting with mathematics. And if there are could you help me find one, maybe two? Please and thank you.

Love,
Rebecca

Dear Rebecca,

Your voice always seems to come through in your writing, and I have to chuckle when I read your letters! I'm thrilled, though, that you're noticing the language. *Esperanza Rising* is definitely full of sensory details.

What do you think of Esperanza now? Does it surprise you when she acts like a brat? Or do you understand it? In some ways I always thought she was spoiled, but under the circumstances I could understand why she reacts the way she does.

Sincerely,
Mrs. B.

P.S. I think your figure skating question has been taken care of.

Rebecca and I have already met about her nonfiction questions and books, hence the P.S. My letter addresses Rebecca both as a reader and a writer. Although the lit log is primarily about reading and I'm delighted she's internalized the inferring strategy, I still point out what she does so beautifully with her writing (and which can be the focus of a writing conference).

OWNING THE LESSON

I collect BLBs on Fridays, so I have time over the weekend to read and respond and get them back to students on Monday (Tuesday at the latest). It doesn't have to be Friday; it could be any day of the week. Or you could spread it out. One of my colleagues makes it manageable by collecting five BLBs per day—alphabetically, so the students know which day their book is due. What works best for you? How is your classroom (and your life!) organized so that you can find the time to respond to each child the way he deserves?

Do the lit logs take a lot of time? Yes. Absolutely. No way around it. I write twenty-five letters back to my students each week. However, I'm not grading book reports, I'm not correcting and recording worksheets—I'm corresponding about reading and thinking and what makes my kids tick! It's an essential part of the way I create the culture of our classroom and assess my students.

WHEN THE GOING GETS TOUGH

Sometimes students have a hard time showing their thinking. We all have students who don't yet think in a reflective way. Susie is being very honest in the lit log letter that follows (you can tell from her first sentence!). It's already October and I have a lot of work to do. Where most of my students at least comprehend at the literal level, Susie hasn't learned how to interact with the text. Her letter reads like most of her stories—disjointed retellings of cartoons or TV shows, which are some important things in her life.

> Dear Mrs. Blauman,
>
> I'm really not thinking of anything. Oh! I finished a book called <u>7 × 9 = Trouble</u>. Was a blast!!! It's about a boy named William. He had trouble with his math problems. Like with his 3s. He was terrible at his 3s. Then he pasted [sic] his test on 3s. Now came the 4s. He studied until he couldn't study anymore. Guess what? He pasted his 4s. Then he pasted his 5s. Then came the 6s. 6s are harsh. But he pasted his sixes. Then came 7s. The 7s were like 2 or 3 chapters. Then there was a hamster named Siggles. In chapter 8 siggles cage door was loose and the hamster got out. Just to let you know there was 10 really long chapters. Anyways Siggles was his good luck charm. But he did get pasted his 8s, 9s, 10s and 11s. But his 12s were really hard. He tried and tried then one day after school he pasted and guess what? He forgot about his little brother. But William got his ice cream cone. Then he ran down to the kindergarten room then guess what he heard squeaking. It was Sqiggles. Then he got two ice cream cones. Then his dad called the school and said to his teacher "Did he pass?" The teacher said, "Yes, He did." Then he got a hamster then he also got to take home Squillgs again. Now squiglles and the other hamster is happy and so is William. <u>7 × 9 = Trouble</u> was great! See ya later,
>
> Sincerely,
> Susie

Whew! Susie's letter sounds like a student talking rapid fire, no? Does this letter reflect comprehension? She knows the main character's name. She knows the problem; she knows some events and the solution. Could she have gotten most of that from skimming through the book? Absolutely. I need to check in with Susie regularly, have her read a section out loud, then tell me what she's thinking about that specific section. When I sit with her in a conference I need her to give me the nitty-gritty of what she's just read—sum it up in one or two sentences. She's also in a lot of needs-based groups, both reading and writing. In writing we're working on "zooming in"—picking one thing and then describing it in detail. For example, I might highlight just one sentence in her letter and then have her write me a new paragraph explaining just that topic.

What would you write back to Susie? Would you write a lot, or just nudge her and then meet with her in a conference? Because we had been writing back and forth for over a month, I knew that my letters made less of an impact than conferring. So after I wrote this to her, I made sure to have a conference with her that day.

To Learn More

See Barry Lane's *Reviser's Toolbox* (2003) for more on zooming in.

Dear Susie,

First of all—aargh! Reading is *thinking*, so I hope you were thinking as you read. It's obvious that you were because you were able to *retell* parts of the book. That tells me that you were reading at a *literal* level. Now we need to deepen your reading—that's what I mean by writing to me about your *thinking*. What connections are you making? What questions are you asking as you're reading? Any predictions? In your next letter to me, I want you to include at least one of those.

Sincerely,
Mrs. Blauman

By January, Susie was writing letters filled with questions—at the literal level, but questions nonetheless. And yes, she was still writing the way she talks, but with more focus on details. Sometimes it's the baby steps!

Constructed Responses

PURPOSE

I added this section in the face of growing pressure for students to perform well on standardized tests. The first year my fourth graders took the Colorado Student Assessment Program (CSAP) test, they were asked to write "constructed responses" to reading selections and writing prompts. They had no idea what that term meant, and I wasn't allowed to explain. They did the best they could, as I watched in frustration. As their teacher, it became my responsibility to

To Learn More

Two helpful books about standardized tests are *Put Thinking to the Test* (Conrad et al. 2008) and *A Teacher's Guide to Standardized Reading Tests* (Calkins et al. 1998).

explain the term and have them practice creating constructed responses. There are numerous test-prep practice books with formulaic prompts galore, but I wanted short, authentic practice for my students, so I added this section to the BLB.

CLASSROOM EXAMPLE: CONNECTING TO CURRENT EVENTS

A constructed reading response often includes summarizing or answering questions by providing specific examples from the text. Both are great skills for students to have.

▶ THE NITTY-GRITTY

You can't afford newspapers or magazines for your kids? With the Internet at your fingertips, there are always applicable articles ready to download and copy. They're only a click away. And why not invite the kids in on the search? Have them pull up articles they think will be interesting or relevant to the class. That could be a classroom job!

My school subscribes to *Time for Kids*—each child gets a copy. The magazine arrives weekly, and I weave the articles into our reading workshop in a variety of ways. Sometimes we read an article together; often I use one in small guided reading groups; other times students read an article independently. (There are numerous other magazines, such as *National Geographic* and *Weekly Reader*, with classroom editions.)

When students are familiar with the format and we've practiced summarizing in class, I introduce constructed responses.

"Remember the day I passed out your BLBs and Reed commented that he didn't get what this section was all about? Well, we're going to find out today. *Constructed response* is a term you need to be familiar with, because you're going to see it on the CSAP test. The test asks for a lot of constructed responses. I could ask you to tell me what you think it means, but I'm just going to explain it to you. I know you understand what it means to respond—you're always responding to my questions. In this sense, it means to write in response to something you've read or a specific prompt. The word *constructed* means you build it—you make it, actually write it. In writing a constructed response, you often have *to summarize*, which is a skill you need to master by fourth grade. We've practiced that—what's in a summary?"

"Your lead sentence should be the main idea of what you've read," states Emma.

"But it should catch the reader's attention," Naomi reminds us.

"Awesome! You're both right. What else?"

"At least three details," Erin adds.

"But it's even better if you explain the details—that makes it more interesting," says Geoffrey. Hooray for Geoffrey!

"I'm so glad you piggybacked on Erin's comment—you both are on the money. And remember, it's even better if you can lift those details right from the piece to prove your point.

"Can you have more than three?" I ask.

"Yes, and you need to end with a conclusion or a sentence that lets the reader know you're done. Those are the hardest for me," acknowledges Jonny.

"Great thinking—and we have all those down on the anchor chart on summarizing, in case you forget!" (See Figure 5.2.)

"Now I want you to take the feature article in *Time for Kids* on Haiti and open your BLB to the constructed response section. Write down the date and the title

THE LANGUAGE OF LEARNING

From this discussion, it's obvious I've modeled summaries (I highlight the lines/detail I want to include) and my students have practiced writing them. I use the word *lift* to describe transferring actual words, phrases, or sentences from the text to the summary or response. Students are often required to explain their answers on standardized tests "using examples from the text." Using the text to support an answer is a precursor of footnotes!

▶ THE NITTY-GRITTY

I set the fifteen-minute limit because our testing is timed and students need to develop the stamina to be able to meet a time constraint.

Figure 5.2 Summarizing Anchor Chart Connecting to Current Events

SUMMARY ANCHOR CHART (CONSTRUCTED RESPONSE)

Lead Sentence
(Main idea to grab the reader's attention)

- Detail
  – support
- Detail
  – support
- Detail
  – support

Concluding Sentence (Wraps up the paragraph so your reader knows you're done)

Students become used to seeing this graphic organizer; it represents the basic outline of a paragraph and reminds them to indent. For this Summary Anchor Chart, the main idea sentence comes right after the indentation–as a "lead" or topic sentence. Then come the detail sentences, with their support, and the concluding sentence.

of the article. Then for the next fifteen minutes I want you to summarize the article. I'm only giving you fifteen minutes because I think you should be able to finish in that amount of time."

The students get to work. On this first constructed response, I want to see what the kids are capable of—establish a baseline—so I stay out of the way as much as possible. The next day, I'll use the document camera to display strong responses, being as explicit as possible, so that the students will write even better summaries next time. Below is Josh's first go at a constructed response. Since we waited until midway through the year to begin these, he already has a grasp of what makes good writing.

> Did you know that Haiti got hit with an earthquake? People say that Haiti got hit with a 7.0 quake that ripped through the country's capital. The earthquake that hit Port-au-Prince was the biggest to hit the region in 240 years. More than 40 after-shocks including a magnitude 5.9 tremor last week. The disaster crushed homes, buildings, and roads. 200,00 people had died and 250,000 people got injured in this insident [sic]. The government gave over a lot of food and money. The quake left over 1.5 million people homeless. After the quake most people are living in tents to survive. It will take years to rebuild Haiti and people are trying to help. Are you?

OWNING THE LESSON

While constructed responses are not my students' favorite things to do, they definitely made a difference in test results. Spending fifteen minutes of class time once a week practicing summarizing and synthesizing well-written articles about current events eliminates surprises when the test rolls around. And the kids become really good at it.

▶ QUESTIONS TO THINK ABOUT

- What curricular or standardized testing expectations are essential for my students to practice?
- How can they practice authentically for short periods of class time and still become independent and proficient at these skills?

Book Clubs

PURPOSE

Chapter 9 discusses the details of managing and setting up book clubs. Overwhelmingly, students say that book clubs are their favorite part of the day. I love book clubs because I get to eavesdrop and observe amazingly rich, in-depth conversations about books. My kids put Oprah's book club to shame!

I offer the students a variety of ways to hold their thinking in preparation for book clubs. Some prefer writing on sticky notes, others use bookmarks, still others write in the book club section of their BLB. In addition, students use the book club section of the BLB to reflect on their book club meetings and the progress they are making, which makes it part of student assessment.

CLASSROOM EXAMPLE

Below, Alie holds her thinking before meeting with her book club to discuss *Esperanza Rising*, by Pam Muñoz Ryan (the headings are Alie's; I didn't add them for the book!).

Questions

Why did Esperanza's mother agree to marry the uncle?

Will they ever get to California?

Will she find out?

Will Esperanza stop acting spoiled?

Inferences

Women were not allowed to own property.

Her attitude will change.

The uncle will do something bad to the mom or Esperanza.

Vocab

Correspondence

Indebted

Vocab (cont.)

Waif

Pining

Two things I want to bring up

It made me mad when the house burned down and when the mom agreed to marry the uncle.
Life was so different back then.

And here are Alie's thoughts the following week:

Questions

Will Esperanza like L.A. very much?

Will Esperanza and Isabel become best friends?

Will Esperanza keep her kind attitude?

When will Esperanza's mom get sick?

Inferences

Esperanza does not like Marta.

Esperanza hasn't done many chores.

Vocab

Groggily

Valise

Two things I want to bring up

Esperanza is changing her attitude.

Marta is really mad.

I had Alie share her pages with her group as an example of organizing one's thoughts, and a couple of members began using the same format. I also encouraged her to record the page number by the vocabulary words, so that the group could turn to that page and read the word in context. Although many of Alie's questions can be answered yes or no, they will trigger deep discussions in the book group.

PAUL EXPLORES HIS BOOK CLUB THINKING IN HIS LIT LOG

Paul wasn't satisfied just holding his thinking in the book club section of his BLB, he wanted to correspond with me about his thinking. He wanted my feedback in addition to the feedback he received from his group.

January 8

Dear Mrs. B,

I now know how you get a heart attack, so you don't have to tell me. Today is the day of book club meeting and I want to know about Guts. I expect it is not a sequel to Hatchet. Anyway, Hatchet is really good, and he has now been there for forty-six days. More than a month! Also I learned something new, I did not know there were any turtles in Canada. One of the most important things is that book clubs are helping me choose better books and it improves my writing.

Sincerely,
Paul

January 12

Dear Paul,

I'm really fascinated by your last sentence. I understand how book clubs might be helping you choose better books—and I'm betting that you're enjoying getting to talk about your reading with others. What I'm curious about is how it improves your writing? Can you explain that a little more?

And how did you find out about heart attacks? I'm glad you're enjoying *Hatchet*!

Sincerely,
Mrs. B

January 15

Dear Mrs. B,

I'm going to answer three questions:

How are book clubs helping with my writing?

Reading books like Hatchet improves my writing because great authors like Paulsen are giving me good examples on Quick Writes or President Paragraphs. His great describing helps very much.

Where did I find out about heart attacks?

A couple of group meetings ago you told us about heart attacks and how they clog blood.

You wrote In Reflections about my reading in my old school and the books that I read took two months. We actually read only two books in my old school, and they were Stone Fox and Sarah, Plain and Tall. We had to answer questions after each chapter, and that really slowed us down.

Sincerely,
Paul

January 16

Dear Paul,

And I'll bet those were really easy books for you. I know both of them and I'd say that you could have finished them in a week or two.

Do you find that you're thinking differently now that you're in book clubs? I also want to push your thinking a bit more—I love how you say that reading great authors like Paulsen pushes your writing. Can you be specific and explain *how*? What are you doing differently or what are you trying?

Sincerely,
Mrs. B

In Kids' Words

I liked book clubs because it made homework something fun to do and not "Oh no, not homework!" It was fun because the books were interesting and fun to read.

—Matthew

Reflections

PURPOSE

So often in education we tend to rush through the material in order to "cover it." At times, it feels as if we're attempting to teach "a mile wide, but an inch deep." (Artemis Ward used this wonderful phrase to describe the Platte River.) When I followed my students from fourth to fifth grade, I was always amazed when I brought up a concept from the previous year and they looked at me with blank faces, as if they'd never heard of it before! I knew I'd taught it. When knowledge is only an inch deep, the potential for retaining it isn't good. However, when we teach a mile deep, children retain the learning.

Taking time to linger and reflect reinforces learning: Students are able to think about their processes—their struggles and achievements. I use the reflection section as a quick check of how students used their time during class. It may be as simple as stopping the workshop five or ten minutes early and asking the students to write a few sentences about the choices they made that morning—how it went, and if there is anything they need to change. I read their responses quickly while I'm answering lit log letters, assessing how students view their use of time compared with how I do, and then I touch base in a conference if there's a discrepancy.

The reflection section is also for stepping back and thinking about the bigger units of study. For example, I may ask students to reflect on their book club, their research project, or even their progress in reading and writing. At the end of a trimester, I may have students evaluate their progress and write how they think they measure against the standards. How would they grade themselves? There are no secrets in my classroom, so their self-assessment should be fairly close to how I assess them as readers and writers. Over the years, I've noticed that my stronger students tend to be harder on themselves. My struggling students tend to inflate their ability and their progress, and I can then talk about their academic level and help them set goals in a conference. Sharing these reflections with parents allows them to see how their child views herself as a learner.

CLASSROOM EXAMPLE

I was going to be teaching my fourth graders in fifth grade the following year, so besides asking them to evaluate their progress this year, I asked for their advice for next year. Here's Ryan's reflection:

> June 8
>
> I have gotten so much better at reading and writing because Mrs. Blauman makes it fun for me. I didn't like writing before this year, but now I love it and I'm good at it. I have really been thinking about Holes the book and whenever I see a deep hole or someone digging, I remember Stanley. My growth has been huge this year. It has gone by so fast. I have learned how to know what book is right for me. I have learned how to talk in book cubs. I want to do them next year. My writing is great. I now can write a book whenever I want to. I couldn't even write three pages of a story, but now I can write five pages. I still have a weakness in ending a piece but I hope I will get better next year.
>
> Mrs. Blauman, I think we need more book shops so we don't have to go to the library every time we're done with a book. We need more reading time. We need more book clubs, too.

Below, Anna reflects on her progress during the second trimester. She automatically connects reading and the writing, sees it as one.

> For me, I'm still trying to get to my goals, reading and writing. I may have changed and grown as a reader, but I still have the problem of reading too fast. I think it helps when you do minilessons because it makes me want to look for great verbs and that stuff I can use in my writing.

Here's Carolyn's assessment of her second-trimester progress:

> I think I am growing in reading in so many ways like I have been reading like a writer and finding phenomenal words. So for my grade I think I am between an A and a B, so in between advanced and proficient. I have been finishing a lot more books now because of book clubs. Why book clubs are helping me is that I am setting goals for how far I have to read and saying which day to try to finish it all. I have changed in a lot of ways like I said, but I have been really proud of myself for changing a ton!

My reading goals are different for me now since I have changed like I said I want to read faster (well a little bit like that) but I have been finishing a ton of books (also because book clubs have been helping me!). I also think that the lit log letters are helping me because I can talk to you about questions in my own book.

And finally, Micha's:

I think I would be between an A and a B because I feel I'm getting more metacognitive and understanding more and more. Book clubs have helped me so much. I think BLBs have helped too because we get your feedback.

I have also grown from minilessons and when you print out pieces and we work the words we don't know. I have reached my goals to put word power words in my writing. When I read picture books and find a word that I like I write it down when I wouldn't before.

When I read these reflections I know my students are reading, writing, and thinking. Look at the quality of the writing and how they use what they've learned about powerful language. These students are making connections and becoming independent.

OWNING THE LESSON

▶ QUESTIONS TO THINK ABOUT

- What do I want my students to internalize?
- When do I want feedback?
- Have I tried something new and am I truly curious how it went? (Ask your students. You honestly have to want their answers and they have to know you do.)
- How can I check myself? Will it inform my instruction?

The BLB as an Assessment Tool

"How do you grade the book lover's book?" Teachers ask me that a lot. First and foremost, I use the BLB as an assessment tool to drive my instruction for each student. I use it to inform my decisions regarding whole-group instruction, small needs-based groups, and individual conferences—to meet my kids' needs.

But I also use the BLB as a tool to mark progress toward meeting the state standards. Are students reading at, above, or below grade level? Literal or inferential comprehension? How is each student using comprehension/thinking strategies on her own? The BLB provides mounds of data. Even better, my students articulate their progress in the reflection section.

But how do I turn this into a grade? That's a tough one, because reading is so hard to quantify.

The vocabulary section is easy. Three words a week is the minimum. Do three well, that's a B. To receive an A, students have to go above and beyond.

Minilessons and lit logs? I hate to quantify these entries, because they're about *quality and depth of response* (which again are reflected in the standards). So how about all or nothing? Complete it to expectations—10 points; no work—0 points. This goes for independent reading, too. Read and follow norms—10 points; mess around, 0 points. Easy to keep track of and cut-and-dried for the students. At the end of grading periods, it's easy to turn these numbers into percentages.

Ultimately you have to work out the grading issue for yourself. What are your reporting guidelines? What are you required to report on? The BLB is the perfect tool for ranking a student's progress against standards—you have the data to support each child's progress.

Final Thoughts

Now that you've had a chance to walk through the BLB, what sections will work for you and your students? You don't have to do them all. Your BLB might simply be minilessons, a lit log, and the books I've read list. That would be a start. How do you envision interweaving reading and writing in your room? How can the BLB help you do this? Is there anything I missed that you think you'd like to try? Make the BLB your own! Remember, it's okay to start small; it gives you room to grow.

Now, what else is in place in my literacy classroom? The BLB is the foundation for much of our reading and writing work and holds our thinking about it in one place, but it doesn't end there. A lot more reading and writing happens throughout the day. Chapter 6 imagines what a workshop might look like in your room. Turn the page. Take a peek.

CHAPTER 6

Making Every Minute Count

When teachers visit my classroom, my colleague Chryse Hutchins (coauthor of *7 Keys to Comprehension* [2003] with Susan Zimmermann) facilitates the lab visits, asking them afterward to describe what they noticed. They often interlock the fingers of both hands, unable to find words that capture what they've seen as aptly as this gesture does. *Seamless* is the adjective Chryse uses, and I confess it's pretty apt. But it took me more than twenty-five years of practice to get to this point.

In this chapter, I show you how to pull all the elements of your reading and writing workshop together into one seamless literacy workshop. The secret is *time*. How to use it. How to feel comfortable spending one day entirely on reading, knowing you'll do writing the next. Daring to spend a few days on writing, confident the kids' reading won't be compromised. You can make every minute count. Forget the flowery ideal of writers writing like mini–Eudora Weltys or reading like pint-sized Rhodes scholars—if we squander the minutes of the day, 'tain't gonna happen.

To make my classroom work, I have to sustain all the principles and practices of the foundational literacy lessons and classroom expectation lessons in Chapters 2 and 3, which set students on a course toward independence, and establish critical rituals and routines so that time in the workshop is very well spent.

How Do I Set Up the Literacy Block?

Teachers are tied to scheduling. Sometimes we control our days, other times our schedule is dictated to us. We're currently caught in a climate in which we are expected to cover more, more effectively, often with fewer resources and less time. Richard Allington (2001) observes, "[Classroom teachers] need uninterrupted time to teach. Kids need time to learn. To read. To write. Uninterrupted learning time" (39). That's why it's imperative to make every minute count. Gone are the days when I could read alongside my students to model what good readers do. Now I model myself as a reader by holding up the books and texts I'm reading outside school. I have to make every minute count.

When laying out your day, start with the blocks of time you have. Allot an hour for reading and an hour for writing, minimum. Sure, you can get it all covered in fifty-minute blocks, but you're going to feel rushed. You want your kids to linger in their learning. If they are going to go deep with their thinking, you have to build in time to linger, reflect, *think*. Do the two hours need to snug up next to each other? No. It's nice when reading and writing flow together, but it isn't necessary. There are still ways to create connections across the day that tie the reading and writing workshops together. (In my example of a typical day in my classroom, my reading and writing workshops aren't consecutive hours.)

WHAT IT USED TO LOOK LIKE

Twenty-seven years ago when I first joined Denver's Public Education and Business Coalition (PEBC), our learning was centered on writing and bringing the writing workshop into our classrooms. For one hour each day, I conducted a writing workshop: an initial ten-minute minilesson, thirty or forty minutes spent writing/conferring, the final ten minutes usually spent gathered around the author's chair. We pushed kids to write, write, write—without a lot of direct instruction on how to make the writing better. The act of writing was celebrated in and of itself. Kids were writing and publishing and telling stories and it was meaningful.

Then the PEBC branched into reading. We dug into the reading comprehension strategies (which we now call *thinking strategies*), and I taught the students how to be strategic and metacognitive about their reading and their comprehension. (Many of the lessons from Chapters 2 and 3 evolved from this work.) I watched my students become better readers and I watched their test scores improve (bottom line, we have to remain data driven). But best of all, I watched my students learn to love to read and write.

The natural progression was to tie reading and writing together. We researched how comprehension strategies were reflected in writing, how writers wrote, how to move back and forth between reading and writing, and how to make the connections clear for the students.

That's how I got where I am. I took one step at a time. Taking the lessons I was comfortable doing and pushing myself to go a little farther, then a little farther than that, then even farther. And that's what I do with my students—start them where they're comfortable and push them a little farther, then a little farther than that, then stretch them as far as they can go. That's what I recommend you do with this book—implement lessons and ideas a little at a time.

A TYPICAL DAY

Every year my schedule is different. Here's what my day looked like last year:

8:00–9:30	Literacy
9:30–10:15	Specials (gym, music, art)
10:15–11:30	Math (students leave my classroom and regroup by ability level)
11:30–12:15	Lunch and recess
12:15–12:30	Read-aloud
12:30–2:30	Literacy, science, or social studies

Luckily, I teach in a building and a district that are committed to giving teachers long, uninterrupted blocks of time. And yes, I use the word *literacy* instead of *reading* and then *writing*. However, you could insert *reading* (or *reading workshop*) in the 8:00–9:30 block and break the 12:30–2:30 block into *writing* (or *writing workshop*) followed by science and social studies on alternate days.

▶ CONSIDER THIS

What does your day look like? Are there ways to manipulate your schedule so that you can build in large blocks of time?

TO LEARN MORE

See these books:

Tovani, Chris. 2000. *I Read It, but I Don't Get It: Comprehension Strategies for Adolescent Readers*. Portland, ME: Stenhouse.

Allen, Patrick. 2009. *Conferring: The Keystone of Reader's Workshop*. Portland, ME: Stenhouse.

Robb, Laura. 2010. *Teaching Middle School Writers: What Every English Teacher Needs to Know*. Portsmouth, NH: Heinemann.

I also have the luxury of keeping my students with me throughout the day except for math and special areas. In many schools, students regroup for each content area—one teacher for science, one for literacy, one for math, one for social studies. If that's your reality, you can still conduct reading and writing workshops; it just means getting to know a whole lot more students (and reading a lot more papers). This is why middle school and high school teachers often abandon the workshop approach, but students with separate teachers for each subject deserve the benefits of a workshop too.

CHILDREN WITH SPECIAL NEEDS

You may also be asking, "What about special needs students? Do they remain in the classroom or get pulled out?" I've taught both ways. Each year, the timing and scheduling differ depending on the students and their needs. In any case, whether the students pulled out have an Individualized Education Program (IEP), are part of a Response to Intervention (RTI) program, or have English as their second language (ESL) (ever notice how much educational jargon consists of acronyms?), if I have set a solid foundation at the beginning of the year, these students know how our classroom operates. They leave and when they return they pick up on what they're supposed to do because they know the routine. I do make sure I don't conduct whole-class minilessons when students are out of the room. I want all my students with me for direct instruction. Are there times when students don't want to leave? Absolutely. But the reality is, we all have students who need extra help or remediation or sometimes accelerated instruction and have to leave our class to get it. Making the transition as smooth as possible is key.

Each year I take my schedule and any mandates (the math block, for example) and make a generic schedule for the day. I don't fill in the minutiae (spelling, planners, etc.). These daily decisions are reflected on the schedule on the whiteboard in my classroom. (For more on yearlong planning and overviews, see Chapter 1.)

The important thing is to carve out uninterrupted blocks of time for literacy. Kids are savvy; we shouldn't underestimate them. If we have to stop in the middle of a lesson in the morning, I know we can pick up where we left off when we return in the afternoon. I give myself permission to teach well and deep and make it meaningful rather than try to "cover" everything and in the process allow nothing to stick!

Setting Up Reading Workshop

An hour each day is optimal, but if you have less, take it and push for more. Predictability is a key component, but how the hour (or the time you have) is broken out needs to be flexible. Time for minilessons, think-alouds, and modeling will differ depending on the length of the book or text and the depth of the discussion. Questions teachers often want answered are "How do I fit it all in?" and "How do I balance working with individuals and working with groups?" Guided reading is mandated for some teachers, and they grapple with how to combine this program's guidelines with teaching strategic thinking skills. As I said at the beginning, I'm offering a framework, which you will adapt to fit your needs.

This	**Versus That**
• Classroom library has a rich supply of books and literature organized for student accessibility.	• Basals and leveled textbooks are stacked and waiting for your arrival.
• Groupings are fluid—needs-based groups, individual conferences, differentiated instruction.	• Leveled groupings don't change; students progress in lockstep with the rest of their group (kids are smart—they know which group is which).
• Students self-select reading material for book clubs at a variety of levels.	OR • One size fits all; all students in class are reading the same textbook.
• Routine is definite but flexible—majority of the time is spent in meaningful, authentic reading and writing; student choice and independence are valued and apparent.	• Hour-long block split into thirds: While you are working with one group (on the lesson from the teacher's guide, complete with script), a second group is working on skill sheets or answering questions (either in a workbook or on a handout) about their reading, and the third group is at activity centers. The groups rotate every twenty minutes.
• A spirit of classroom community and student independence is evident; students hold themselves and their classmates accountable.	• You're constantly putting out behavioral "fires" (could it be because students are bored?).
• Students have choice and buy-in.	• Class is predictable but with absolutely no choice.

WHAT IT LOOKS LIKE

I wish I could tell you that every day in a reading workshop looks the same, but if I did I'd be lying. My reading workshop changes as we focus on a series of specific comprehension strategies. When I introduce a strategy, we spend a lot more time on group work as I model. As the students become more adept at the strategy, I gradually incorporate more independence so there is less whole-group work. By the time we are finishing up a strategy, my minilessons are extremely short—usually just a quick status of the class for accountability. This progression and evolution are shown in Figures 6.1 through 6.4.

The pyramid in Figure 6.1 represents the typical gradual release strategy. At the top of the pyramid, you are doing most of the work, modeling thinking. Many teachers do the majority of their strategy instruction here, and students remain dependent on them. The goal is to get your kids working independently, so this stage should last only a couple days to a week. In the middle of

Figure 6.1 Typical Gradual Release Strategy

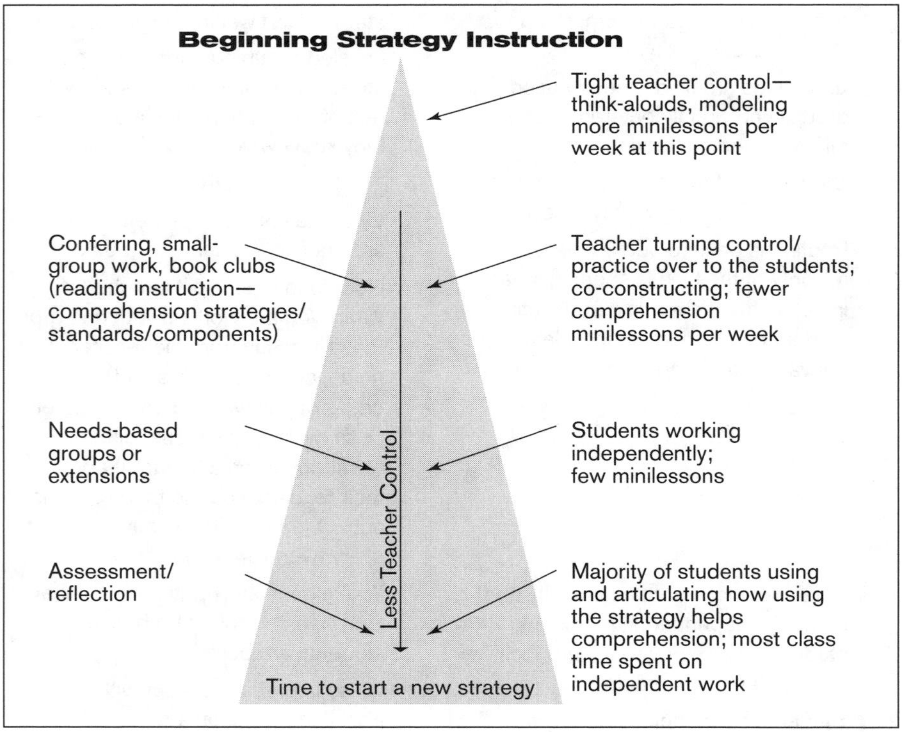

the pyramid, you are co-constructing learning, releasing responsibility to the kids, while monitoring and assessing. A perfect example is when my students are working in the minilesson section of their book lover's book while I'm teaching. We're in it together.

As students become more independent (the bottom of the pyramid), very little of the workshop time is spent on minilessons; students are working independently most of the time. Where am I? Conferring or pulling together needs-based groups. When the majority of the class is using a strategy independently, it's time to move on to another strategy (or in the case of writing, to another unit of study).

While the comprehension strategies are intertwined, when you start out it's more manageable to choose one strategy and teach it well. Figure 6.2 shows how that might look in a classroom. Choose a strategy, model it, co-construct learning, and release responsibility to the kids. An important point to remember is that you must assess your students' knowledge prior to starting a study. If they already know and use the strategy well, move on to another.

Figure 6.3 captures how you match your instruction to your students' needs. What background knowledge do they possess when they enter your

Figure 6.2 Comprehension Strategies Intertwined

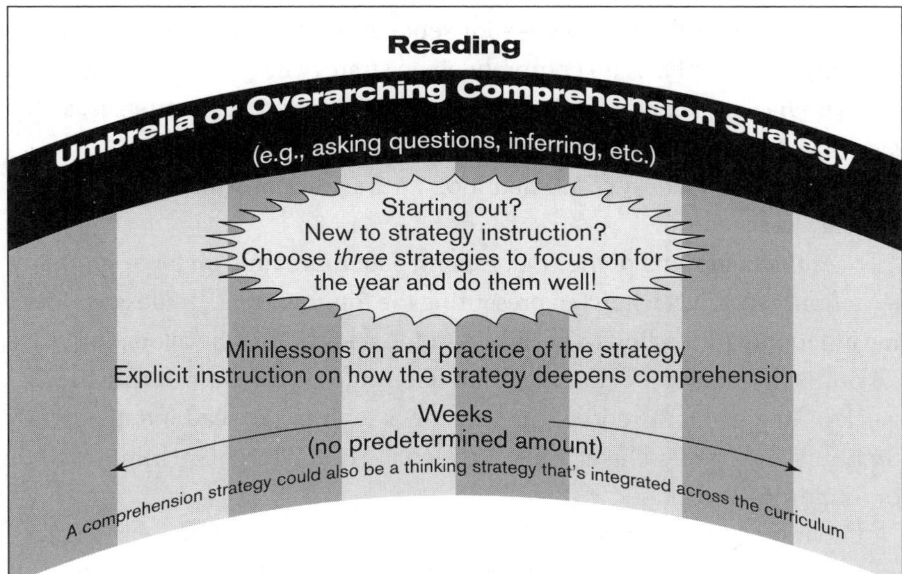

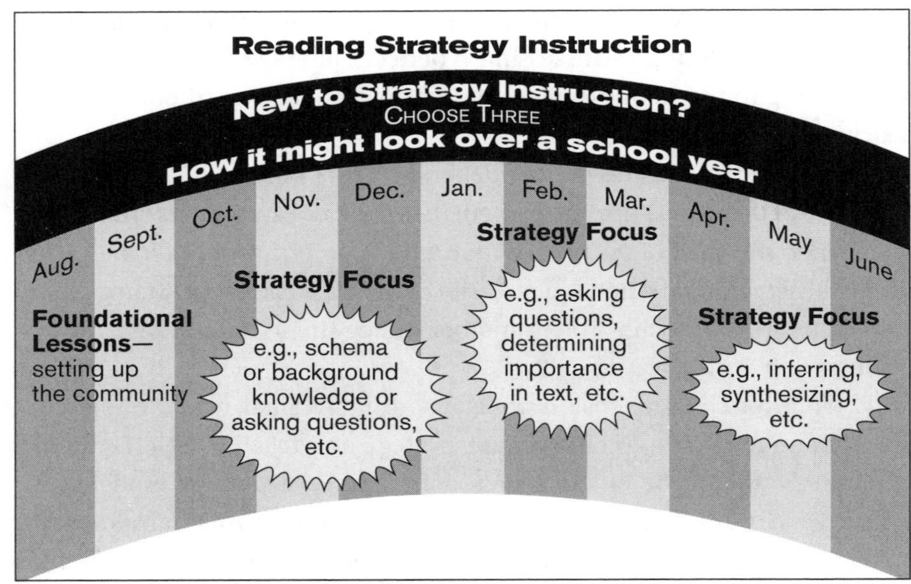

Figure 6.3 Reading Strategy Instruction

class? What strategies do they know? Which strategies will help them improve as readers? Use your students to guide your instruction. Remember, start small and build. As the strategies become part of your repertoire, you will find yourself teaching them all year—not separating them. If your school has a buildingwide emphasis on comprehension strategy instruction, you will find that you have to spend less time instructing the individual strategies, as the kids have background knowledge.

Figure 6.4 takes a combined look at the gradual release method and strategy instruction.

At the beginning of the year, I spend a lot more time on large-group instruction, especially when I'm presenting the foundational minilessons. Also, for independent reading to be successful, I need to start by allocating small amounts of time for it—no more than ten or fifteen minutes during the first week of school. By the end of the year, my students can read independently for hours, but I generally set aside between thirty and forty-five minutes three or four times a week.

While my students are reading independently, I am either working with small groups or conducting individual conferences. My small-group work is

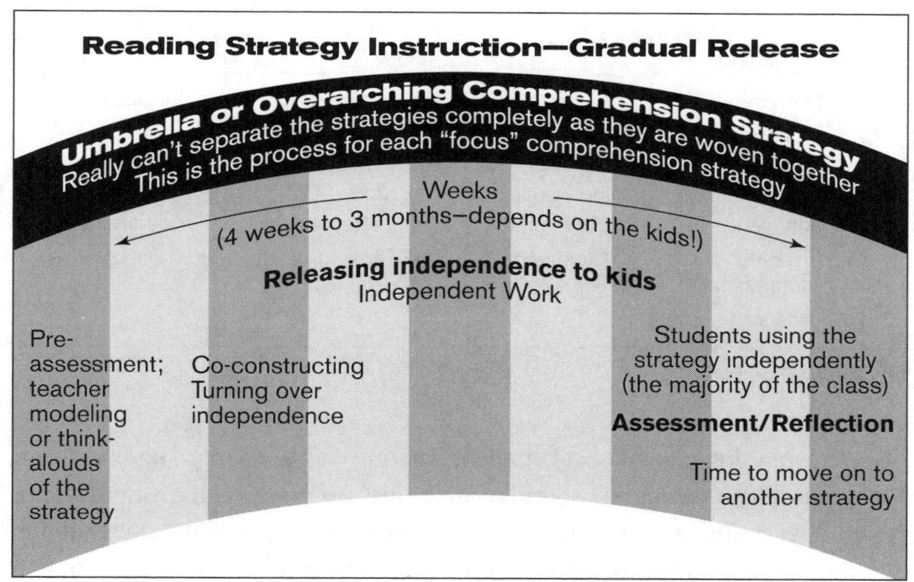

Figure 6.4 Combined Gradual Release Method and Reading Strategy Instruction

what I call "guiding the reading" and is usually needs based (at all academic levels). The groups are fluid and change depending on students' needs. However, my struggling students, who tend to need more direct instruction/remediation, meet with me at least once a week.

Nevertheless, each day has some predictability and is broken into three parts.

- *Focus lesson.* This could be a minilesson, or I might simply take a status of the class for accountability purposes. At the beginning of a unit of study, there may be days when the focus lesson takes up pretty much the entire reading workshop.
- *Independent practice.* Most often students read independently while I work directly with students individually or in small groups.
- *Closing moments.* To ensure accountability, I introduce some sort of closure activity. It may be peer conferences or individual reflection. It can take two minutes, ten minutes, twenty minutes, depending on the activity.

One option for a weeklong schedule is shown in Figure 6.5; again it's just a frame! I tend to spend more time conferring, because I can teach each child

Monday	Tuesday	Wednesday	Thursday	Friday
• Minilesson • Independent reading/ individual conferences • Closure	• Minilesson • Independent reading/small-group instruction (varies as the year progresses) • Closure	• Minilesson • Independent reading/ individual conferences • Closure	• Minilesson • Independent reading/small-group instruction • Closure	• Minilesson • Independent reading/ individual conferences • Closure

Figure 6.5 Overarching Weekly Organizational Chart

directly what she needs. However, there's no one way to do this. Depending on the needs of the students, I spend more or less time on small-group instruction. I spend time at the beginning of the year getting to know my students and their needs before I decide what my overarching weekly organization will look like.

To Learn More

Fletcher, Ralph, and JoAnn Portalupi. 2001. *Writing Workshop: The Essential Guide*. Portsmouth, NH: Heinemann.

Graves, Donald. 1994. *A Fresh Look at Writing*. Portsmouth, NH: Heinemann.

Ray, Katie Wood. 1999. *Wondrous Words*. Urbana, IL: National Council of Teachers of English.

Ray, Katie Wood, with L. Laminack. 2001. *The Writing Workshop: Working Through the Hard Parts (And They're All Hard Parts)*. Urbana, IL: National Council of Teachers of English.

Setting Up Writing Workshop

Unlike reading workshop, my writing workshop has a more predictable weekly schedule throughout the week. It is divided into the three sections suggested by many of the experts in the field of teaching writing (Graves 1994; Fletcher and Portalupi 2001; Routman 2005; Ray 2001).

- Minilesson or focus lesson (including status of the class)
- Independent work/practice
- Closure (including sharing)

Again, the amount of time spent in these three areas changes depending on where we are in a unit of study. When I'm launching a study on writing, there is more whole-group time, but as I release responsibility to the students, the majority of the time is spent immersed in the writing process. When students have more class time to write, I often build in more time at the end of class for them to confer with peers. While my students are working independently, I am either conferring with individuals or helping small needs-based groups.

Figures 6.6 and 6.7 mirror the reading workshop charts. The writing workshop focuses on a unit of study or a specific writing topic instead of a comprehension strategy. The key to bridging reading and writing is to use the same books to teach both reading and writing. The comprehension, or thinking, strategies are another bridge. For example, if students are working on sensory images/visualizing in reading, they may be writing descriptive pieces or poetry during the writing workshop.

I admire Katie Wood Ray's insight about the writing workshop.

> In a writing workshop, one of the main goals teachers have is to help students find good reasons to write. These teachers feel that nothing else matters if students aren't finding writing projects in which they can become deeply involved. . . . They see the writing process as a tool they can give their students to use when rocking the world, not just as something to learn to do. That knowledge at the forefront of teaching, that knowledge that writing is this amazing, powerful tool you can use to rock the world, *changes everything*. (Ray 2004, 4)

I want my students to bring this passion to their writing lives and to have the power to "rock the world." I want to give them choice and power in their writing lives. I want my students to be aware of the process writers go through (see Figure 6.8), but I'm also very explicit that this process is messy

Figure 6.6 Writing: Another Way to Organize Time

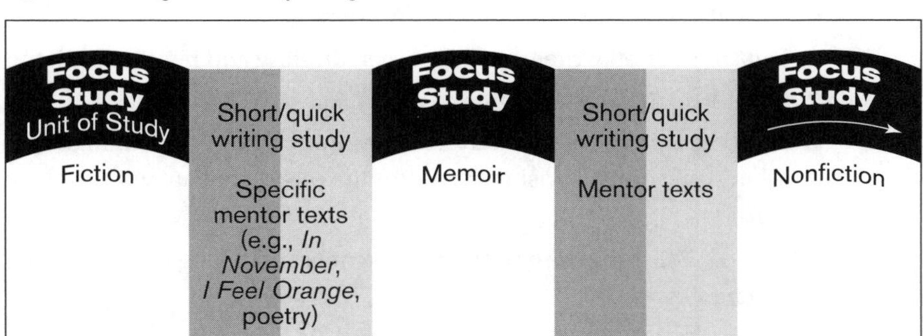

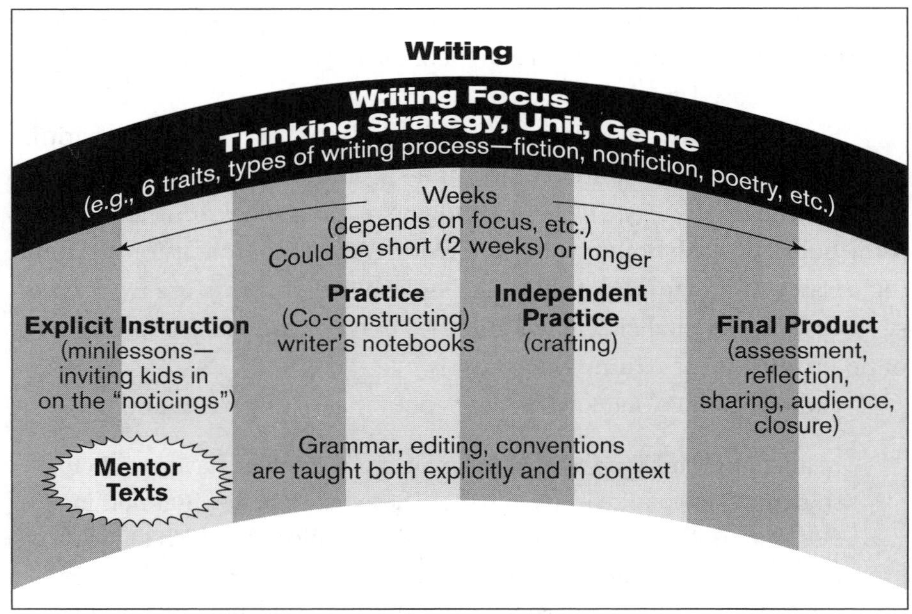

Figure 6.7 Writing Focus Chart

and often requires going back through stages again and again. I also want my students to know that writers practice—*a lot*—and that not everything in a writer's notebook is published but only truly worthy work. The stages of the writing process are:

- *Practicing, rehearsing, envisioning.* The prewriting stage—immersing yourself in similar texts and deciding what the final product will look like (*envisioning*). What other published text will your piece look like? A picture book? A poem? A chapter of a novel? An editorial? Students need to know what they're creating.
- *Drafting.* (Often writers circle between drafting and revision until the text is the way they want it.)
- *Revising.* Looking at the draft with new eyes, adding or deleting text, asking questions. Revising is only for the pieces that are worthy of revision.
- *Editing.* Polishing the grammar and syntax and taking care of the mechanics.

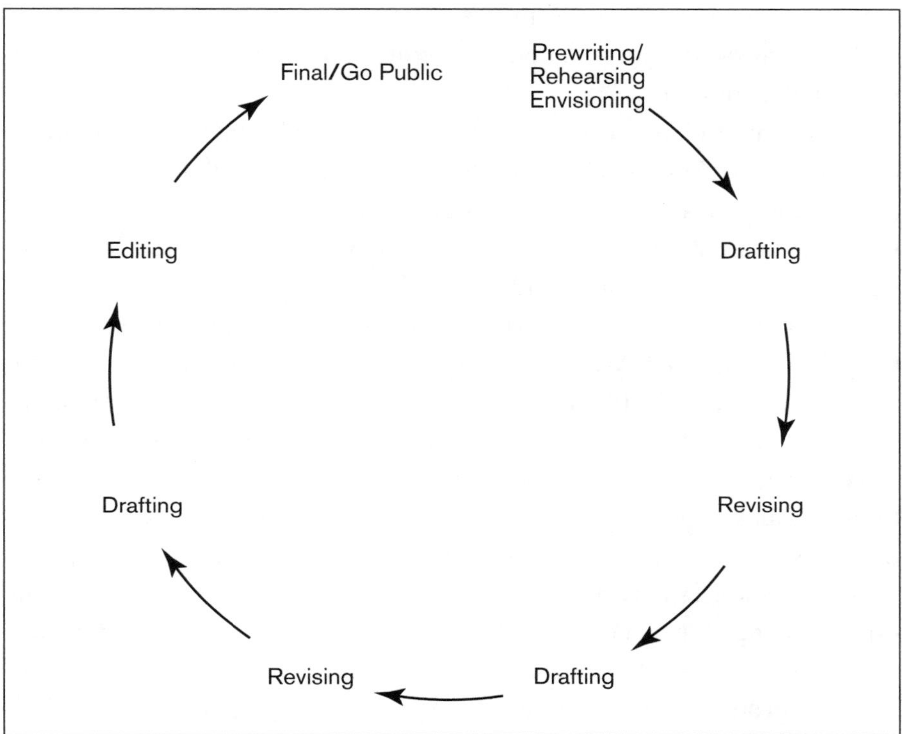

Figure 6.8 Stages of Writing Process

- *Publishing.* Taking the piece public. This is such an important part of the process. If the kids are only writing for you, what's the point? How are students going to share their finalized writing with a larger audience?

WHAT ABOUT FUNDAMENTALS LIKE GRAMMAR, MECHANICS, AND SPELLING?

These skills are important and need to be mastered; they truly are the foundation on which the structure of writing is built. And it's usually spelling and mechanics that students are judged on first, no matter how amazing the content of their writing.

I explain to my students that these are foundational skills, but unlike the reading process or the writing process, there are rules—and once you master the rules, you're set. (If our elementary students truly mastered these basic skills, they'd need a lot less instruction in these areas as they progressed through the grades.)

I tell my students, "Learn it now and learn it well, and you will be ahead of the game. Why put it off? I know this stuff isn't fun, but it's important to be able to edit your own work and not always depend on spell-check. When you're older, it's often your writing that will get you a job interview. So as your writing teacher, I'm going to hold you accountable this year."

And how do I do that? From informal student writing at the beginning of the year, I immediately know who can spell and who can't. I gather a lot of information about how students use mechanics. I also pretest. I want to know who has mastered what skills—punctuation, capitalization, grammar. From there I decide on a plan of action. My pretests lead to differentiated instruction. Why make students practice a skill they have already mastered? If the entire class is weak in a mechanics area (quotation marks, for example), I provide whole-class instruction and practice. If only a few students lack the skill, I pull together a needs-based group for direct instruction while the rest of the class is writing. We meet as many times as needed to achieve mastery.

I hold students accountable for correctly using grammar and mechanics in their writing across all content areas. When a student turns in a final draft, it must be perfect, but even daily work needs to reflect grade-level expectations and have basic words spelled correctly. I work on editing skills in writing conferences, and when students are finalizing pieces, I serve as their copy editor.

To Learn More

For effective warm-up activities see:

dailylanguageinstruction.com

Anderson, Barbara. 2003 (revised edition 2010). *Daily Language Instruction, Grade 4: 30 Weeks of Editing and Proofreading Tasks*. Morrison, CO: Hogback Press.

Daily Geography Practice. 2004. Various grade levels. Monterey, CA: Evan-Moor.

Rituals to Make Every Minute Count

Monday, the third week of school. The morning bell has rung, and I hear the students trooping down the hall. I'm ready for another phenomenal week. The schedule for our day is on the front whiteboard, the homework assignments for the week are on the back whiteboard, and warm-up work is on top of students' desks. I wait by the classroom door, ready to greet the students as they enter.

Hays, always the first to arrive, slings his backpack on one of the hooks outside the classroom door and bursts in, making a beeline for me. "Well, the Broncos stunk it up again, didn't they? But Air Force was totally awesome. Hey—how'd your Huskies do?"

"Lost. I think it's going to be a long year," I answer with chagrin. (And indeed, the University of Washington Huskies, my alma mater's football team, go on to lose every football game that year.) Hays and I already know that part of our morning ritual will be discussing sports or politics. He needs to visit with me before he can move on to his desk and get to work. I point him in the direction of his desk as the other students file in.

Some head directly to their desks to unload their backpacks, others head over to me, a folder in hand. "It's signed," each says, holding it up for me to see. On Fridays, all work is sent home in a "communication folder" (see Figure 6.9). Students write a comment about the week on the record sheet on the front (I add comments if necessary) and return the folder on Monday (minus all their papers) with a parent's or caregiver's signature. "Put them in the tote on top of the mailboxes," I direct.

Still others meander over to the shelf where the cafeteria menu is hung and place their "popsicle stick" in the container matching their lunch choice. There is a low hum in the room as students settle in, saying hi to classmates

Figure 6.9 Cover of a Communication Folder

Communication Folder

Student Name ______________

Date	Comments (Teacher/Student)	Parent Signature (Comments Optional)

and sharing a bit about their weekends. Jinu, the class "technician" this week, is turning on the class computers. Erin, the "electrician," is turning on all the classroom lamps.

Reed and Taylor stand at my side, talking over each other, Reed recounting how his lacrosse team did over the weekend, Taylor sharing the results of her gymnastics tryouts. After they head off to their desks, Naomi breezes into the room, holding up her current book for me to see ("You just have to read it when I'm done!").

"Happy Monday, guys! If you're not already seated and working, I'd like you to settle in and start on your warm-ups—both language instruction and geography. The schedule is on the board and we'll have group after the pledge." This reminder sends the stragglers to their seats, and I walk among the desks, looking over shoulders, redirecting students' attention, or just saying hi. This is just the second week of warm-ups. I introduced this routine the previous Monday, so we're still very much in practice mode. (A completed DLI warm-up is shown in Figure 6.10.)

▶ THE NITTY-GRITTY

Warm-ups start the day in a predictable manner and focus students. Plus, there's no time lost to short practice sessions on editing, proofreading, and geography later in the day. What are some basic skills you could weave into the beginning of your day as a warm-up? I also periodically send home editing worksheets for kids to complete at home. Having parents support these skills at home frees time for me to work on writing. I meet with students who don't have appropriate parental support in a study group or give them time to complete the sheets during the school day.

"Okay, you've had about ten minutes to settle in and work. We'll be going over these in two minutes, so make sure you're ready." A couple of students get to work at the last minute; others already have their noses in books, anticipating independent reading.

After two minutes, we discuss the answers to the warm-ups and I instruct, using the document camera. This week's editing lesson is a review of capitalizing proper nouns; the geography lesson is on globe lines. The students correct their own work—this is a learning experience.

I know what you're thinking: *She starts the day with worksheets?! What happened to authenticity?* My classroom has changed over twenty-five years of teaching. Some of this is due to standards, accountability, and the reality of standardized testing. While I am not a proponent of worksheets, they're sometimes necessary. Editing and grammar skills are a huge component of our state (and many other states) tests. Students need to be able to edit and proofread—it's a basic skill. In addition to these warm-up exercises, I teach skills in context and have my students practice them in their writing. How-

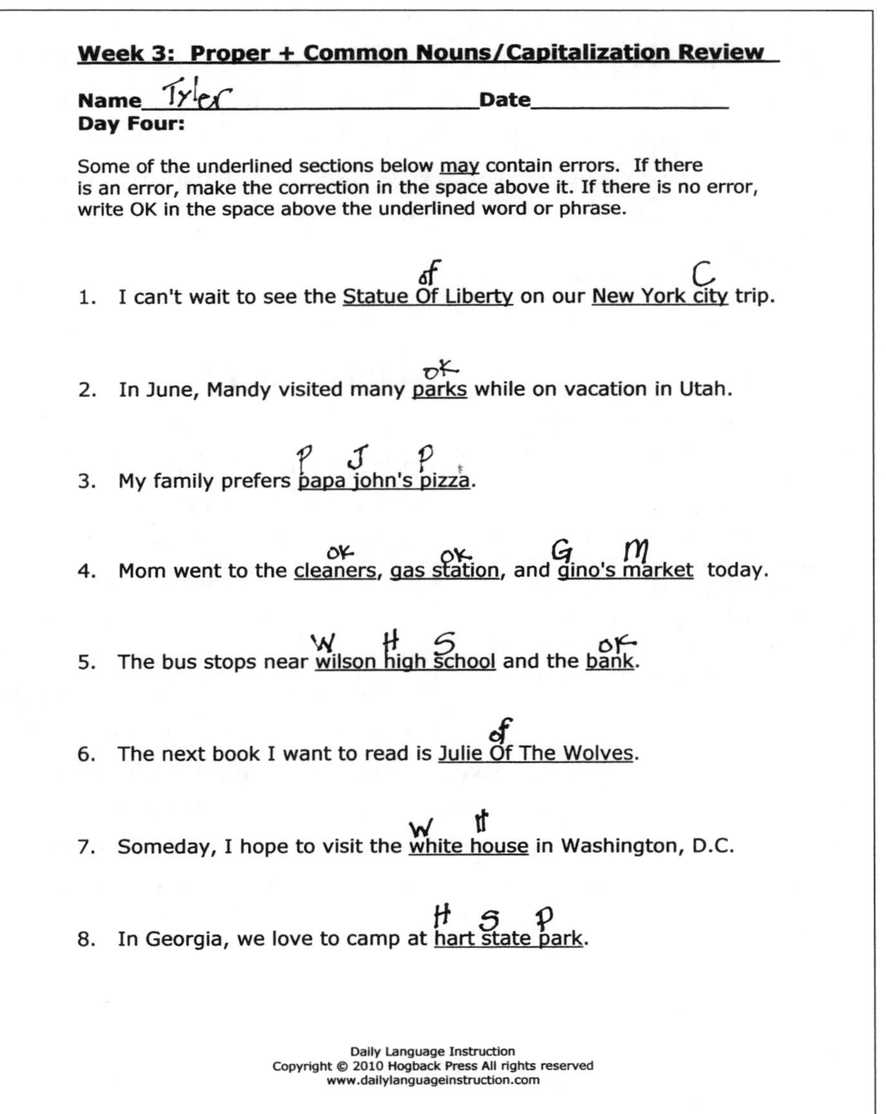

Week 3: Proper + Common Nouns/Capitalization Review

Name_Tyler_________________**Date**_______________

Day Four:

Some of the underlined sections below may contain errors. If there is an error, make the correction in the space above it. If there is no error, write OK in the space above the underlined word or phrase.

1. I can't wait to see the Statue Of Liberty on our New York city trip.

2. In June, Mandy visited many parks while on vacation in Utah.

3. My family prefers papa john's pizza.

4. Mom went to the cleaners, gas station, and gino's market today.

5. The bus stops near wilson high school and the bank.

6. The next book I want to read is Julie Of The Wolves.

7. Someday, I hope to visit the white house in Washington, D.C.

8. In Georgia, we love to camp at hart state park.

Daily Language Instruction
Copyright © 2010 Hogback Press All rights reserved
www.dailylanguageinstruction.com

Figure 6.10 A Student's Direct Language Instruction Warm-Up

ever, there are uncontextualized editing questions on the tests, and students need to be able to recognize particular formats and conventions. Worksheets address these specifics quickly and give students a bit of practice, all within ten minutes or so. Since I need to make every minute of the day count, why not use this time before the pledge and announcements to focus on some literacy or geography skill?

The payoff? My students score well on the state test's editing questions (those ten minutes a day add up) and the rest of the day is free for authentic work. Some words of caution, however. There's a plethora of blackline masters and workbooks that promise to be the standardized testing "magic bullet." You need to be savvy; choose wisely. What's the best match with your state standards, district curriculum, and your kids' needs? Less is better; make it worthwhile!

MONDAY GROUP TIME

I ask students to stack their corrected worksheets in the center of their table. As I pick up the stacks, I instruct those students to move quietly to the group area. The kids quickly realize that those who follow directions quickly and quietly get the best locations, and I'm able to manage the traffic—not all twenty-five students are moving at one time.

▶ THE NITTY-GRITTY

There are many professional books on the market with tips on how to manage "morning meetings" and similarly designated gatherings. We have "group" once a week, on Mondays, during which we share our weekends and launch our week of learning together. It's an integral aspect of building our community, a realization I came to after teachers who had participated in a four-day observation lab said they couldn't wait to go back to their classrooms and institute Monday group time. They viewed it as a key component of our success.

"Good morning! I can't believe it's already the third week of school! Our schedule for today is on the board." Although the schedule is fairly predictable, I want the times and activities recorded; it's especially helpful for students who need visual reminders. I go over the following schedule.

8:00–9:15	Opening
	Group
	Reading
9:15–10:25	Math
10:30–11:15	Gym
11:15–11:40	Read-aloud
11:40–12:25	Lunch/recess
12:25–2:30	Fill out planners / homework
	Spelling pretest
	Literacy (reading/writing workshop)

"We're holding our jobs for one more week, then next week we'll change. I'm still president this week, so that I can model precisely what you will do when you hold this position. Jack, I know you're paying close attention to all this, since you assume the role of president next week! You get one more week of being vice president to watch and observe."

I should interrupt here and talk about classroom jobs, which are listed on a chart that hangs prominently in the front of the room (see Figure 6.11). During the first week of school, I introduce the jobs—and the job descriptions. I try to create jobs that make classroom management the responsibility of the students, thus reinforcing that it's *our* room. Students have been terrific over the years at making suggestions for additional jobs to add to the chart.

To Learn More

Routman, Regie. 2003. *Reading Essentials.* Portsmouth, NH: Heinemann.

Miller, Debbie. 2008. *Teaching with Intention.* Portland, ME: Stenhouse.

Ray, Katie Wood. *The Writing Workshop.* 2001. Urbana, IL: National Council of Teachers of English.

Some of the jobs are self-explanatory: teacher's helper, messenger, mail deliverer, lunch boxes, librarian, chalkboard supervisor, floor janitor, coat custodian, gardener, substitute-at-large. Others require some explanation.

- *President.* Calls students to line up, leads the line to its destination (so I can walk beside students and monitor), and checks planners and homework for parent/caregiver signatures. The class interviews

Figure 6.11 Job Chart

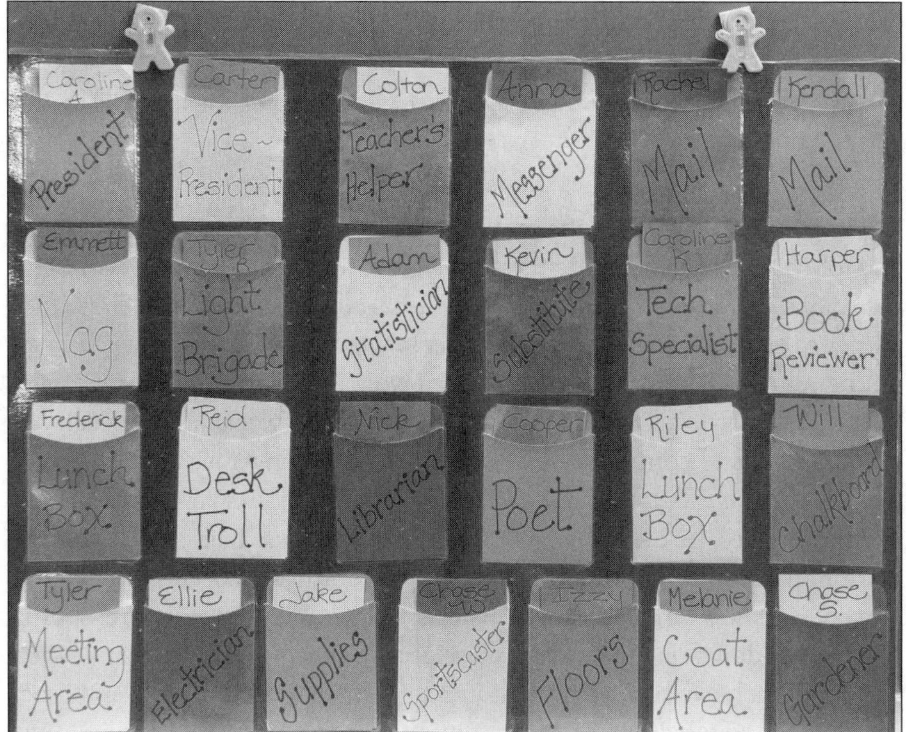

each new president and then writes about her. (The vice president steps in if the president is sick and assumes the president role the following week.)

- *Nag* (the only time this is a positive!). Writes any announcements or reminders on the whiteboard and reminds me of things I might forget (administrative announcements, passing out papers from the office at the end of the day).
- *Humorist.* Tells a joke sometime during the week (we all need a little levity!).
- *Statistician.* Comes up with a question for the week for students to answer and graphs the responses.
- *Tech specialist.* Takes care of the computers.
- *Book reviewer.* Reviews a great book!
- *Desk troll* (a favorite!). One day each week, comes in at recess and checks students' desks. Clean desks receive rewards (usually a Jolly Rancher tucked inside), so-so desks receive nothing, and messy desks get marked for a makeover.
- *Poet.* Shares a terrific poem and then posts it on the board.
- *Meeting area monitor.* Keeps our meeting area clean and organized.
- *Supply sergeant.* Checks that we have everything we need and reminds me when we're running low.
- *Sportscaster.* Shares sports results at our Monday meeting.

We run through the jobs on the chart in order, reviewing expectations and touching base with students to make sure jobs are being done correctly. Some jobs are Monday jobs. The *humorist* starts our week out by telling a joke (if they're prepared; if not, they share later in the week). Our *book reviewer* recommends a great book; the *poet* shares a favorite poem that gets hung on the board. The *sportscaster* shares sports news from the weekend, then calls on other students to contribute sports news as well. Denver is a sports kind of town. We've got the Broncos, the Colorado Avalanche (hockey), the Nuggets, and the Rockies. We even have two professional lacrosse teams: the Colorado Mammoth (indoor) and the Denver Outlaws (outdoor). Soccer? The Rapids. Add college sports and recreational sports, and we have a lot to share. Sportscasters who don't want to report professional or college results can share their own sports achievements. Throughout the year, we hear about weekend soccer matches, football, lacrosse, basketball and baseball games, swimming, tennis, gymnastics, skiing. If it's sports related, it gets shared. This is a terrific way to establish community and a phenomenal way for me to learn about my students and their passions outside school. (Also, I love sports, and this is where I establish credibility with my boys.)

After we finish sharing, I revisit the previous week and set the stage for our upcoming week. Because my students have already been gathered in the group area for a half hour, I don't continue with a minilesson but rather take an independent reading status of the class and then begin conferring with individual students while the remaining students dip into their books.

▶ THE NITTY-GRITTY

What skills and strategies were elicited in this lesson?

- Settling in and getting to work
- Practicing mechanics, grammar, and geography
- Building community (visiting with students as they enter the room, sharing during group/job session) (A bedrock belief: Know your students—and let them know you as a person outside of school.)
- Entering the room, moving from desks to group area and then back to desks for independent reading
- Modeling and practicing listening and grand conversations
- Scaffolding independence/responsibility
- Being accountable and communicating with parents (communication folders)

SPELLING

To be honest, I have grappled with best practice in spelling instruction for years. With twenty-plus years of teaching under my belt, I've seen programs come and go—generic workbooks and individualized lists. I've read the research, especially Diane Snowball's work, and I still haven't found the magic bullet—or that manageable piece that fits into the time frame (and time constraints) of a school day. Snowball and Bolton (1999) advocate individualized lists of misspelled words from student writing. That is a huge undertaking when combined with everything else I'm doing. So I've compromised. Our district has a list of "no excuse words" that is part of each grade's scope and sequence—each year a few more words are added. I give these as a pretest at the beginning of the year, and students include the words they've misspelled on their individual spelling list. These are also words that I expect my students to spell correctly in their daily writing, and I hold them accountable.

We also have a spelling program—one size fits all, but there are still ways to differentiate! I pretest, and students who score 90 percent or better don't have to participate. Instead, they create an abbreviated spelling list of either "no excuse" words or vocabulary words from their book lover's book (see below). If students already know how to spell words correctly, why waste their time doing the work and taking a test covering something they already know? Why not push them to learn new words?

I don't give spelling instruction every day. I provide short bursts of direct instruction two or three times a week, either during the ninety-minute morning literacy block or in the afternoon (cutting into my science/social studies hour).

I do expect some authentic spelling practice. Besides being able to spell words correctly, I want my students to be able to find misspelled words in their own writing. I also want them to take risks. So I make this deal with them. When they give me a piece of writing to edit, I expect them to have circled misspelled words (excluding "no excuse" words, which they should have corrected themselves). I give them the correct spelling for circled words, thus encouraging them to risk using great words they don't know how to spell. (This approach also means I don't have students following me around the room asking how to spell things.) However, if *I* circle a misspelled word, they have to look it up in the dictionary—an incentive to proofread carefully.

If students really struggle with editing, I confer with them and directly teach specific skills—again, it's all about teaching the writer and meeting the individual writer's needs!

Shopping for Books

A final routine I establish is how to use our classroom library. Before I do this lesson, I lay the groundwork by establishing a community of readers and presenting lessons on how readers choose appropriate books. Students also have their "someday" list in the back of their book lover's book. Once these elements are in place, we're ready to "shop" our classroom library. This lesson takes thirty minutes, and I do it at least once every trimester. As the students mature as readers, their tastes change and they notice new books.

PURPOSE

Richard Allington (2001) writes that "classrooms with a larger supply of books had kids who read more frequently; classrooms with a larger supply of books usually had more kids reading books they could manage successfully" (54). He goes on to say, "I would recommend at least 500 different books in every classroom with those split about evenly between narratives and informational books and about equally between books that are on or near grade-level difficulty and books that are below grade level" (55). To make the point even stronger, he writes, "Children from lower-income homes especially need rich and extensive collections of books in the school library and in their classrooms if only because these are the children least likely to have a supply of books at home" (57).

Well-stocked classroom libraries are essential to create a rich, literate environment with abundant student choice. Whether the books come from the school library or belong to the teacher, there needs to be a lot of them. When my students walk through my door for the first time, I usually overhear someone whisper, "She must have thousands of books in here." I probably do—I haven't counted, but it's close. Through book clubs (like Scholastic's), donations, and purchases, I've created an impressive classroom library. Some books are on shelves—poetry, nonfiction, and books that integrate with our social studies and science units. Novels are stored in plastic tubs. (Books I will use for minilessons are off-limits.) The books are not organized by level, although in many classrooms I visit, they are. *There's no one way to organize a classroom library.* The books in mine are organized by genre, author, and text sets. After our "shopping day," students who wish to can come in at recess and reorganize and relabel tubs. I want every aspect of our room to reflect my students for that year.

HERE'S HOW IT GOES

At a break in the day, or before students come in, I pull all the tubs off the bookcases and place them on desks. The room becomes a sea of books. I ask students to bring their book lover's books and pencils and join me in the group area.

"I know I went over all the parts of our book lover's book, but there's one section I want to revisit today before we go shopping. Remember how I told you about the book I read, *The Reading Zone*, by Nancie Atwell [2007]? And how teachers always get lots of great ideas from different books? Well, Nancie wrote about 'someday' books and she has her students record them in a reader's log. I read that and decided to create a someday list to add to your book lover's book. I tried it with last year's class and it worked great. You also know I want you to select books deliberately and thoughtfully. It's been awesome to watch you gravitate toward books that your classmates are recommending or trying authors that I suggest. I also see a lot of you heading to the basket of recommended reading up front.

> ▶ **THE NITTY-GRITTY**
>
> There is a large basket of recommended books at the front of my classroom. At the end of each school year, I ask students to contribute to this basket at least one book, pulled from our classroom library, that they think is a "must read." Next year's students start the year with a good supply of recommended books.

"I've noticed that some of you have already entered titles you might want to read on your someday list. That's what it's for—when you need a new book but are unsure where to go. At my house, my someday lists are piles of actual books. I have my pile of 'fun' reading, a pile of professional books, and a pile of kids' books. I always have something to turn to.

"Today you get to look through all the tubs of books. Make sure you pay attention to the label on the front—some are organized by genre, some by author. If you find any books that are misplaced, put them back where they belong. If you find a book you want to read right now, take it. In this box [I hold up a box of index cards] there's a card that has your name on it. Fill that out whenever you borrow a book from me—I don't have to check it out for you. However, I do need to initial your card when you return the book. That way I know it's back where it belongs. So take any books you want, but make sure to check them out.

> ▶ **THE NITTY-GRITTY**
>
> This checkout system is also tweaked from Atwell's *The Reading Zone* (2007, 38). On each index card are two columns: date and title. When the student returns the book, I cross out the title and initial the cross-out. Simple, and the kids do the work!

"Also pay attention to the sticky notes inside the front covers. See what other kids have to say. You may find some books you think you want to read later in the year. If a book interests you, jot the title down on your someday list. You may also want to write down the label of the tub in the location column, so you'll be able to locate the book when you're ready to read it!"

I explain my expectations for our thirty-minute shopping spree—no more than two students at a desk, three-inch voices a must, sharing books and great finds encouraged! Then the students head off to "shop." As they peruse the books, I circulate, pulling and recommending books (even in the first trimester, I've already gotten some inkling of students' interests).

> **▶ LESSON LOGISTICS**
>
> Before I instituted the someday list, my avid readers would hoard books, piling them on their desk. They'd end up with so many books on their desk there was no room to work. I love it when kids have a backup book ready to go, but not a tower of books.

Students usually explore the books for about twenty minutes this first time. When we're done, the kids replace the book tubs on the bookcases and we meet briefly, sharing some of the books we found and telling what we noticed about the organization of the classroom library. I remind the kids to check out the books they've selected and ask who wants to join a team to reorganize the shelves and tubs during recess.

OWNING THE LESSON

This is a perfect time to think about how you want your classroom library organized and how you want students to access it. From my consulting work, I'm also aware that not all classrooms have books and that not all classroom libraries (or libraries in general) are created equal.

▶ QUESTIONS TO THINK ABOUT

- If I don't have books, how can I get them into my room?
- If I have leveled books, how do I want to present them to the kids?
- How do I want to keep track of my books?
- What message do I send kids if I *don't* have books in the room?

Before I started using the checkout system, former students who were cleaning their rooms before heading off to college would sheepishly stop by to return books they'd found with my name in them. At least the books made it back! And when I taught in economically impacted schools, the size of my classroom library shrank drastically—but I knew my students had some books at home!

I also have a "shopping list" posted in the room, headed *These are books I'd like Mrs. B. to buy*. Kids write titles, authors, their name, and a brief reason *why* I should purchase that book for our classroom library. And I always ask the kids if there are any titles they'd like me to get with the free choices and bonus points that accrue on our Scholastic book orders. We also have a large basket in the front of the room with a tag heralding "new arrivals" in which I place new books after I show them to the kids and give a brief book talk (one clever teacher I know uses a baby basket, complete with bottles and rattles!).

Sometimes I come across a book that seems a perfect fit for one of my students. I put it on the student's desk with a note saying I think he might find it interesting and asking whether he'd like to read it and review it for the class (always optional). For example, Brett was into extreme sports, and I thought Gary Paulsen's *How Angel Peterson Got His Name* had Brett's name written all over it. Brett devoured the book and did such a great book review that the class insisted I read it aloud. Since that year, Paulsen's book has been a must-read in my classroom—my boys love it and the girls enjoy it, too. I know it's a hit, because it is never on the shelf—it's constantly checked out.

CHAPTER 7

Conferring

The Current of Talk That Holds the Workshop Together

I pull my stool up next to Jinu, who is sitting in a comfy chair. It's the second week of school, and I'm still trying to figure Jinu out. He is a young man of contrasts. Korean is his main language, and the language spoken at home, and yet he reads English books avidly. His favorite series is the Warriors. Every day he has a new one in his hand. From his lit log, I know he comprehends at the literal level, but his entries tend to be short, and I'm wondering if this signals that he's not understanding at higher levels.

Today he has a new book and when he told me the title earlier, I was a bit surprised—it's Rudyard Kipling's *The Jungle Book*.

ME: How's it going?

JINU: Good. I ran out of Warrior books, so I decided to try something new. I got this book at the library. My dad takes me to the library a lot.

I've already discovered that literacy is valued in Jinu's home. No wonder he always has a new book!

ME: I've gotta know how you chose this book. I have to tell you, I've never had a conference on *The Jungle Book*!

JINU: I like cartoons and I like the Disney *Jungle Book* cartoon. You know, there are some things that are the same, like the characters and their names, but the book is a little different. And there are way more stories in the book.

ME: How so?

JINU: Well, I got confused in a couple parts.

ME: Can you show me?

JINU [*flipping right to the page*]**:** See that—that word, *thou*! My tongue is getting really tricky when I see *thou*!

ME [*laughing; I love his comment about tricky tongues*]**:** What does *thou* mean, do you think?

JINU: I went back a bunch and figured out that it meant *you*. That's weird. But I'm guessing that since this book was written a long time ago, that's the way they talked. They sure didn't do that in the movie!

ME: Good thinking. Anything else that confuses you?

Jinu says no. I ask him to read a short passage (without any *thou*s) and then ask him to tell me what he's thinking. It's obvious from his response that he is having very little trouble understanding this book. I jot down notes on my recording sheet.

ME: You've done a terrific job today and I've learned a lot about you as a reader. When you get confused in a book, I want you to mark the spot with a sticky note. That way, when I come to confer with you, I can do my best teaching. The other thing I want you to do is to make sure you're writing about your thinking in your lit log. So when you're done reading each day, I want you to pause and ask yourself, *What do I want to hold onto in what I read?* That way you'll have something to write about. Okay?

JINU: Okay.

ME: Anything else you need before I leave?

JINU: Uh huh. What did you write down?

ME [*showing him my notes; there are no secrets in my classroom*]**:** See? I've got the title and date and that you read fluently and knew the vocabulary. I wrote that you had a strong literal retelling and that you truly understand the text, that you are using background knowledge. I wrote *thou* to remind me of your confusion. I also wrote what I taught you—that I want you to mark confusions and think about your reading. How's that?

JINU: Pretty cool.

Conferences as Mirrors of Our Teaching and Learning

It *is* pretty cool. Conferences are windows into my students' thinking, so I can intervene with a great, doable next move for a young reader like Jinu. They also allow me to "tilt the mirror," get some light bouncing between reading and writing in kids' minds. Our discussions reflect what they're thinking and what I'm teaching. It's an opportunity to listen, talk, teach, reflect, guide, nudge, and know my students.

More generally, conferences are a current of talk and thinking that holds my literacy classroom together. Previous chapters have shown you the lessons and the classroom setup that make it possible to have this one-on-one time with students: they know the rules and can stay productively engaged while I'm conferring with other students. Previous chapters have also given you the foundational lessons for cultivating students as *resourceful* readers and writers—again, so I can confer. Conferences get meaningful talk flowing through and around all the elements of the workshop.

Think about yourself as a learner. When you are excited about something, or confused, what is your natural inclination? You want to talk to someone. Reading isn't done in isolation; after finishing a terrific book, you need to discuss it. Writing is also social. We check with others to make sure our thoughts come across clearly and that we're communicating what we want. I wrote a spirited letter to the editor of our local paper in response to an article about the national standards. But before I sent it off, I read it aloud to a friend to get her input. Similarly, one of my students wrote her mom a love poem. It wasn't Mother's Day or anything, just wonderfully out of the blue. But she ran it by me. Conferring is a natural act! It's not merely a "school thing." The conference flows from this human need to talk.

What makes a conference different is that the talk is purposeful. The example conferences in this chapter all have a *purpose*. In fact, three *P* words provide the key to successful conferences:

- *Purpose*
- *Patience*
- *Practice*

I also want to give you two principles to keep in mind, roles to play as you read this chapter and when you confer with your students.

- *You're an investigative reporter.* Remember the *who, what, when, where, how* of building a journalistic piece? When you confer with students, you want to focus on one point of need or leave them with one thing to try, but it doesn't mean you aren't actively seeking a *handful* of insights. Keep an open, questioning stance, looking for clues: *Who* is this child—his personality, his interests outside school? *What* does his expression or comments or questions tell you he is trying to get better at right now? *What* do you know as his reading and writing teacher that he needs to improve? *When* can you follow up with additional scaffolding beyond this five minutes together? *Where* can you find texts that will be perfect for his next step in reading or writing? *How* can you ensure that he will use and connect what you teach him to his independent work?

- *You're a rock star.* (Okay, maybe that's my fantasy, not yours.) What I mean by this is that in this one-to-one time, elementary students hang on your every word, tune into your tone, worship what you say about their strengths—and may be more open to learning than at any other time of the day. They do look up to you, especially when they trust you and know there is a purpose for your conferences. They do think you know far, far more about literacy and life than they do, so don't disappoint! Give them your undivided attention. Even on a day where you're tired and not at the top of your game, keep conferring sacred for furthering trust, mirth, and learning. You might even be the only one in a child's life who is cheering her on. No matter what, come to the conference with high expectations and honesty. Kids always know.

Teachers and students need to be aware of the purpose for each conference. Talk needs to be meaningful—a means to an end. Phenomenal conferences don't happen overnight. It takes a lot of patience. Remember "you have to go slow to go fast"? You have to give kids time to learn how to talk and listen. And patience ties in to that listening. You can't be in a hurry. You have to be patient and wait. Some kids take a while to gather their thoughts and then talk. Wait time is essential. Patience is key. Then there's practice. Lots and lots of practice. And modeling. All those anchor charts from Chapters 2 and 3 are crucial for great talk to happen in your classroom. Let's look at how my conferences evolve during "a year in the life."

Status of the Class

I use a status of the class form to record what my students are reading and writing. I also use the form to record conferences. While I store these forms in a three-ring binder, I put them on a clipboard for easy access during the day. Checking status of the class has become a norm for me, and I often forget how crucial it is for the success of my workshop.

This point was driven home to me while I was consulting in a school after I wrote the first draft of this chapter. We had been working on reading comprehension, and I had mentioned status of the class early in our work together in August. When I returned later in the year, teachers were doing wonderful comprehension work, but when I asked how they knew what the students were reading daily, the teachers couldn't say. I hadn't been explicit about the importance of the status of the class form. After I did some demonstration teaching using the form, teachers immediately said it was a missing piece in their workshop. The status of the class is powerful.

> ▶ **TRICK OF THE TRADE**
>
> I use the same form for both reading and writing. I just copy it on different-colored paper so I can keep them separate: pink for reading, yellow for writing.

On a single reading status form, I can:

- Record what students are reading and check in with them on a daily basis
- Watch for reading patterns (Are students choosing to read a different book every day—"snag and grab"?)
- Notice if a student is spending too much time reading the same book
- Observe whether students are choosing books at the appropriate level
- Notice whether students are choosing a wide variety of genres
- Strengthen the community of readers (When students hear the title of a book a classmate is reading, they may want to read the book, too.)
- Hold myself accountable for knowing who is reading what
- Hold my students accountable for their independent reading
- Facilitate smooth, quiet transitions back to independent work

Using a writing status form, I can:

- Monitor topic choice
- Follow students' progress through the writing process

- Note students who request writing conferences
- Hold myself and my students accountable

The status form is also a place for me to record:

- With whom I confer
- Notes on individual conferences
- Notes on possible minilessons or needs-based groups

Even better, it only takes at most five minutes to check the status of the class, and all this information is in one place! Students quickly realize that my status check lets me know what they are doing each and every day. They also know this is when they are to tell me if they need a conference or some other kind of assistance. There are fewer interruptions and more thoughtful, independent students: they have to plan ahead. Figure 7.1 is an example of a form completed in August.

STATUS OF THE CLASS, AUGUST: LISTENING TO AND LEARNING FROM MY STUDENTS

"It's time for independent reading, so I'd like you to take a minute and think about the book you're going to be reading. Or perhaps you're going to be writing your lit log letter to me. Think of how you're going to use your time. And remember that as you're reading, I'll be conferring with some of you, so be prepared to tell me how it's going."

Silence for a full minute. That feels like an eternity the first couple of times you do it.

After a minute I say, "Now I'll call your name and you can tell me what you're doing. As soon as you answer, go ahead and get your materials and settle in. Brett?"

"Harry Potter number 3."

I write down his response on my status sheet and move to the next name. "Emma?"

"*The Tale of Desperaux,* and I think I'll work on my lit log letter."

"Sounds good. Make sure to take your book lover's book and pencil with you so you don't have to get up and move once we start."

▶ THE NITTY-GRITTY

At the beginning of the year, since we're not yet focusing full force on a strategy, I use my conferences as both informal assessments *and* as a means to establish relationships with my students and begin to know them as readers and writers. This knowledge will inform my instruction—and help me individualize it—for the rest of the year. It also establishes the trust and rapport that allow me to push my students and allow them to feel safe enough to take risks.

STATUS

Date August/ Sept.

Lessons: – notes to self – vocab is showing up! slow down * notice words!

Mon.	Tues.	Wed.	Thurs.	Fri.
	vocab post-its		choosing the correct book!	*meet w/Xavier next week-check up

Conferences:

Mon.	Tues.	Wed.	Thurs.	Fri.
Henry. Maddie Jinu	Geoffrey Johnny Grace Iliana		Dexter Emma Qmarah Dray	Xavier Lucie Thomas

Henry	Maddie	Geoffrey
Silverfin Fluent and strong retell- beyond literal. Asking questions * Needs to notice new vocab.	Island of the Blue Dolphins Empathy - puts herself in Karana's shoes This is a just right.	Tracker Not one of his Favorites, but will stick with it. Can't relate but predicting what will happen.
Dexter	**Xavier**	**Emma**
Diary of a W. Kid Easy! Need to push him. Loves humor. No new words he doesn't know.	Goosebumps Literal retelling Fairly fluent- knows how to pronounce words but not necessarily meaning-Work on vocab.	Harry Potter #7 Fluent & strong comp. Just right. Lots of inferences/?'s.
Jinu	**Lucie**	**Qmarah**
Warriors Loves this series- devours them Likes the humor and the cats. Strong comp & fluency. Vocab.	Flush Going to abandon. Doesn't like the book. Check in - next week.	Goosebumps Loves scary. Continue to work on fluency- interfering w/ comp. Literal comp. No inferential main idea

Figure 7.1 Completed Status Form for August

I continue through the list, jotting titles on the sheet. If a child doesn't answer or gives a blank look, I quickly move on. No time wasted. After I've gone through the entire list, I return to the children who hadn't made a decision or weren't paying attention. Generally by the time I get to the end, they've figured things out. This is a great inducement to be ready next time, because those called on last have last pick where to sit in the room. A status check generally takes only a couple of minutes and by the time I'm done, the class has settled in to read.

Which means I am now ready to confer. I pull up next to Jack, who's reading number 3 of the Diary of a Wimpy Kid series.

THE LANGUAGE OF LEARNING

In this initial conference, I'm informally assessing Jack as a reader. I want to know how he approaches reading and his interests. I listen as he tells me about his book so I can assess his literal comprehension. I take an informal reading inventory and fluency check as he reads orally. And finally I ask him to tell me what he's thinking after he's read. In this first conference, I may not teach Jack as much as he teaches me. But the next time I sit with him, I will know how to instruct him better as a reader. And Jack may not be aware of it, but he is doing more talking than I am. I am mostly listening–and learning.

ME: How's it going? Is there anything you need?

JACK: Good. No, nothing.

ME: Okay, since this is our first conference, I want you to tell me how you chose this book and if it's easy, just right, or a challenge.

JACK: I love Diary of a Wimpy Kid books and Reed let me borrow this. He says it's a good one. Oh, I guess it's maybe between an easy and a just right.

ME: Why do you say that?

JACK: Because it's really easy for me to read and I get all the words.

ME: Hmm. I'm wondering if it might be too easy for you. Can you tell me about it, and then I'll have you read a little.

STATUS OF THE CLASS, NOVEMBER: CONNECTING THE MINILESSON TO CONFERRING

On the front whiteboard is a list of independent activities—almost a menu—from which students can choose:

- Reading—choice book
- Lit log letter
- Reading—research

The list is short, but the students have some choice over how they will spend their time, and more of their time is spent working independently now. Stamina has improved, so students have no problem working from thirty minutes to an hour. Since they are doing meaningful work, there are few behavioral issues, if any.

I finish a reading minilesson on questioning using Eve Bunting's *So Far from the Sea*. "Today in your independent reading, I'd like you to pay attention to the types of questions your book creates in your mind. You can use either your choice books or books you're reading for your research. And as I come around to confer with you, I'll be asking you to tell me about those questions. Let's take a minute and you decide how you'll use your time, then I'll do a status check."

Later I approach Trinity for a conference. She has said she'll be reading for her research topic, which I know is Alcatraz. She has a pile of books at her side and one open in her lap.

ME: How's it going? Anything you need from me?

TRINITY: I'm fine. I really like my topic. Now that I'm reading about it, I really want to go see Alcatraz.

ME: That would be pretty neat. At the end of the minilesson I told you guys to pay attention to your questions. Can you tell me what questions you're asking or how they're helping you?

TRINITY: I really wanted to know about the guys who got sent to the island, and I wanted to know why they decided to put the prison there. Did you know that a few people tried to escape but they're not sure if anyone ever got off successfully? I want to know more about the guys who tried. I also want to know who the Bird Man of Alcatraz was and why the prison got shut down.

ME: Wow! That's a lot. You know what I'm noticing right now as your reading teacher? You are asking questions that set a purpose for you. You're reading to find out more. What I want to know is what you do when you find the answer.

TRINITY: I think about it. And I think these are some of the things that I'll put in my research. I want to write about the interesting stuff and the people.

ME: Sounds great. I'm going to let you get back to it. Do you need anything else from me?

Trinity, already engrossed in her book, doesn't even shake her head as I start to leave. While I haven't explicitly pushed her to do something new in her reading, I've implicitly encouraged her to hold on to the answers to her questions and begin to frame where she'll go with the writing she'll be doing about her topic in the future.

STATUS OF THE CLASS, JANUARY: MOVING STUDENTS TOWARD INDEPENDENCE

The kids have come back from winter break full of energy, eager to get going. I feel it in the air. They're excited about book clubs, inquiry (research) projects, selecting poetry, and so on. They're going to be working on meaningful tasks!

The choices on the board for working independently are:

- Independent reading
- Lit log letter
- Book clubs
- Research notes

Instead of a minilesson, we sit down together in the meeting area and quickly discuss their choices. Because book clubs will be meeting, I'll spend time eavesdropping on the groups but I still get in a few conferences.

"I'd like you guys to take a look at the list of choices and think about how you'd like to use your time. Since we will be spending most of the time working independently, you may want to choose two things to work on—and let me know both of those. You also might need a conference. If you do, let me know when I do the status check—just say, 'I'd like a teacher conference.'" Sydney asks for a teacher conference, and I write a *1* by her name so I'll get to her first.

Later, when I approach her, I let her take the lead.

ME: Hi.

SYDNEY: Hi. I just really wanted to share with you some cool stuff I've found out. Remember how we were reading from *Somewhere Today* as a possible mentor text for nonfiction, and it was talking about the size of an eagle's aerie? Well, I've been reading about swans, and their nests are even bigger than that! [*Sydney regales me with amazing facts of swan nests and how sometimes pikes can eat the babies.*]

ME [*finally getting a word in*]: Whew! I can tell you're totally into your topic. And what's cool is that you are determining importance in text. Tell me what you need from me.

SYDNEY: Nothing, I just wanted to share.

ME: Okay, then let me ask you–what are you going to do with all that information? Is it important to remember? Especially since you're taking notes right now.

SYDNEY: Oh, I get what you're asking. I'm putting this down in my notes–see right here is my big question about birth and young and so I can put the information here. I'm also writing down my connections to the eagle's nest because I was so surprised. And I'm also putting down about the pikes because that just makes me sad. [*Her notes are shown in Figure 7.2.*]

Sydney is reading strategically, taking notes, and getting ready to write. She's integrating reading and writing!

STATUS OF THE CLASS, APRIL: INDEPENDENCE IN ACTION

The options on the board for working independently are now:

- Independent reading
- Book lover's books
- Book clubs
- Research
- Writing project—fiction

At this point in the year, the students have a passion and energy for the work they're doing. I present a short minilesson and get out of the way.

As students respond to my status check, I remind them to be specific. If they are going to read, I want to know the title. If they are going to be writing, I want to know the title of the piece and where they are in the writing process.

When everyone has settled in to work, I sit down next to Conor. He's told me he's working on his writing and that even though he'd already begun a piece, he's back at the prewriting stage. I want to know why.

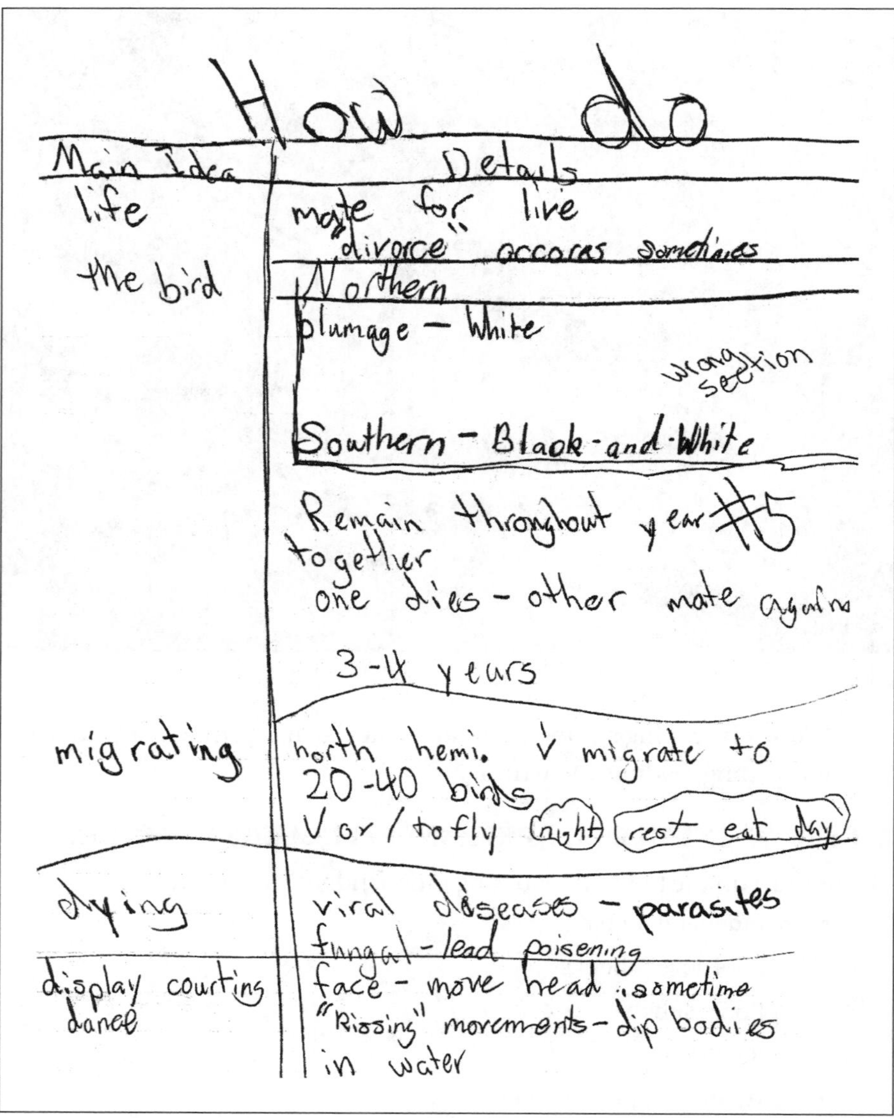

Figure 7.2 Sydney's Notes on Swans

ME: How's it going? Do you need anything?

CONOR: Yeah, I started over—I just didn't like my first piece.

ME: Tell me about it. What happened?

CONOR: Well, I was trying to do fiction and I was using *Diary of a Wimpy Kid* as my mentor text. I wanted to do something funny. I tried, but every time I wrote something it just didn't sound right. Then I had a conference with

Figure 7.2 Continued

Scott and he didn't laugh. He just said that he didn't get the jokes. Plus, my drawings stink.

ME: Fiction is tough. That's why the fiction unit comes at the end of the year. We all read so much fiction, but it's really tough to write. Whenever I write it with you guys, I have a new appreciation for fiction writers. But you've done something terrific as a writer–you realized it wasn't working for you, you checked with an audience who confirmed that it wasn't working, so you decided to start over. That's the best thing about writing—we can change it or start over. We can't do that with talk. So what are you thinking now?

CONOR: I still want to do something funny, but I want it to be something I get. So I've been thinking about my dog. And then I thought about your dogs and all the trouble they get in and I thought I could do a short story about a dog getting in trouble. Kind of like a mix of the picture book *Marley* and the novel. But it would be my dog and his troubles. I'm just trying to figure out if I should write it from the dog's point of view or if I should tell about the dog.

ME: You have time. Why don't you think for a while? Or maybe you could write the lead from both perspectives and see what you like better. Are you doing any planning?

CONOR: Yes, I'm writing down the ways he gets in trouble.

ME: Sounds good. What else do you need from me?

CONOR: Can you check back tomorrow?

ME [*making a note on my conference sheet*]**:** Absolutely.

Conor knows the writing process. He knows how to envision what he wants to create—what the end product will look like. He has a sense of audience. He has a purpose. He's drawing on his own experience. He understands point of view. What Conor needed right then was to be listened to and validated. And then he needed the time to think! So I got out of his way.

TO LEARN MORE

The following professional books all have wonderful things to teach about coming to know students through talking and conferring.

Allen, Patrick. 2009. *Conferring: The Keystone of Reader's Workshop*. Portland, ME: Stenhouse.

Anderson, Carl. 2000. *How's It Going? A Practical Guide to Conferring with Student Writers*. Portsmouth, NH: Heinemann.

Graves, Donald H. 1994. *A Fresh Look at Writing*. Portsmouth, NH: Heinemann.

Robb, Laura. 2010. *Teaching Middle School Writers: What Every English Teacher Should Know*. Portsmouth, NH: Heinemann.

More Conferences in Action

As you've seen, conferring is a form of direct instruction: there is nothing indirect about it! While students are working independently, I focus on making every minute count for every child. I put my core beliefs into action: provide honest feedback, teach every child at his or her level, push as far as he or she can go.

I both assess and teach while conferring. I record anecdotal notes to drive future individual, small-group, and whole-group instruction. Are students reading texts at their independent level? Are the majority of them using comprehension/thinking strategies independently? What are their general writing strengths and weakness? I teach my students how to improve their reading and writing by doing what real readers and writers do.

To become comfortable and skillful at the art of conferring takes time. It also requires a lot of listening—the students need to guide you. Finally, you need to be able to think on your feet. My conferences are short—no more than five minutes, even a writing conference—and my goal is to teach one thing. That's it: one thing. That way my students remember what they're supposed to practice and I don't overwhelm them. I keep it simple!

TALKING ZAVIER OUT OF A CHALLENGING TEXT

ME [*sitting down on the floor next to Zavier*]: How's it going?

ZAVIER: Okay, I just started this book [*holds up* The Lightning Thief, *by Rick Riordan*]. A lot of kids are reading it, so I wanted to, too.

I know this book is going to be more than a challenge for Zavier. While we've spent class time on how to choose appropriate books, Zavier is still attempting to read what his peers are instead of reading at his level. Rather than tell him the book is too hard for him, I need to get him to realize this on his own. I want him to take control of his learning.

ME: So tell me about the book? How far are you?

ZAVIER: I'm in the middle of the first chapter and it's about a boy and there are lots of mythical creatures in it.

ME: Can you tell me the boy's name? You know readers really need to remember the characters' names. That's an important part of comprehension.

ZAVIER: I'm not really sure what his name is [*he starts flipping back through the chapter*].

ME: Okay, I'm really curious. How did you decide that this was an appropriate book for you?

ZAVIER: I picked it because it looks and sounds good.

It's obvious to me that Zavier hasn't applied any of the strategies from our anchor chart on how to choose appropriate books!

ME: Why don't you go to the page you're on and read a little to me?

Zavier reads from the text. His reading is fairly fluent, with few miscues, but there are many words on the page that I know he doesn't understand.

ME: Thank you. You read that fluently, but I'm wondering if there are any words that are getting in the way of your understanding.

Zavier goes back through what he has read and identifies six words that he doesn't know. We discuss their meanings.

ME: Even if you can pronounce the word, if you don't know it, shouldn't you still put your finger down for the five-finger test? What do you think about this book? Is it a good fit?

ZAVIER: I really want to read it. But yeah, I don't get some of the words. But I really want to read it.

ME: You need to decide: Is this a book you can stay with and think with, or are the words going to get in the way? You have a huge job to do. After one chapter, you must decide if this is a book for you. How about you keep reading and I'll go confer with some other kids, then I'll come back and check in.

The kids know that when I say that, I'll always be back! After about twenty minutes, I return and sit down.

ME: So what do you think?

ZAVIER: I really want to read this book, but I'm not getting it. Maybe I should try another book.

ME: I think you're right. Here's the cool thing, though. Books wait—so you can always come back to this one and read it later and really understand and enjoy it. Or we can get it for you on tape so you can listen to it at home. [*Although Zavier has realized this text is too hard, I'm not sure he will find an appropriate text. This is my opportunity to continue to explicitly teach and guide him.*] The other thing, Zavier, that I want to teach you as your reading teacher is that when readers always try books that are way too hard, their reading doesn't improve or get better. And my job is to help you become a stronger reader. So, do you have another book you might want to read, or do you need help?

ZAVIER: No, not really.

ME: You want some help? We could go shop the shelves together.

ZAVIER: Yeah, I'd like that.

We go to the classroom library and I guide him toward books that are appropriate for him. We pull three titles and he goes back to peruse them and decide which one he wants. He still has choice, and now he can interact with the text successfully.

TRINITY EXPLORES HER WRITER'S NOTEBOOK

We met Trinity and read one of her phenomenal poems in Chapter 1. Is she a gifted writer? Absolutely. But even great writers need direct instruction.

ME: Hi. You asked for a conference. What can I do for you?

TRINITY: I want to write a poem and I'm not sure how to put it all together. I just can't seem to get poetry out of my mind.

ME: Tell me a little more about what you mean.

TRINITY: Well, I've been doing all the quick-writes from our reading pieces. See, here's what I wrote after we read the September piece [*she flips to that page in her notebook*].

Untiteled

By Trinity G.

The leaving of Autaum can be described in many ways. Like the crisp sound the leaves give us when the they leave the wind whistleing branches. Or when the soft powdered blanket of snow tucks.. in the harvest for winter. Or could it be the little changes in are selfs. Body temputure becoming colder as the winds waft thrugh are hearts and souls. Caring us back to the begianing of a new season.

And here's what I wrote after some of the fall poetry you gave us [*she flips to this, too*]. I have a lot of stuff in here that I like, but I want to write a new, really great poem. But I don't want to completely start over.

Auatm is a part of us. the place we rember in the briskly cold vinter. The place that trigers are hearts and eyes open to the beuty of Mother earths children. the place children gather to thank the brilliant colored leaves for giving them shade during the heated sumer. The place Mothers and Fathers work to admire. The place Mother earth crys a tear of happiens wich turns into and blanet of snow as if to tuck her children in for vinter. Autuam is ~~place I like to call home~~. A place of love.

ME: You know, you are really using your writer's notebook so well. Ralph Fletcher [*The Writer's Notebook*] has written that sometimes in our notebooks we have crystals and that we need to dig for them. Trinity, I think your notebook is absolutely filled with crystals. What do you think you could do? What do you want to do? [*I think she already knows what she wants to do, she just needs my permission.*]

TRINITY: I'm kind of noticing that I have pieces in all my different writing that I could kind of put together. Can I take out stuff I've already written and make something new?

ME: What do you think? Why do you think we keep a writer's notebook?

TRINITY: Okay, you're saying that I can. I wanted to check.

ME: I'm glad you figured that out, because that's what a writer's notebook is for. But think about this: If you just combine a lot of stuff, is that enough? Or is that just a start?

TRINITY: I think I need to fix stuff and add to it. But I have a lot that I like already.

ME: As your writing teacher, I suggest you go back through your writer's notebook and either highlight or mark the lines or the parts that you really like and then think how you could use them together. Would that work?

TRINITY: I think so.

ME: Before I leave, would you show me a line that you'd really like to use? [*Trinity finds a line she loves and shows it to me.*] I absolutely agree. Now the trick is going to be how you combine all this. I also have to tell you that you are reading like a writer and writing like a reader. As I look through your notebook, that is absolutely obvious. Is there anything else you need before I leave?

TRINITY [*after thinking for a minute*]**:** I think I'm okay, but would you check in with me tomorrow?

ME: Absolutely.

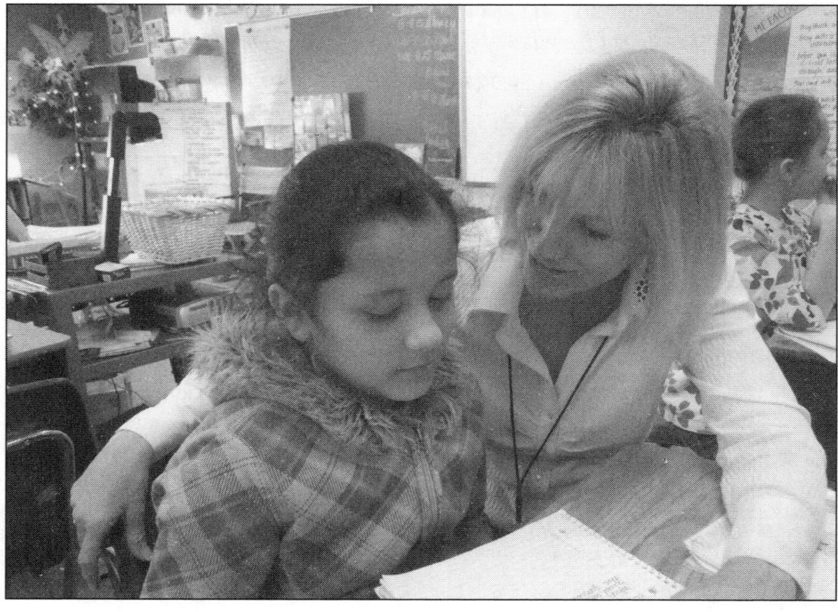

Introducing Conferences

> **THE LANGUAGE OF LEARNING**
>
> Starting this way lets students articulate what they need to learn and gives me the opportunity to truly *listen*.

Before I start conferring with the students, I explain conferences to the whole group. An initial discussion with my class about how I'll confer with them might sound like this.

"I'm always going to start out my conferences with something like, 'How's it going?' Then I'm going to ask you, 'As your reading teacher—or writing teacher—what do you need from me?'

> **▶ THE NITTY-GRITTY**
>
> Here I'm assessing how students are using strategies independently. I'm also gathering information I'll use to pull together needs-based groups.

"If we are studying a specific comprehension strategy (questioning, for example), I'm going to ask you how you're using that in your reading, and how it's helping you as a reader. Or if we are working on something specific in writing, I am going to ask you how you're doing that.

"Sometimes I may ask you to read to me, so that I can check your fluency and how you're doing with vocabulary words. Sometimes I may just have you tell me about your reading. You'll probably hear me ask you to tell me about what you're *thinking* as you read and *why*. You know how much I love that word.

"Finally, before I leave you, I will teach you one thing that will help you as a reader or writer, and I will expect you to practice that. You'll notice me writing down comments on my clipboard. I'm taking notes what you're doing really well and what we need to work on. And of course you may ask me to read you what I write. Remember, there are no secrets here." (Many times the kids do ask to read what I write, and thus they begin to internalize that our literacy journey for the year is going to be a collaborative one!) Figure 7.3 list the things I check for during reading and writing conferences.

As I confer with students, I'm instructing not only the child I'm sitting next to but also the students close by. Kids eavesdrop! I'm glad they do: They listen and learn. I want them to hear the way I talk, because I expect them to replicate this type of meaningful talk when they begin to confer with each other.

Another trick I've discovered through trial and error is to confer with only one child at a group table or in a cluster of desks. I directly touch that child but have an effect on the others. Then I get up and confer with a student across the room. Why across the room? Behavior management. I want the

Skills I Check for in a Reading Conference	**Skills I Check for in a Writing Conference**
• Fluency • Literal comprehension • Inferential comprehension • Use of comprehension strategies • Appropriateness of text • Internalization of reading level • Vocabulary • Retelling • Summarizing • Synthesizing • Goals • Recommendations for future reading	• Organization–beginning, middle, end • Rich details • Knowledge of genre • Use of the traits • Use of the skill or concept I am teaching directly in class • Transfer of vocabulary • Conventions of standard English • Using authors and texts as mentors

Figure 7.3 Checking Skills During Reading and Writing Conferences

▶ CONSIDER THIS

As I look through this list, what could I add? What skills am I not teaching in my classroom?

kids to pick up on the fact that there's no sequence to where I go. If I do five five-minute conferences (a half hour by the time I've written my notes and moved from place to place), I can work at five different tables and my words will have reached almost all my students.

What about the students who have trouble staying focused? Do I go confer with them then and there? *Absolutely not*; that just reinforces the negative behavior. Instead, I confer with a nearby student, possibly snapping my fingers or giving "the look" to indicate that the misbehaving student needs to straighten up. If the student continues to be disruptive, I finish my conference and then tell the troublemaker, "You're breaking my heart! How can you be doing this when we're all working so incredibly hard? What do you need from me to help you settle down? Or do you need to leave the room until you can get yourself under control and then come back in?" It works.

Figure 7.4 lists the principles to follow in order to conduct effective conferences. Figure 7.5 lists some helpful prompts that should build on students' responses to move them forward, and which then leaves them with a job to do.

- Sit right next to the student at the same level.
- Let the student guide the conference.
- Teach *one* thing.
- Teach the *reader*, not the reading.
- Teach the *writer*, not the writing.
- *Wait, wait, wait!* Be patient.
- *Listen.*
- Keep it short–five minutes max.
- Mirror the child–give feedback.
- Trust the student. Be honest, so they trust you.
- Be genuinely curious–you'll be amazed at what you find out.
- Be patient with yourself. (Yes, this does take practice!)

Figure 7.4 Principles for an Effective Conference

▶ TRICK OF THE TRADE

I watched Patrick Allen use this (Figure 7.5) with a student and since then I've tried it in my classroom. It works, maybe because it gives the student more time to reflect. When you ask a student a question and they answer, "I don't know," respond, "Well, if you did know, what would you say?" Ninety percent of the time they'll tell you! Try it!

Figure 7.5 Conference Prompts to Help Students Construct Meaning

CONFERENCE PROMPTS TO HELP STUDENTS CONSTRUCT MEANING

- How's it going? What do you need from me?
- What are you thinking as you read that page?
- You've just done a literal retelling. Read the passage again and tell me what you see differently. How did your perspective change?
- So what do you think I want you to do?
- Remember how we share with one another in our group discussions? That's the same sort of thinking you need to leave behind in the margins of your book.
- Find one sentence you really like. Look at it like a writer. Why do you like it? How can you use the same technique to make your writing better?
- What did you do to fix your understanding?
- Walk me through how you figured out this word. What can you take away from figuring this out that you can use in future reading? (One word can make a huge difference in comprehension!)
- As your reading teacher, do you think that I think you understand this page? Why not?
- How did you choose __________?
- When did you decide __________?
- What's holding you back?
- How did you figure that out?
- Is there anything else you need from me to be successful?

Teaching Kids to Talk

I begin teaching kids how to talk on the first day of school—before we discuss expectations, even before they put their supplies away. After welcoming the kids, I tell them a bit about myself. Then I direct them to turn to the student next to them, introduce themselves, and talk about their summer, what they hope the school year will be like, or anything else that's on their mind.

"You do need to introduce yourself, first and last name. And you need to pay attention. Because when we're done, you will stand up as a pair, introduce your partner to the class, and share one thing you learned about her or him. If you need to take notes to help you remember, that's fine. I'll give you ten minutes for this. One person starts, then after five minutes I'll say *switch* and the other person takes her or his turn. And it's okay to ask each other questions."

This is a great icebreaker, and nobody is left out. (If there's an odd number of students, I interview the one without a partner.) After ten minutes, I ask for volunteers to stand and share. It's a great way to practice talk and immediately makes it clear that talking—and listening—will be valued in our classroom. Plus we get to learn a little about each other in a fairly short time.

Other ways we share and talk in our room include:

- *Table talk.* Desk/table groups talk about a topic.
- *Turn and talk.* Students turn to a neighbor and talk about a specified topic. Doing this during a minilesson gives every student a chance to talk as I eavesdrop. It makes group discussions manageable and less time-consuming.
- *Partner shares.* Two students discuss their reading or their writing. Partner shares are the perfect way to start the year. I often have students meet with the same partner for the first week or two.
- *Four-way shares (compass groups).* Steph Harvey and Anne Goudvis (2000) coined the "compass" designation: just as a compass has four directions, four students sit across from each other at eye level. Once students are comfortable and successful with partner shares, I begin using compass groups. Sometimes the kids choose the groups; sometimes I assign members.
- *End-of-period table shares.* This is often the reflection activity at the end of a workshop. Students at a table or part of a desk group share what they went through, how they used their time, or what they learned. Talk solidifies learning!

A Fifth-Grade Table Share in April

After reading two poems, one by Langston Hughes, the other by Emily Dickinson, and "leaving tracks in the snow" about their thinking, students sit down for a ten-minute quick-write. I write in my journal for five minutes—I always write with my kids for the first five minutes and no one may interrupt me—then move around the room, glancing over shoulders to read or kneeling beside students to check in or ask, "How did you do that?"

After ten minutes, I ask the students to discuss quietly at their tables how they decided to write what they did and how it connected to our literacy work for the day. After students at each table share their thoughts, I ask who wants to share their writing. (This sharing is critical. It's fabulous to hear the different voices and ideas.)

I'm surprised when Todd raises his hand. Todd is a great student, but never one to call attention to himself, and his responses are generally at the literal level. Todd stands up and reads the following.

Dead with the Wind

The wind blows. The sand curls up like a giant wave. The wind blows. The tumble weed rolls along like a wheel on a car. Nothing but silence is in the air but the shrill whistle of the wind. There once was noise. The zipping whistle of the bullet. The wham of the cannon. The shrieking cry of the man who was shot then dead silence again. And thats how it stays. The cold of the war is over and peace stays after the war to make sure none of the spirits are in the wrong hands. Peace spreads easily like flowers, but it can be killed if you aren't careful. And then the ugly weeds sprout and bring darkness to the land.

By: Todd

When he finishes there is an audible gasp from the lab visitors in the room. How did he do that? Even I don't know where it came from, so I ask: "How did you do that, so that I can do the same thing in my writing?"

Todd has blended his inquiry report on the cold war with the poems he read. "I tried to capture the random way Dickinson wrote with the power of Hughes and use the information from the cold war." (Many, many thanks to Chryse Hutchins for capturing his exact words.) Whew! When in doubt, ask—and listen.

Lingering Questions

- Do I have a Todd in my class? How will I find out?
- How much time during the school day is spent on purposeful talk?
- How much time do my students spend talking?
- How much time do I spend talking?
- Is listening valued and practiced?
- What can I learn about my students through conferring?
- What can my students learn about reading and writing through conferring?
- Does the thought of conferring scare me? (It's okay if it does. It's difficult at first, but with practice it gets easier—and the payoffs are worth it!)

CHAPTER 8

Demonstrate, Do It, Eavesdrop, Confer

The quality of your talk with students is instrumental in helping them live the connection between reading and writing. Through conferring, we exchange our thinking about the texts we read and the texts we compose. A literacy workshop is one big "think fest." It's not about reading or writing per se—it's an instructional venue in which students are eager to use their intellect and imagination.

Taking a four-part approach to conversation is another way to build the trust and independence necessary to *sustain* high-level thinking, reading, writing, and talk. In other words, you need to get out of the way! I've mentioned this concept in passing, but this chapter presents a template of sorts. This sequential flow is key to helping children advance, because it puts students in the driver's seat. It's my version of the gradual release model (Pearson and Gallagher 1983). Using it, you turn your classroom over to the kids, so they are engaged, *practicing* what you teach rather than passively listening.

This four-part pattern encourages students to participate and gets them in the habit of being generous with their thinking—during lessons, conferences, and book clubs and in their own writing. The sequence is:

> *Demonstrate*: Model and think aloud during a minilesson.
>
> *Do it*: During and immediately after the minilesson, invite kids to interact with the text and "do" the strategy.
>
> *Eavesdrop*: Listen as children turn and talk during the minilesson or while they are working on a strategy together.
>
> *Confer*: Push independence while kids are working independently.

Through it all, you're also assessing students' use of the strategy. The book lover's book (BLB) facilitates the process as kids interact with you and work hard alongside you.

In a way, the pattern reminds me of the box step in ballroom dancing. Step, forward, side, back—you get this basic choreography down in your teaching, and then, like an expert dancer, you add and adapt to suit your class. Waltz, fox trot, jitterbug—in an effective literacy workshop, you can change the moves, change the tempo, on different days. You might savor a read-aloud one day and forget writing entirely. But to stay with the dance metaphor, what I encourage you *not* to do is to stand still—that is, don't demonstrate most of the day. Teachers admit that's the phase they get most stuck in, because they are afraid of things falling apart if they give up control.

I'll show you how this sequence works by focusing on how I teach just three of the seven metacognitive strategies (see Figure 8.1): using schema, asking questions, and making inferences (the heavy lifters in helping children become strong readers). Once you've studied these examples, think through your own reading strategies instruction. If you are just starting out, you may want to start small and focus on *just three* your first year. When you're comfortable with these, take on the rest. Your ultimate goal is to integrate all the strategies so children are able to use them flexibly as they read, but you don't need to cover all of them at once.

To Learn More

To teach reading comprehension strategies well, you need to know what they are and how they work. These three great books give you that background, as well as useful lessons to use in your classroom.

Keene, Ellin Oliver, and Susan Zimmermann. 2007. *Mosaic of Thought: The Power of Comprehension Strategy Instruction*, 2d ed. Portsmouth, NH: Heinemann.

Harvey, Stephanie, and Anne Goudvis. 2007. *Strategies That Work: Teaching Comprehension for Understanding and Engagement*, 2d ed. Portland, ME: Stenhouse.

Zimmermann, Susan, and Chryse Hutchins. 2003. *Seven Keys to Comprehension: How to Help Your Kids Read It and Get It!* New York: Three Rivers Press.

Strategies that help you "listen to the voice in your mind that speaks while you read"

- *Monitoring meaning*: knowing when you know, knowing when you don't know
- *Using and creating schema*: making connections between the new and the known, building and activating background knowledge
- *Asking questions*: generating questions before, during, and after reading that lead you deeper into the text
- *Determining importance*: deciding what matters most, what is worth remembering
- *Making inferences*: combining background knowledge with information from the text to predict, conclude, make judgments, interpret
- *Using sensory and emotional images*: creating mental images to deepen and stretch meaning
- *Synthesizing*: strengthening meaning by combining understanding with knowledge from other texts/sources.

Figure 8.1 Seven Key Comprehension Strategies (Zimmermann and Hutchins 2003)

When I'm deciding which ones to delve into deeply, I take into account state standards and requirements and the grade-level curriculum. But while I'm doing an in-depth study on one strategy, many of the others come into play as well. So we're really talking all of them, all the time. With practice, you'll get to this point!

Using and Creating Schema

PURPOSE

I begin the year with a study of background knowledge. But it needs to be meaningful background knowledge—connections that enhance and deepen understanding rather than lead the reader away from the text: *How does this help you as a reader? How is this helping you understand the text?* Background knowledge gives students huge hooks on which to hang their new learning. Building vocabulary, taking notes, navigating the textbook—activating and building background knowledge undergird it all. It is a skill students will use through college and beyond.

DEMONSTRATE (1)

To introduce background knowledge, I talk about it in terms of *making connections*. At this point, students' faces light up and they point to the board that proclaims *It's All About Making Connections* and comment on the footprints that stretch around our room.

"Okay, I get it. It's not just about leaving tracks in the snow, is it? Those tracks go all around the room," Lucie says.

"Good observation. It's about connecting all our learning so that we can keep building on it. Those connections create that hook we can hang new learning on."

Students usually see that there are *text-to-self* and *text-to-text* connections, but I often need to nudge them to include *text-to-author* and *text-to-world* connections. A word of caution, especially with text-to-self connections: Right from the get-go, I stress that any connections they make must help them understand the text. I constantly ask, "Why did you make that connection?" followed by, "And *how* does it help you understand this text better?" You have to help kids see the difference between random connections to their lives and more significant, illuminating connections.

Figure 8.2 is an example of an anchor chart a class and I co-constructed during a week in which we explored background knowledge.

By fourth grade, students generally have experience with background knowledge (at least if thinking strategies are a school-wide focus), so we touch on it and practice, then move on. Our investigation generally lasts a couple weeks. However, it can take longer. If students come to my room with no exposure to this strategy, I slow it down, spend as many as six weeks if necessary.

▶ THE NITTY-GRITTY

In the second edition of *Strategies That Work*, Stephanie Harvey and Ann Goudvis insist: "Whether we are questioning, inferring, or synthesizing, our background knowledge is the foundation of our thinking. We simply can't understand what we read without thinking about what we already know" (2007, 17). Text-to-self connections are also important in visualizing, creating sensory images, making inferences, and monitoring meaning and comprehension—you can't understand when you don't have a hook.

DEMONSTRATE (2)

In third grade, I spend a bit more time exploring the idea that what students bring to the text and their reading helps them understand. One of my favorite books I use to help me do this is *The Wednesday Surprise*, by Eve Bunting. In the book, a little girl teaches her grandmother to read as a surprise for her

What We Know About Background Knowledge

- Connections to what you already know
- Helps you understand/comprehend
- Helps you remember
- New learning
- You can use nearby words to help you understand (context)
- Know something already
- Word level
- Sentence level
- Whole text

Text-to-self

Text-to-text

Text-to-author

Text-to-world

Figure 8.2 Anchor Chart: What We Know About Background Knowledge

father's birthday, but it's not evident until the end of the book that it's the grandmother who is learning to read. Students are always caught by surprise when the grandmother stands up and begins to read, to the delight of the family. We discuss how students' background knowledge—and their own connections—add to this sense of surprise, this "gotcha" moment.

Figure 8.3 is an anchor chart based on a discussion of *The Wednesday Surprise*. Creating it allowed me to informally assess the students' skill at summarizing (the left-hand column) and the kind and depth of the connections they made (the right-hand column). Although the right-hand column isn't explicitly headed *Connections*, it's that column that pushes student thinking. As the year progresses, the right-hand column becomes much longer.

DO IT: TURN RESPONSIBILITY OVER TO THE KIDS

While I still demonstrate during this step, the students also demonstrate by recording their thinking in the minilesson section of their BLB.

My good friend and phenomenal teacher Mary Pfau gave me *The Librarian of Basra: A True Story from Iraq*, by Jeanette Winter as a gift a few years ago, and I've been using it with my students ever since. The story, based on a real woman and event, links the power of reading and writing with world events.

What It's About (Literal Knowledge)	What It Makes Me Think or Wonder (Inferences)
The grandma learns to read, and her seven-year-old granddaughter, Anna, taught her. Anna taught her grandmother to read to surprise her father for his birthday. Grandma would come over every Wednesday to practice. They totally surprised the entire family.	Why didn't the grandmother ever learn to read? Was she too busy when she was younger? Was she an immigrant? Surprised when it was Grandma who learned to read. Reminds me of spending time with grandparents. Bag of books connects to another book—Can You Read to Me, Mama? Why was the bag so heavy?

Figure 8.3 Anchor Chart: *The Wednesday Surprise*

It tells how, as Basra, Iraq, braces for war, a librarian asks the people in the town to hide 70 percent of the books in the library in their homes. When a fire destroys the library, these books are saved.

This book raises powerful text-to-world connections and gets students thinking. Figure 8.4 is the anchor chart my class and I co-constructed during a minilesson on this book. Nicole's thinking as the lesson unfolded is shown in Figure 8.5.

EAVESDROP: LISTEN AND READ TO INFORM TEACHING

I eavesdrop on kids' thinking about the text by listening as they turn and talk and by reading the lit log letters, reading responses, and reflections in their BLB. Doing so is another way I assess how students are using the strategy *independently*.

Following are some examples of responses after students read *Number the Stars*, by Lois Lowry (a fourth-grade anchor text).

> The Holocaust was a truly horrible thing. It really helped to build my background knowledge, but I will, and everyone will still have one lingering question...why would anyone be so bad, be so mean as the Nazis were? Before we started studying the Nazis and the Holocaust, we were just reading the book and not understanding how bad it really was. No big deal! They are just going to the camps! We had no idea. We saw the picture of the crematorium and thought it was their home, but boy were we wrong!!! It blew my mind that they

The Librarian of Basra

Before

Iraq—war—Saddam Hussein

- Has something to do with Osama Bin Laden (Cole)
- Taliban/al-Qaeda—Afghanistan
- Three tribes fighting in Iraq (Jonny)
- Middle East (Davis)
- Ties to 9/11
- Library is important (Triple Creek Dam—text-to-text)

During

Text	Connection
Basra	"I hear it on the news all the time, important."
Sand swept	Desert/pictures I've seen
Library	Meeting place—important; it's important in Iraq, too—not unique to the U.S.
Muhammad biography	
700 years old	U.S. isn't even 400 years old!

After

Lingering thoughts, connections, etc.

- Where are the books now? (four years later)
- Was/has the library been rebuilt?
- Amazed at how important books are in Iraq
- Woman librarian—that's still surprising about Iraq

Figure 8.4 Anchor Chart: *The Librarian of Basra*

burned people in there! I couldn't believe that they would do such a horrible thing, but if you want world domination, you must really want it to be that bad. I bet most of the soldiers didn't even want world domination, they were just following Hitler's orders because if they didn't they would be killed! At the beginning of Number the Stars, I didn't, and no one did know how bad this was and now that we have read, and learned, and learned some more, and learned some more, we now realize that it was a big deal to go to the concentration camps! I LOVED this unit about the Holocaust!!!!!

—Madi

The Librarian of Basra

Before: In war, Iraq, Saddam Hussain, 3 tribes fighting, middle east, ties to 911, Libr. im.

During text	connection
library	Kobel is meetingplace too.
Questions	in U.S. too.
Muhamed Bio 700's	US. isn't even 300 yrs.
Rumors	rumors reality
hide books	wicked brilliant idea
fireburns library	good they moved books
library	literacy

After: lingering thouts, connections, etc. Where books now 4 yrs. later. What happend to restaraunt. Women librarian WOOhw. Why stile fighting, library been rebuilt?

Figure 8.5 Nicole's Thinking

Background knowledge helps me understand Number the Stars better because we know what relocating means and if we didn't know we wouldn't know where they sent the Jews. Also it helps because we might not know what the Holocaust was so we might not know how much danger the Rosens were in and if we didn't have background knowledge we wouldn't know who the Nazis were and how dangerous they can be. Also in the beginning I didn't know what a concentration camp was. The concentration camps were in the book it was still useful to know what they were. Also it helps because we would not know that the Nazis were taking the Jews and we would think the Jews were in no danger and we would read the book thinking that everyone was in no danger except when the Nazis come in their apartment and pull on Ellen's hair not caring about her. That's why you probably need background knowledge because you won't understand it and you will see it at a different point of view. That's how background knowledge helps you read this book better.

—Spencer

THE LANGUAGE OF LEARNING

Both Madi's and Spencer's reflections demonstrate the depth of their learning. As I meet with these students in conferences, I can check to see how their thinking *changes* as they read. For good readers, thinking often changes as schema are developed. Thinking changes *before*, *during*, and *after* reading, and I want to be explicit about this. I can also stress the importance of asking questions before reading—in fact, before launching any new learning—to facilitate building background knowledge. My goal is for these students to take what they've learned in their reflections and apply it to their independent reading. By eavesdropping, I match our conferences with these students' need to be pushed to a higher level.

CONFER: BRING OBSERVATIONS BACK TO STUDENTS

Finally, through my individual conferences with students, I listen to them explain how they are using the strategy in the book they are reading. For example, as we study the strategy of schema, I want the students to articulate whether it's a text-to-self, text-to-text, text-to-author, or text-to-world connection and *how* this connection helps them understand the text at a deeper level. It's all about articulating how.

Asking Questions

PURPOSE

My students are exposed to questions from the moment they walk through the classroom door. They know I am curious and want to know how and why they think and learn. Curiosity is contagious. Young children overflow with questions. I remember both my son and daughter as toddlers driving me insane with their constant questioning and need to know. Kids go to school still questioning—primary students exhibit the sheer joy of learning about the world. But often something happens. The questions get squelched. Maybe it's because sometimes kids aren't listened to or they think their questions don't count. Or maybe it's the result of questions in textbooks and on worksheets whose answers don't matter much.

I need to retrain them to realize that their thinking and questions matter. My core beliefs really enter in here, because kids have to feel safe and trusted and able to take risks in order to ask phenomenal questions. And they need to know that their questions will be respected and answered honestly or that I will point them in the right direction to find the answers, that they will be listened to and their thinking valued.

Independence and choice wouldn't occur in my students' and my classroom without our ability to ask questions—questioning leads to rich, deep thinking. Questions prompt great book club discussions, questions frame our research studies, questions allow me to push my students to their highest potential.

There are numerous books on questioning and lots of different ways to organize questions or place them in hierarchies (Bloom's taxonomy, for one). I want my students to know the difference between *literal* questions, sometimes called "questions on the page" (I call them "smack-me-upside-the-head-I-can-find-the-answer-right-in-the-text" questions—and of course I smack my forehead as I say that, which tends to make an impression) and *inferential* questions, sometimes called "questions in your head." I explain inferential questions as those you can answer by combining what's in the text (the clues) and what you know (your background knowledge). Inferences *always* need to be tied to the text. Inferences that aren't tied to text pull readers out of the text and impede comprehension.

DEMONSTRATE

Chryse Hutchins (coauthor of *7 Keys to Comprehension* [2003]) uses the analogy of "thick and thin" questions (Harvey and Goudvis 2000, 2007) when she works with students and teachers. Kids get this analogy because it's so concrete. Chryse uses a template (see Figure 8.6) that makes it even more concrete—the space allotted reinforces the concept. Students are quick to realize that literal questions tend to be thin and inferential questions are thick. Clarifying questions—questions that begin with *when*, *where*, and *what*—are generally thin questions; they can be answered in just a few words. Questions that start with *why* or *how* are thick questions.

Name:

Text:

THICK AND THIN QUESTIONS	
Thin questions from the text:	
Thin question	*Answer*
Thick questions from the text:	
Thick question	*Answer*

Figure 8.6 Thick and Thin Questions

I use Chryse's analogy in my classroom and students grasp it quickly. As we read through textbooks (science and social studies textbooks are *resources* in my classroom), we discuss whether the questions at the end of the chapters are thick or thin. Students realize that the majority of these questions are thin, with one or two—those requiring students to apply the material they've read—being thick.

Thick questions lead to the best thinking and discussion. Book clubs center around thick questions, research notes center around thick questions—the classroom revolves around thick questions.

DO IT (1)

I use Eve Bunting as a segue between building text-to-author connections and asking good questions. I also model the asking questions strategy using Chris Van Allsburg's books (see the minilesson on *The Stranger* in Chapter 4).

I usually start with his *The Garden of Abdul Gasazi* because it's his first book (and the main character is a dog—kids love the dog).

"We've started looking at questioning as we've been reading some of Eve Bunting's books—she's written some books that we really had to think about. Today, I'm going to share another of my favorite authors who prompts readers to ask great questions. His name is Chris Van Allsburg. What's cool about him is that he's the illustrator, too, so his pictures enhance, or help us understand, the story.

"This is his first book. Let's look at the cover and think what it might be about, but also think of questions that arise just from looking at the picture." On the front cover is a garden with a topiary. Students raise their hands and share and I record some of the questions on our class anchor chart. Students really want to know why the bushes are shaped like animals, so we take a moment and discuss that (an example of building their background knowledge).

"Here's one more thing I want you to know about Van Allsburg. In this book, one of the main characters is Fritz, the dog. Van Allsburg had a dog like that, so now he puts the dog in every picture book he writes, but he kind of hides it."

"Like in Where's Waldo?" Scott wants to know.

"Exactly. It's fun to go through the book and see if you can find it. In this book, though, the dog is everywhere."

With that, we begin to read the book, stopping and asking questions, which I record on the chart. At the end of the book, Van Allsburg leaves the reader hanging. Was Fritz the dog really turned into a duck by the magician, or did he simply make his way home? Van Allsburg leaves the hat as a clue, but it's up to the reader to write the ending. Every year when I get to the last page, students think that it can't be the end.

"Come on, there has to be one more page!"

"Nope, that's it. He's leaving us hanging, isn't he? What are you still thinking now that the story is over?"

Then we record our lingering questions, which are numerous.

▶ THE NITTY-GRITTY

If there are certain authors that you love to teach year after year, find out about them and share the information with the kids. It makes reading come to life even more, gives a window into the writing, and helps you weave writing instruction into your literacy workshop.

Once we've finished recording our thinking, I circle back. "Let's go back through all the questions that we asked and see if they were answered by Van Allsburg. Let's code them. *L* means they were answered literally—we can find the answer right in the text, we could lift out the words to write the answer. *I* means we had to infer the answer. Van Allsburg gives us clues in the text and then we have to add our own thinking to come up with the answer. And finally we can code it *NA*, for not answered—sometimes our questions aren't answered."

The students and I go back through our questions on the anchor chart and code them. After this, we discuss how that helps our understanding of the ending of the book. Figure 8.7 is an example of an anchor chart from this lesson.

DO IT (2)

After the lesson on *The Garden of Abdul Gasazi*, I bring in other books by Chris Van Allsburg and continue to model the strategy of questioning, at the same time building background knowledge and using text-to-author connections. With each new book, I give the kids more responsibility—they record their thinking in the minilesson section of their BLB, for example (see Figure 8.8), instead of my attempting to capture all the thinking on the anchor chart.

EAVESDROP

Besides assessing student's independence, the lit log section of the BLB is an excellent place to check for understanding and usage. Take this entry by Lucie:

> Dear Mrs. B,
>
> I have finished Found, only 1 chapter left. I'm wondering if Jonah is going to pick the future or the past? I'm itching to know what Jonah is going to pick. The last pages are getting better and better! I love Things Not Seen. It answers your questions in the next chapter. I like how it zooms in and it doesn't have a long intro. Bobby is very smart sometimes. Why don't they tell anybody or any of their relatives? I'm wondering is his mother going to die? Is he going to become friends with that blind Alicia? Can't wait to read the rest of Found.
>
> Sincerely,
> Lucie

The Garden of Abdul Gasazi

by Chris Van Allsburg

Strategy: Questioning

(Coding, done after reading: L = literal, I = inferred, NA = not answered)

Before

- How old is the dog? NA
- Who is the boy? Alan–L
- Who is Abdul Gasazi? Retired magician–L
- Why are the hedges trimmed to resemble shapes (topiary)? NA
- Is the boy Abdul Gasazi? No–L
- Who is the man on the cover? L
- Boy's name? L
- Why is the garden involved in the title/story? I
- Dog? Magic? I
- How big is the garden? NA/I

During

- What's going to happen? I
- Why did Fritz run? I
- Where is Fritz? L
- Who will find Fritz first? Alan or Abdul? L
- Is the duck really Fritz? I
- Will Miss Hester be mad? L
- How long will the spell last? I
- Will he ever find his hat? L
- Why did Abdul Gasazi play the trick? I

After

- Which animal was really Fritz? I
- How did Fritz get the hat? I
- Did Fritz really turn into the duck? I

Figure 8.7 Anchor Chart: *The Garden of Abdul Gasazi*

The Wreck of the Zephyr

by Chris Van Allsburg

Author Connections (How does this deepen our understanding of the text?)

- Dog is going to show up in a picture (V.A. has one)
- Clues
- Leaves you with questions at the end
- Reader has to figure out the ending (using the strategies of questioning and making inferences)
- Illustrates and writes—pictures help with comprehension
- Inferential writer

Before

- What is a zephyr?
- Did it get wrecked in a storm?
- Why is there a sailboat on the front?
- Is the Zephyr a boat? A person?
- Is the wreck bad?
- Is anybody in the boat?
- How will it wreck?
- What's the "twist"? What will Van Allsburg do to surprise us?

Figure 8.8 Anchor Chart: *The Wreck of the Zephyr*

Inferring

PURPOSE

Human beings infer all the time—when we observe social cues, when we laugh, when we cry. So when we tell kids that making an inference is reading between the lines, they don't get it. Honest students will say, "I'm looking between the lines as hard as I can and I just don't see anything!" We have to be explicit.

Primary students infer all the time. They create stories from the wordless picture books they read. They know exactly what is happening in the story by looking at the pictures in *Good Dog, Carl*. They read comic books and laugh—they get the joke.

As students move up through the grades, inferring becomes more sophisticated. Some students, though, claim they're making an inference when they are simply guessing, and their guess is pulling them out of the text. I always push the words *why* and *how*, because inferences are always tied to the text. *Why did you make that specific inference? What in the text leads you to think that?* And then, *How did making that inference help you understand the text better?* These are key questions, no matter the grade level.

DEMONSTRATE (ASSESS CLASS KNOWLEDGE)

When I introduce inferring, I often talk about social cues with the kids. How do we know when someone is mad? He clenches his fists, she grits her teeth, he turns red, and so on. How do we know when someone's sad? She cries, his mouth droops, she doesn't laugh. When authors describe how a character is feeling without actually naming the emotion, we—the readers—have to infer what's going on inside that character. We may also discuss that when we laugh at a comic strip, we're inferring; when we read and feel an emotion, we are inferring.

To hold our thinking about inferring at the beginning of the unit, we create a class anchor chart.

Making Inferences

- When we're visualizing, we're inferring.
- When we're answering our thick questions, we're inferring.
- When we come up with the nitty-gritty, we're inferring.
- When we understand character's feeling and emotions, we're inferring.
- If we go back and reread and it's not right there in the text, we're "reading between the lines."
- We have to understand to infer.

We add to it as our thinking deepens.

I also want the students to understand that as readers we take our background knowledge and combine it with the author's words to create an inference. Inferences are always tied to the text. That's an important difference between an *inference* and a *prediction*. When we predict, we are drawing on our own background knowledge and thinking—it isn't always tied to the text. For example, before beginning a book, students may predict what it's about by looking at the cover illustration and reading the title, but these can be misleading. We infer when we make meaning from the text and the pictures within the book.

DO IT (1): CO-CONSTRUCT MEANING

In connection with our study of the Holocaust, we also read Roberto Innocenti's *Rose Blanche,* a beautiful picture book in which the atrocity is seen through a young German girl's eyes. The last pages of the book switch from first-person to third-person narrative, leading the reader to infer that the young girl dies. This haunting book makes kids think. Although our main focus was inferring, the students needed to draw on background knowledge in order to do so. Figure 8.9 is the anchor chart Talia created in her BLB.

Following is Talia's synthesis after finishing the book. It's another example of how it is almost impossible to teach the strategies in isolation. Talia is using many strategies simultaneously to understand the text. Her synthesis helps her reflect and solidify her learning and acknowledge how her classmates helped.

When you finished the book I felt so bad. It is a good but sad book. The way the author makes it a realistic fiction story is very cool. Knowing that this really happened is an awkward feeling. It is hard to believe it but lo and behold it's true.

When we first started this project, I thought I knew a lot about the Holocaust, but when we got deep I realized it was a harsh, disturbing, and cruel time.

Why did the author not tell who the other army was? Is there a special way to tell that she was shot, or did he just do it?

I like it how Will [another student in class] said it went from first to third person because she couldn't finish the story because she was shot.

THE LANGUAGE OF LEARNING

Talia's notes and synthesis show that she is interacting with the text in a very sophisticated way. She is an advanced reader. As her teacher, I want to make sure she is using the strategies when she is reading challenging text independently but also (even more important) that she understands *how* they help her construct deeper understanding. In a conference, we may discuss how her thinking about Rose Blanche deepened her understanding and how she thinks she might transfer this to her own independent reading—the ultimate goal!

DO IT (2): TURN THE WORK OVER TO THE STUDENTS

After I had read *Rose Blanche* aloud to a class of fifth graders, I asked the kids to respond independently. Their responses demonstrate different levels of sophistication and analysis. Each is grappling with the text in his own way, another reason we need to be very choosy about the books we teach.

Rose Blanche

Connections	Questions	Inferences
Swastika/Nazis		
Wink in German different than the treatment in Denmark	WHY?	
	Is the mayor not Jewish? Is the mayor a Nazi?	I think that the Nazis are taken people in the trucks to the concentration camps.
		The Nazis are going to do something bad to the kid
In a movie clip was told Nazis took 1000 kids in trucks to concentration camps.	Why doesn't the mom go look for ROSE?	
barbed wire	Will Rose get caught?	Rose is going to get caught & forced into the camp.
	Does she know that it is a concentration camp	Giving food to concentration camps. Rose knows the way because goes there almost every day.
	Are the soliders taking it? Why are the hurt? Who would hurt them?	she was taken to a camp the girl was killed.

Figure 8.9 Talia's Anchor Chart in the Minilesson Section of Her BLB

During the end of this book, I was MAD that the soldiers had shot her, I mean she was only trying to help the prisoners in the concentration camp. But that would have been very hard on her mother probably, that was a sad book, the mood was sort of dark and depressing. I wonder what the concentration camp really did look like, when Mrs. B read about the big, tall, wooden house thing it sort of made me think about what it must have been like to be captured in war and be starving like that. So I guess I will still think about the book and what it was really like.

—Katherine

Rose Blanche was walking in the foggy forest. A shot was fired. She was shot. Wasn't she? Her sad mother waited and waited for her. She didn't come back!

This book was depressing. A nice little girl that delivered food to prisoners was shot. Who fired the shot? Allies, Germans, Americans? Who knows?

What happened to the prisoners, are they still there? If the bullet just whizzed by Rose, and didn't kill her, would she still have the confidence to feed the prisoners?

—Sean

I think that a war was about to happen there. That explained why everyone ran away. When Rose went to the Concentration Center, the kids weren't there. I don't get why they weren't there. The soldiers were German and their enemies. I believe that the war was going to happen there, but unfortunately Rose was in the middle of it. If only Rose had not gone there she would still be alive. Rose was shot and killed instead. The picture at the end was of the flower that Rose was holding when she got killed. In a way, the flower symbolizes a happy thought. Rose was a good thought because she gave her food to the needy kids. The leaves beside the purple flower were dark green. Those symbolize the evil in the world at the time.

—Rachel

THE LANGUAGE OF LEARNING

Rachel came up with her symbolism comment on her own. It's not something we had discussed. But the comment was fodder for a future classroom discussion and a great segue into teaching about symbolism.

▶ THE NITTY-GRITTY

Two phenomenal nonfiction books I use to help me teach the asking questions, activating schema, and determining importance-in-text strategies are Kathy Wollard's *How Come? Every Kid's Science Questions Explained* (1993) and *How Come? Planet Earth* (1999). Both are chock-full of well-written, interesting articles that answer questions students often ask. These books are also a terrific way to integrate science and social studies with literacy.

Moving to Independence: Offering Choice

The four-phase instructional pattern discussed in this chapter—demonstrate, do it, eavesdrop, confer—is one more element in how I get students to feel confident about and comfortable with articulating their thinking and prepare them to roll up their sleeves and participate. This mind-set, along with all the literacy lessons of the first part of the year, prepares them to handle more choice.

It's February and my students are gathered up in the group area. I'm not presenting as many minilessons but instead turning the majority of our literacy workshop over to the students, allowing them to choose how they use their time. It's part of the gradual release approach I've modeled and we've practiced. Students began by selecting one of two choices, and I've gradually expanded that to three, then to five, but students still know they are accountable for their time. On the board I've written:

Choices for Literacy Workshop

- Independent reading
- Lit log letter/vocab
- Preparing for book clubs
- Note taking for research
- Writing project

"You have been doing such a terrific job with using your time well. I appreciate it when I'm able to trust you to make good choices so that I can eavesdrop on book clubs. Why do you think you're doing so well with this?"

Reed's hand flies up. "Because we've practiced and we know what to do."

"And it's not worksheets. I hate worksheets," Ellie comments. Any time there is an opportunity to reflect, Ellie reminds me just how much she hates worksheets (although we rarely do them!).

I prod, "Why does it make a difference if it's not worksheets?"

"Because they're boring," Ellie answers.

She's right, but I add a qualifier. "I tend to agree with you, but sometimes we have to do them. Why do you think you guys are able to stay focused for over an hour, though, without my having to ride herd on you?"

Lots of hands go up; I call on Naomi. "Because we're choosing and we're working on stuff that's important to us."

Amen.

As the year progresses and I get to release responsibility to the students, all my core beliefs come into play. We would not be at this juncture if I did not truly live by these beliefs. When students are engaged in meaningful work—work that pushes them—behavioral problems decrease. When expectations have been modeled and practiced, behavioral problems decrease. When students are able to make choices, the classroom hums.

"I have five choices on the board. I'll be meeting with two book clubs today. We'll start with *Esperanza Rising*, take a ten-minute break, and then the *Hatchet* group will meet. If you're in one of those groups, half your time will be in book clubs and you'll need to be preparing.

"Because we have such a long period, I want you to choose two things you might work on today and then let me know what those are when I take a status check. That way, as you're finishing the first thing, you'll already know what you'll be working on next. Take a minute and decide. I'll be calling the *Esperanza* group up in ten minutes, so make sure you're ready."

Because it's February and the students have had almost six months of practice, the transition is seamless and they get right to work.

Some years, I let kids make these kinds of choices in November or December, especially in fifth or sixth grade or if it's my second year with that group of kids. Some years, kids aren't making these choices until April. But we always get there. Knowing the kids is the key to when.

I know it's time to release responsibility to the kids when students are following the structures we have in place with little or no direction from me, when they've internalized our anchor charts (especially the ones about what makes good listening and great conversations), when they are using a wealth of comprehension strategies/thinking strategies independently, when stamina is natural and they can maintain focus for long periods of time.

Start small. At the beginning allow *two* choices. When students are successful with those, add another. And be explicit about what your classroom will look like and sound like. When I first introduce choices, I often take the last few minutes of the period and have the kids write a one-sentence reflection on how they used their time. It's a way to hold them accountable and for me to check whether we're in sync. There are a number of rubrics and forms that help students document how they use their time, but I like to keep it short and simple—a quick sentence in their BLB.

We need to step back and let the kids do the work. When students know how to use strategies, how to hold their thinking, and how to talk and listen, they're ready for book clubs, which is the topic of the next chapter. Not Oprah's book club, but classroom book clubs as they have evolved over the years, always with student input. Are you ready to eavesdrop? What the kids have to say might surprise you!

CHAPTER 9

Book Clubs

Bringing Out Students' Best Talk and Thinking

Throughout this book, I've coached you to "model, guide, and step aside" so that students become more independent in the classroom. Book clubs are the ultimate expression of students' rich, self-generated, self-monitored thinking, the payoff for the front-loading you've done early in the year. Students can really fly with their thinking as you sit on the sidelines and marvel.

When I met him, Smokey Daniels (author of *Literature Circles* [2002]) told me that in his workshops he shows a video clip of a book club discussion in my classroom (it's on the *Strategies That Work* DVD [Harvey and Goudvis 2000]) to demonstrate how teachers need to get out of the way. I'm sitting outside the circle of conversation, observing, only occasionally joining in. I'm an "eavesdropper," listening in on the students' conversations and learning from them.

Student-driven literature conversations *are* the be-all and end-all. So much of the literacy work students and I have done together unfurls, like a big, colorful flag, in these conversations. And students love them, citing book talks as the most vital, memorable practice of the year (the book lover's book [BLB], conferring, and using mentor texts are semifinalists). Taken together, these classroom practices are the game changers. And it's no accident that these are the venues where *students talk, share, and are listened to.* Everything I've discussed in this book so far—foundational lessons, anchor charts, talk, listening, the BLB, writing, reading—comes together in book clubs.

Book Clubs	**Versus Reading Groups**
• Students select books.	• Teacher chooses books.
• Groups are fluid, not static; students "opt in."	• Groups are static and usually homogenous.
• Class sets norms.	• Teacher sets rules.
• Groups are student driven/student led.	• Groups are teacher directed.
• Students mark text, hold thinking, and ask their own questions.	• Students are passive; they answer the teacher's questions and complete "canned" end-of-chapter worksheets.
• There is student buy-in.	• Students are "doing school."
• Talk is rich and authentic.	• There's a test on the book at the end.
• Time is built in for reflection/assessment.	

Which classroom would you rather be a student in?

Generally, I start book clubs in November or December, after we've completed the foundational lessons, gotten our literacy workshop up and running, and studied an anchor text. The exact start time depends on the students' grade level and needs. Many teachers I work with don't begin them until January or February. Trust your instincts.

As you see in the first column of Figure 9.1, the key to successful book clubs is front-loading: foundational lessons, reading comprehension strategies, conferring, and anchor texts. The rest of the year is divided into three zones representing gradual release. In zone 1, I'm more active (taking notes, instructing when necessary), and book clubs meet one at a time. In zone 2, kids have more responsibility; two book clubs meet simultaneously and I move back and forth, eavesdropping on the conversations. The kids have deeper conversations and need me less. By zone 3, I've worked myself out of a job! All the book clubs meet simultaneously and all I do is listen. Student talk at its best!

Figure 9.2 depicts what a typical week might look like when you're launching a book club (the lessons on this chart are laid out later in this chapter). Figure 9.3 presents various possibilities for plugging book clubs into your literacy workshop during the following weeks.

Frontloading	Zone 1 Nov.—Jan.	Zone 2 Feb.—April	Zone 3 April—June
 The Key to Successful Book Clubs • Foundational lessons • Conferring • Anchor texts	• Introducing and launching book clubs • Round 1 of book clubs (*I use this to eavesdrop, instruct, and assess, so I'm present at each book club.*) • *Reflecting* on the process • If book clubs finish early, students may choose to stay together with a new book or "take a break"	• Reflect/revise: What do we need to do to make book clubs even better? • Round 2 of book clubs: Repeat the launch (*What* is your purpose? Genre, theme, author, kid choice?) • Run two book clubs *simultaneously* (releasing responsibility) • *Deeper* conversations	• Reflect/revise: Turning more responsibility over to the kids • Goal is independence • All book clubs meet simultaneously • Deeper conversations

Figure 9.1 The "Key" to Successful Book Clubs

Monday	Tuesday	Wednesday	Thursday	Friday
Lesson What is a book club?	**Lesson** Revisit and finalize book club norms	**Lesson** Round 2: Making choices	**Lesson** • Introduce the books and members • Explicitly review club norms	**Lesson** Reflect on how the previous day went Make changes if necessary
Lesson Beginning to explore book club norms **Teacher** Have book choices ready!	**Lesson** Round 1: Narrowing the choices **Teacher** • Collect and compile choices • Narrow down books	**Teacher** • Collect and compile choices • Create book clubs (talk to individual students if they don't "fit" into any of the groups)	**Teacher** • Meet with book club 1 (20 mins.) • Meet with book club 2 (20 mins.) • Reflect: Ask students to reflect on how it went	**Teacher** • Meet with book club 3 (20 mins.) • Meet with book club 4 (20 mins.) • Reflect: Ask students to reflect on how it went

Figure 9.2 Launching a Book Club: What a Typical First Week Might Look Like

Monday	Tuesday	Wednesday	Thursday	Friday
Reader's Workshop	• Meet with book club 1 • Meet with book club 2	Reader's Workshop	• Meet with book club 3 • Meet with book club 4	Reader's Workshop

OR . . .

Monday	Tuesday	Wednesday	Thursday	Friday
Reader's Workshop	• Meet with book club 1 • Workshop	• Meet with book club 2 • Workshop	• Meet with book club 3 • Workshop	• Meet with book club 4 • Workshop

OR . . .

Monday	Tuesday	Wednesday	Thursday	Friday
Reader's Workshop	Reader's Workshop	• Meet with book club 1 • Meet with book club 2	• Meet with book club 3 • Meet with book club 4	Reader's Workshop

OR . . .

whatever works for *your* classroom

Figure 9.3 Book Clubs over the Following Weeks

An Example to Whet Your Appetite

EAVESDROPPING ON A CONVERSATION ABOUT GARY PAULSEN'S *HATCHET*

The boys in the *Hatchet* book club drift up to the meeting area, some sitting on the couch, others pulling up chairs around it to form a circle. This is their second meeting, so they know the drill. They don't wait for me; they plunge into their discussion. They know I'll pull my stool over and sit outside the perimeter of their circle and take notes.

Will announces, "I think I know what the secret is. Remember how last week we noticed how Paulsen kept repeating 'the secret'?"

Nick jumps to what he's been thinking about. "It made me feel real good when he found berries and the bear didn't attack. That was way different from what you see in movies."

Dropping the topic he just broached, Will piggybacks on Nick's comment to share something in the book that *he* enjoyed. "My favorite part so far was when the porcupine attacked Brian. It was the only actiony part."

Jorge adds, "It was weird how I could kinda feel what Brian felt at that point."

The other boys nod their heads in agreement.

"On page 77, Paulsen's writing sort of lets you into Brian's emotions and thoughts," Matt observes.

"Yeah. It makes something really bad turn into something good." Nick adds.

"What do you mean?" asks Will.

"Well, if it wasn't for the porcupine, he wouldn't have discovered the spark. He did that by accident," says Nick.

"You're right. He did get something good from the bad," Joey agrees.

"I still think it was pretty cool that you could feel Brian yank out the quills. I marked it on p. 81." Frank begins to read the section he marked as everyone follows along in his own book.

This elicits more discussion. Will predicts that Brian will throw the hatchet again and that will help with the fire.

Then Nick changes the subject. "I wonder what Brian will do when he meets the bear again. Do you think he'll meet the bear again?"

"And what about the wolf?" adds Frank.

There is a short discussion about Brian and the animals he encounters, and then Will steers the conversation back to fire. "I want to know how Brian is going to make fire." The group discusses how to use sparks to create a sustainable fire.

Then they wonder what will happen in the upcoming chapters. "He's got to get food. He's hungry and he can't just live on berries, other animals are eating them too," Nick says.

"But I have to say what I thought about the secret before we end," Will insists, circling back to his original thinking, which is important to him.

This is my cue to jump into the group and "teach" a little. "May I come join you for a bit?" I pull my stool in, so I'm no longer an observer. "Will, since you're making a prediction about the secret, would you hold on to that topic and bring it back up when we meet next week? I also want to ask you guys what were the conflicts that showed up this week?

THE LANGUAGE OF LEARNING

I allow the book club to run on its own as much as possible. However, if there are teachable moments or important points to make, I ask if I may join the group. Since the entire class had been working on "conflict," I want to make sure it is explicit here.

"After you guys decide how far to read for next week's meeting, I'd like you to open up to your book club section in your BLB and record your thoughts about when Brian tried to make fire. I want you to be able to go back and reread what you were thinking."

The boys decide to read to chapter 14, page 127, for the following week. Then they record their thinking in their BLB and move back to their desks. Most of them immediately open *Hatchet* and begin to read.

THE *HATCHET* CONVERSATION CONTINUES

As the boys gather the following week, they agree they will finish the book by the next meeting. They again start with their favorite parts. This is typical. Groups usually spend five or ten minutes "mucking around" before the conversation "goes deep."

Once more, Will leads off. "I thought it was really cool how Brian made the bow and arrow and tried it the next day in the water and it worked."

"Yeah, before he made the bow and arrow he had the spear, so he was able to get birds," Nick adds.

"He changed in this part. Remember how Brian thinks back to when he was in school, things aren't what they seem." Frank has touched on something important, and the boys continue to discuss how Brian has changed.

"I got frustrated with Brian though when he was trying to make the fire. It was obvious that you need oxygen to make a fire. And what's up with him always thinking about hamburgers?" Alex muses.

"Wouldn't you be hungry? I think I would want hamburgers too. And there's no way he can get a hamburger where he is," answers Will.

The topic of fire fascinates the boys; they are amazed at the length of the chapter and how Paulsen wrote about it in such detail. Joey comments, "I bet by just reading this book we'd be able to survive."

Next the talk turns to the plane that flies over. "I didn't realize that Brian had been in the wilderness for forty-seven days. That's cool that Paulsen just skipped all the boring stuff and it's been forty-seven days. On page 122 it says Brian's been there forty-seven days," says Will.

"I thought it was weird and sad when the plane went by and Brian said it 'took my hope away,'" adds Matt.

"Why would the plane not be looking for him?" asks Joey.

The boys toss this around and when it's obvious that they aren't going to solve it, I jump in. "After forty-seven days, do you think Brian's family or the searchers have any hope? What do they probably think?"

"Oh! Yeah, they probably think he's dead!"

Next the group discusses how the bow and arrow exploded; then Will returns to the topic he introduced the week before. "I want to finish the book this week. I'm thinking that when we finish the book we'll find out what the secret is."

"They might not ever tell you," Frank cautions.

Chris adds, "Brian kind of let go of the secret in this week's reading. I thought it was important that when he looked at the reflection in the water, Brian knows he's changed."

"But the secret is the thing that is destroying his mind," Will insists. He thinks for a minute and then adds, "Oh, wait, Brian is finally letting it go when the plane went over."

The boys flip through the book to the end before they return to their desks. They ask me if they need to read the epilogue.

"Well, what is an epilogue?" I ask.

"Is it like something that happens after the story?" suggests Jorge.

"That's right. And knowing that, do you think it's important to read? If the author wrote it, should the reader read it?"

They all agree that they should read it and head back to their desks to find out what will ultimately happen to Brian.

As the boys have been discussing their reading, I've been capturing their thoughts, transcribing them as fast as I can. I use these anecdotal records to monitor their comprehension. Do these boys understand the text beyond the literal level? Absolutely. And are they having fun reading the book and discussing it? You bet. And so am I—what could be better than eavesdropping on rich, powerful discussions about great books!

Book Club Questions	**Versus**	**End-of-Chapter Questions**
• It makes something bad turn into something good. . . . What do you mean by that?		• Where was Brian when the plane crashed?
• How's he going to make fire?		• What was the first thing Brian did after the crash?
• What's up with the hamburgers?/ Wouldn't you be hungry, too?		• Where did he make his shelter?
• Why wouldn't the plane be looking for him?		• What did Brian find to eat?
		• How do you think Brian feels?

Where is comprehension stronger?

More crucially, where is the *quest* for comprehension stronger?

NOT YOUR PARENTS' BOOK CLUB

Are you or have you been a member of an adult book club? They're often maddeningly superficial or rambling and, let's face it, more about socializing with friends than participating in deep discussions. I've been in some where the food and drink are more important topics than the book! Often reading the book isn't even a requirement for participating.

Compare that to the conversations these boys are having. It's messy, at times disjointed, but deep and meaningful. And the discussion and direction came from the kids, with only a little help from me. They construct meaning together. Year after year, my students return to *Hatchet.* Doesn't matter if I'm teaching fourth, fifth, or sixth grade. They want this book. While some years the book club may be all boys, often it's a mix of girls and boys. And the conversation is always deep. Paulsen wrote a powerful novel, and the students appreciate this. Rich writing elicits rich conversations around deep thinking. I want to show you how to have kids take the wheel and steer themselves into deep, meaningful conversations.

The Evolution of Book Clubs

Kids have also helped steer my thinking about book clubs. Their reflections and input have guided me over the years. Your students will do the same for you. Remember, little is set in stone. Give my ideas your own slant. Also, notice that there are no assigned jobs; these are free-flowing book clubs (but with a lot of structure in place). And as you saw in the discussion described earlier, I step in when I want students to go deeper or connect their exchange to something we've discussed. This is an important leitmotif—*you gotta jump in and teach.* It's okay for book clubs to become a "guided reading" book club from time to time.

BEFORE OPRAH, THERE WAS ME (AND LOTS OF OTHER TEACHERS)

Yes, I was doing book clubs long before Oprah. I was even doing book clubs before the first edition of *Literature Circles* (Daniels [1994] 2002) was published. I wish I could take credit for creating my version, but my kids did it. My students and Scholastic book orders get the credit.

Whenever I placed book orders, I ordered multiple copies with the free points, so more than one student could enjoy the book. Naturally friends often chose the same book. However, students couldn't talk during independent reading, and the brief time I allotted for conferring with peers wasn't long enough for in-depth discussion. And they wanted to read certain parts together out loud. So a couple of the girls asked if they could come in at lunch and eat and talk about their book. How could I say no to that? And it caught on. I started to notice handwritten sign-up sheets taped to the board. "I'm reading *Island of the Blue Dolphins*. Does anyone else want to read it with me? We could meet at lunch. Sign up below."

The kids signed up. A lot. And I was having kids in for lunch. A lot. They loved it, but it made sense to me to do it with the whole class.

So we chose great books—ones I had multiple copies of—and the kids formed groups and read the entire book by the established deadline. Then each group met (I supplied pretzels!) and we talked about the book. Just like adults do. Then I asked the kids to reflect. What went well? What didn't? What would they change? I asked them to help me teach better. Boy, did they help! Overwhelmingly, students wrote that they wanted to talk about their reading *as they were reading*. They didn't want to wait until the end. I had noticed them talking with other kids in their group throughout the process, but when they stated it so baldly, how could I not listen? They wanted guidelines, a framework to operate under, but they still wanted to be in charge of their own discussions.

We started meeting once a week: four different book clubs, two class periods a week (twenty to thirty minutes for each club). That left three days to work on other reading. I admit, at first I have the groups meet one at a time. I like to eavesdrop on the conversation and transcribe what's being said. Also, I use book club discussions as an assessment, and I can't do that as well if all the groups are meeting simultaneously. However, some of the best teachers I know run book clubs simultaneously and it's seamless and beautiful. (I discuss lots of different looks at the end of the chapter.) That's the joy of it. There isn't one correct way—make it fit your classroom. And by the end of the year, all my book clubs—no matter what grade level—meet simultaneously as I move from group to group. By then the kids are running them independently.

USING AN ANCHOR TEXT TO MODEL BOOK CLUB EXPECTATIONS

I truly believe that anchor novels (see Chapter 4) are the cornerstones of successful book clubs, because reading them gives students lots of practice marking text and holding their thinking. Students see me modeling my thinking, and they have the opportunity to discuss their own thinking with their classmates. They need to hold on (and record) their thinking over a longer period of time. Sustaining their focus like this translates into deeper thinking in book clubs.

Does this mean you can't introduce book clubs without first reading an anchor novel as a class? Of course not. The critical prerequisites are that students know how to mark and hold their thinking and how to discuss their thinking with peers without your direction.

Setting Norms and Expectations

PURPOSE

When I began setting up book clubs in my classroom years ago, my students not only wanted longer, more frequent meetings, they also asked for guidelines—parameters to work under.

Teaching professionals are always creating norms—for staff meetings, staff development, and so on. *Norms* has a different connotation than *rules*. Norms are created together and have group buy-in. If I want book clubs to run smoothly, I need student buy-in. Our book club norms evolve throughout the year. We create our initial anchor chart (I nudge and guide, embedding my expectations in the norms we create as a class, or add my own expectations explicitly) and then revisit it periodically, making additions or changes as necessary.

HERE'S HOW IT GOES: DAY 1

"How many of you know someone who's been in a book club? Or maybe you've even been in a book club."

Hands fly up in the air, and I call on a few students to share their experiences.

"What happens in book clubs?"

"You talk about the book, of course," answers Dexter.

"But people eat a lot at book clubs, too," adds Lucie.

"You're both right. We're going to start book clubs, but ours will look a little different from what you've probably seen. For instance, we'll be meeting every week to talk about our reading. And we won't be eating as much as at adult book clubs."

"Can we bring our snacks?" asks Ellie.

"Absolutely. That would make it authentic," I laugh.

At this point, I relate the history of book clubs in my classroom (just as I've done for you!) and then I turn to the idea of norms.

"You know, the teachers at this school have norms that we've created for our meetings. Be on time, listen, stuff like that. They're kind of like rules, but they're more like expectations of how we'll act and treat one another. And we articulate them to make sure that our meetings run smoothly and that everyone understands. I'd like to create our class book club norms. The expectations that we'll all follow. For example, I could start by saying that in order to have great book clubs, we have to live by our rules of listening—the ones we have on our class anchor chart. What do you think?"

"That makes sense," Naomi agrees, "but we should also add our anchor chart for what makes good conversations."

I've already written down the date and "book club norms" on a piece of chart paper, and I start to record our thinking. Students start making suggestions, which we discuss as a group. Then I add them to the chart. (A final version of a book club norms chart is shown in Figure 9.4.)

The years when students get stuck, I throw out ideas. One thing I always bring up is no side conversations. Think about it: In adult book clubs, this happens all the time. Two people sitting next to each other start their own private conversation, which tends to derail the larger, group discussion. Plus it's rude! I am explicit about this: "No side conversations."

Another point I bring up is how we know when someone hasn't read the material. Kids are great at explaining how they know. And every year they add the expectation that you have to read to be able to participate. Do they hold their classmates to this? You better believe it! They stick to their guns—tough love! I have watched students madly trying to finish their assigned reading in order to participate. It means too much to them.

A final norm I add—it's my expectation—is that when the students gather for book club, they must have some way to hold/mark/record their thinking. Having read an anchor novel together, they have had a lot of experience writing about their thinking as they read. I expect them to continue to do this in their book club. That's their ticket into the group. I'm adamant about this. Harvey Daniels has a terrific way of giving credit—if students come with recorded thinking, they receive 10 points. If they come with no written record,

Book Club Norms

- Listen (refer to chart!).
- Practice/live by our rules of good conversations.
- Respect one another's opinions.
- Don't change the subject until it has been totally discussed (thoroughly).
- Eye contact—sit in a circle.
- Pay attention.
- Be there on time.
- Come ready to discuss—hold your thinking:
  - Book club section in BLB
  - Sticky notes
  - Bookmarks
- Bring your book.
- Have to talk/share thinking/go deep!
- Everyone discusses (flexible)—go deeper—piggyback (no one hogs conversation, though).
- No excuses! You must read!
- Make the commitment to reflect/review prior to the meeting.
- No side conversations.
- Ask questions.
- Leave reading ahead up to the individual book club, but no spoiling it!
- Hold emergency meetings if necessary.
- Mrs. B. will give five to ten minutes before to prepare.
- Rest of class should be working—quiet and considerate (responsibility).
- Group/class needs to be respectful.
- There will be ten minutes in between groups.
- Move quietly.

Figure 9.4 An Anchor Chart of Book Club Norms

it's 0 points, even if it's obvious they've done the reading. It works. Plus it ensures that students mark specific pages to refer to in their discussions.

You'll also notice on the chart that the students have asked for ten minutes to prepare for a book club meeting. Allowing students time to collect their thoughts is a way to ensure success.

When it looks like we're winding up the list, I say, "Okay, this is a great start. This is our rough draft. Tomorrow we'll revisit this anchor chart, and you can add anything you want or that we might have missed. And then we'll go through each norm and vote and then I'll finalize the chart."

HERE'S HOW IT GOES: DAY 2

"So, did anyone think of anything else they'd like to add to the list?" I begin. If any students raise their hand, I add their thoughts.

"Now we're going to go back through each norm and vote. Is it something that will help our class? Can you follow that norm?" I read each norm, we discuss it if necessary, then take a vote. Later I rewrite the chart and post it in our room.

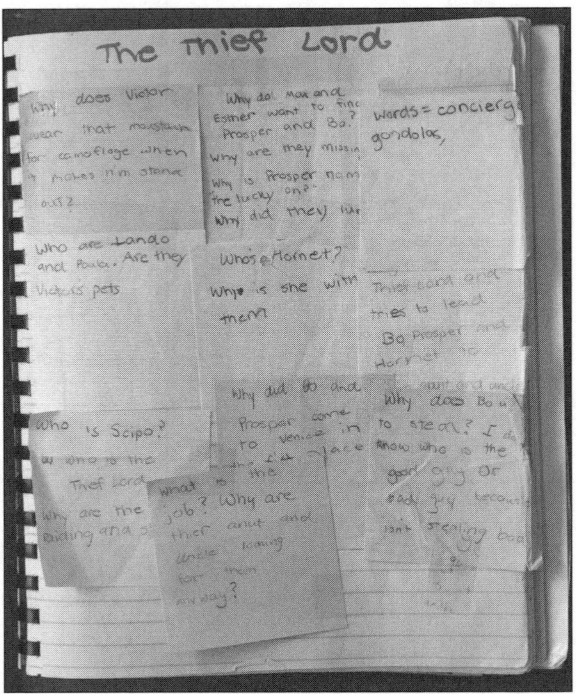

Student's BLB book section with Post-its reflecting her best thinking

Notice how many of the norms build on or refer to the foundational anchor charts from Chapters 2 and 3: Students know how to hold their thinking. However, making it explicit on the chart holds them accountable. Most students prefer to use sticky notes. However, simply slapping a sticky note on the page isn't enough. Students must write their thinking on it. Another favorite is to use a bookmark and capture thinking and page numbers for each week. One year, a student made special bookmarks for her group each week—each week the bookmarks reflected a different aspect of the book!

Groups usually call an emergency meeting only when the members want to read more than they originally decided. Students go out in the hall, have a quick discussion, and then let me know what they decided.

Probably the one area that causes the most disagreement is whether or not students should be allowed to read ahead. Instead of making it a norm, we leave it up to the individual club. Most of the time, students ask their classmates not to read ahead—no matter how hard someone tries, he always inadvertently spoils the story for the rest of the group.

HELPING STUDENTS HAVE PRODUCTIVE BOOK CLUBS

Questions to Help Students Organize Thoughts Before and After Discussion	**Typical Responses**
• How are you preparing in your head for book club? • What ideas will you offer the group for discussion?	• Thinking about the anchor chart, thinking about my favorite part, thinking which sticky notes I want to share most, what I'm confused about, new words I don't get, what I'm thinking about the characters, what surprised me.
• Why have you marked certain spots with a sticky note? How will you take the readers in your group back to those words?	• Important parts, confusing parts, exciting parts. Sections where our anchor text questions got answered. Parts where I'm making predictions or inferring. Marking new vocabulary words—we'll go to that page and read the word in context and maybe someone in my group will know what it is, or Mrs. B will help us (or the dictionary!).
• How will you help the discussion go deeper?	• By not just retelling. To listen to the others in the group and piggyback on their thinking. To look for the deeper meaning in the book. Make connections and inferences and ask really thick questions.
• How are you, as a reader, keeping track of the characters?	• If I'm really into the book, it's easy to keep track. Sometimes if there are a lot of characters, I might need to write down the names of the ones that aren't as important. Talking about them with my book club really helps me remember.

Questions to Help Students Organize Thoughts Before and After Discussion	Typical Responses
• What are the nagging questions you're hanging on to?	• If I have a huge nagging question, then usually Mrs. B. will ask me to be the keeper of that one and to bring it up in group. I write down my huge questions on sticky notes and when we're getting ready for group, those are the things I want to bring up first.
• How does this new, factual information inform and connect with your book club book?	• Helps me to understand it better. Helps me to visualize and also to determine what else could be important. I can also share it with my group.
• How do you feel you fit in the group? • What do you like about book clubs? What doesn't work? • What did you learn about yourself as a reader?	• Responses to these questions vary! Often students make these reflections at the end of the year. I use this feedback to structure future book clubs. The answers to these questions also facilitate discussions about how we all get along!

CHOOSING BOOKS

First, you have to know your students and their reading abilities and choose books (a wide variety) that are a good match. If you teach fifth grade and have students reading at the second grade level up through junior high, this can be quite a task! Second, sometimes *getting* the books is the most difficult part of conducting book clubs. If you're lucky, you have access to multiple copies of novels in your building. Or you begin to build up your own classroom library (Scholastic book orders are terrific for this). Or you might check the books out of various libraries (including those in other schools in your district). Try to start with a lot of choices—eight to ten novels. Then have enough copies for the kids in the book club and one left over for you.

It all comes down to *purpose*. What is your purpose for the book club? Is it to teach a genre or a particular author? Is it to integrate the content area? To work on a specific reading comprehension strategy? To read well-written books? You have to have a purpose in mind before you go searching. One caution: To have great discussions, you need great books—books that are well written and require thought. Figure 9.5 lists a number of books that are appropriate for book clubs. These are only the tip of the iceberg.

General

Esperanza Rising

Becoming Naomi Leon

Hatchet

Things Not Seen

Things Hoped For

Because of Winn Dixie

Summer of the Monkeys

Where the Red Fern Grows

Pictures of Hollis Woods

Savvy

Fig Pudding

Native Americans

Sign of the Beaver

Julie of the Wolves

BearDance

Canyons

Island of the Blue Dolphins

Toughboy and Sister

Fantasy

Dragon Rider

Knights of the Round Table

Thief Lord

by Avi

Who Was That Masked Man, Anyway?

The Barn

Smuggler's Island

S.O.R. Losers

True Confessions of Charlotte Doyle

The Secret School

The Good Dog

Windcatcher

Westward Expansion

The Secret School

Trouble River

Mystery

Castle in the Attic

The Indian in the Cupboard

Mrs. Frisby and the Rats of NIMH

Westing House

Historical Fiction

Angelica

The Witch of Blackbird Pond

Blast to the Past series

Figure 9.5 Some of the Many Books Appropriate for Book Clubs

How to Set Up a Book Club, Launch It, and Keep It Going

Okay, you've posted the norms, kids are excited, and you have the books. Now it's simply a matter of matching the right book with the right kid, right? Here's where it gets tough, and many teachers just assign students to groups and assign books to the groups. These are still book clubs, but the kids don't have choice and are much less likely to buy in to the experience. *If* you've chosen appropriate books at the right levels it works. I *trust* the kids to choose the right book for them. Seriously. I do. But I have them make *three* choices, so I can help them a little. That's why it's incredibly important to have so many books at the start.

The following fairly short minilessons (ten to twenty minutes, depending on how many books you bring!) help my students narrow their choices.

INTRODUCING CHOICES

When I introduce the books, I just want the kids to be aware of the books and the levels; I don't want them to commit. I want their input. I talk briefly about each book. I read the title, the author, and the cover blurbs. I mention the level of the book, how long it is, how large or small the typeface is. Then each child writes down the titles of the books they're interested in on a sheet of paper. That's it—only the books that they would like to read.

I collect the sheets and make a quick tally of the titles. It's clear which books need to be reshelved and which ones have made the cut. (I make sure that all my reading levels are still covered.)

MAKING CHOICES

I instruct the kids to take out a sheet of paper, put their name at the top, and number it 1, 2, and 3. Then I talk about each book that's still in the running. The kids get to hold copies of the books and look through them. We've already discussed how important it is to choose wisely—to choose a book you want to read (not one your best friend wants to read), to choose a book that fits your reading ability.

Then I ask the kids to list their three choices. I also tell them that I can't promise that they will get their first choice; they may end up with their second or even third choice. And I ask that they don't write down a book that they've already read. Then I collect the sheets.

Next comes the fun part—finalizing grouping and books. (I do try to give kids their first choice, but it doesn't always work out.) Here's what I do:

1. Decide how many book clubs I want. Four or five is manageable.
2. Sort the sheets of paper into piles by first-choice book. Sometimes this works out perfectly, other times I have to move to second and third choices.
3. Look at the numbers! The minimum for a book club is three. Four is better. On the other end, I would have to say from experience that any group bigger than eight is unmanageable. But if I have ten kids

who want to read the same book (and I have enough copies), I'll divide them into two groups. One group reads more each week, the other group reads at a slower pace.

What about the kids who read significantly below grade level? We all have those groups. They need more teacher support—the book club becomes almost a "guided reading" club. I make sure I have an appropriate novel for these students to read.

What about the student who wants to read a book that's above his level? That happens too. And that's where honesty is absolutely essential. I talk with the student and discuss where he belongs. Often children with learning disabilities are able to understand and think at a higher level, but their disability makes harder text inaccessible without support. In certain cases, I allow students to listen to the book on tape while following along in the text and marking their thinking. (One year I had a student who was determined to be a part of the *Hatchet* book club. His mother agreed to read the book with him, and he was an integral part of the discussions. He truly knew and understood the book.)

What if a child writes down three books that aren't chosen? That happens, too. Again, I go to the student, discuss which book clubs are available, and let her choose. I also tell her she may borrow any of my books to read independently and present the possibility that one of her original choices may make the cut during the next round of book clubs.

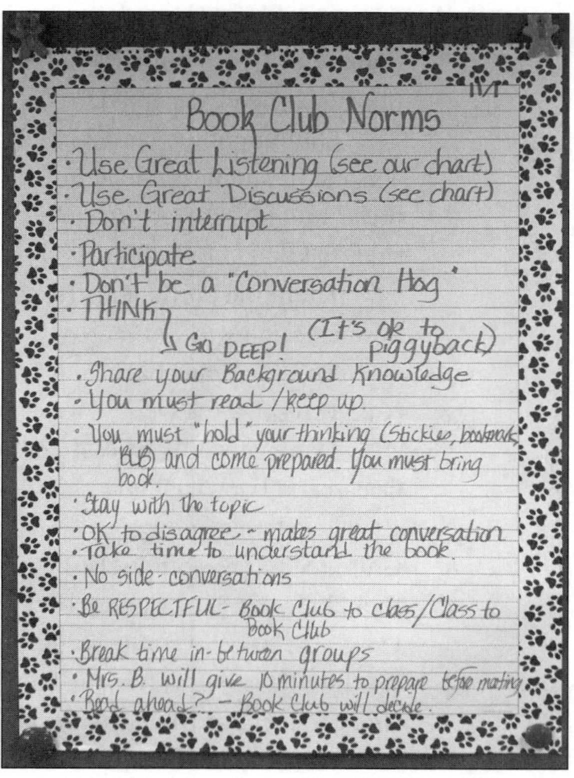

LAUNCH MEETING

Book groups have been chosen, and now it's time to put the books in the kids' hands. But it's not simply a matter of passing out the books and saying, "Go for it." During their first meeting, each book club needs to access background knowledge, articulate questions, and set a purpose. Each launch meeting takes between twenty and thirty minutes. (Which means four book clubs can be launched in two days.)

I call a group to the meeting area, pass out the books, and instruct the kids to read the cover blurbs again and look through the book. While they're doing this, I start a T-chart that looks like this:

Then the kids start throwing out what they know and what they're wondering, and I record it on the chart. This helps me assess how much background knowledge they have and helps establish a purpose for reading the book. As we read, students can refer to this anchor chart and see which questions have been answered.

Sometimes the launch meeting leads to a teachable moment. One year a group of students chose *Julie of the Wolves,* by Jean Craighead George. As these students shared what they knew and asked questions, Danielle finally said, "Okay, I get that Julie is trying to get to her friend in San Francisco—it says that in the blurb. It also says that she's trying to walk. What I don't get is how she's going to walk across all that water from Alaska to San Francisco."

This took me aback, and I didn't answer for a moment. Finally, I asked, "Can you show me what you mean?"

Danielle said, "Well, if you look at a map, Alaska is out in the Pacific Ocean and I don't get how she's going to cross the ocean."

Teachable moment. On maps Alaska is not part of the contiguous United States. It's out in the ocean next to Hawaii, and that's where Danielle thought it was. That was her background knowledge. Because of her question, I was able to incorporate some map-reading skills and clear up her misconception. If we hadn't had the launch meeting, she would have read the book with a lot of confusion. Talking is so important.

The launch meeting also lets me push the kids to deeper questions, and if they're missing key elements, I can explicitly instruct them. Just because this is a student book club does not mean that I don't teach!

Figures 9.6–9.10 are examples of book club anchor charts that have been created during launch meetings.

THE LANGUAGE OF LEARNING

Notice "Mrs. B needs to help here"? The kids knew they didn't have background knowledge about Quakers and were asking me to front-load it for them, create a "hook" on which to hang new learning. Also, I record why the students chose this particular book. It helps me understand their personalities and deepens the purpose for reading.

The Witch of Blackbird Pond by Elizabeth George Speare	
What We Know	**Questions**
Kit—main character	Why such a shock?
Going to New England—coming from the Caribbean	Why is Kit living with Quakers?
Head of house doesn't like Kit	Who is this? Dad?
Kit—orphan	
Goes to live with relatives	What happened to Kit's parents?
Quakers—religion (Mrs. B. needs to help here)	Why are her relatives strangers? Why/how is Kit a prisoner?
"Midwife"	Does Kit have siblings?
Why we chose:	What's her age?
Ariel: "Kit keeps her head up high"—interesting	Who is the witch?
Caitlyn—witches, mysteries	Is the witch real?
Tracy—blurb	Do the Quakers think Kit is a witch?
Danielle—interesting—Kit gets through struggles	Will they hurt her?
Erin—sister read it/played school	Who's William?
Nicole—title, blurb	What's the disease? (Mercy)
Raina—blurb—Wow! First page—mysteries	

Figure 9.6 Fifth-Grade Book Club Anchor Chart: *The Witch of Blackbird Pond*

Things Not Seen by Andrew Clements	
What We Know	**Questions**
Main character—Bobby Phillips, fifteen	
Becomes invisible	How does Bobby become invisible?
His dad is a physicist	What is a physicist?
Alicia—blind	How do they meet?
Found out about Bobby being invisible	"Before it's too late"—before what happens?
Can't go to school, etc.	Setting—where?
Why we chose this book:	What do Bobby's parents do with him?
Erin—likes mystery books; not boring; makes you want to find out more	What are "dangerous consequences"?
Lucie—mystery	What does "time is running out" mean?
Ellie—likes scary and mystery	Is he fading away?
Cooper—last year read first two chapters; got bored; thought with a group it'd be better	Can he walk through things?
Trinity—mysterious kind of story in it; when you read the back, you have to read the book	What can Bobby do because he's invisible?
Emma—good blurb; likes title	What does "he has no life" mean?
Hayden—mysteries	
Dexter—cover	

Figure 9.7 Fourth-Grade Book Club Anchor Chart: *Things Not Seen*

THE LANGUAGE OF LEARNING

This group is lifting lines from the cover blurbs to direct their questions. They are paying attention to the teasers that the publishers are writing to catch their attention. These questions will help focus their reading.

Knights of the Round Table by Gwen Gross	
What We Know	**Questions**
Castles King Arthur Magical land —dragons —witches —wizards —giants Knights of the round table in wars Great fighters Arthur got the sword out of the stone, lots of people tried—got to be king People (historians) think there probably was a king Arthur in England 1500 years ago Arthur won many battles Old—told by storytellers in many lands	What is it about? How do the wars start? Why are they knights of the round Why do they fight? When do all the magical things happen? Why do they need knights? Why are they mean? Do they fight over a sword? How come Arthur is the only one to get the sword out? Do the castles get destroyed? Why do they want to get the sword out of the rock? How'd it get there? Will there be little stories or one big story? Setting? When was the story made up?

Figure 9.8 Third-Grade Book Club Anchor Chart: *Knights of the Round Table*

THE LANGUAGE OF LEARNING

In the *Knights of the Round Table* chart, the questions tend to be more literal, in keeping with the lack of sophistication of the group members and the text.

Hatchet by Gary Paulsen	
What We Know	**Questions**
Brian—main character —thirteen years old —crashes in wilderness —one engine plane —pilot has heart attack and dies Setting—Canada wilderness Parents—divorced Brian going to see his dad Brian has a secret (tearing him apart) Has a hatchet Newbery Honor Book	Does Brian find his way to his father's house? Will he get out of the wilderness/survive? How? How does he eat? Does he get supplies from the plane? Does he meet anybody? What are his experiences? What is the secret? Why? When will Paulsen let us know? How will it help? Will his hatchet break? Does he stay in the wilderness until the final book?
Why we chose this book: Joey—mysteries; "How does he get out of the wilderness?"; survival (theme!) Alex—read Brian's Winter and liked it Matt—adventure Will—didn't like the other choices Jorge—interesting Nick—interesting; wanted to see what Brian does Chris—interesting; will he survive?	

Figure 9.9 Fifth-Grade Book Club Anchor Chart: *Hatchet*

Island of the Blue Dolphins by Scott O'Dell	
What We Know	**Questions**
Island off the coast of California (setting)	How old was she when she was deserted?
Island looks like a big fish	How/why did she become deserted?
Karan (girl)	Is she ever going to find a boat?
Spends eighteen years alone on island	What does she make her shelter out of?
Karana makes weapons, shelter, food	What food does she eat?
Weapons used to fight wild dogs/ protect herself	How many shelters does Karana make?
She waits for a boat	What happens with the wild dogs?
Blue dolphins/otters/sea elephants	What kinds of weapons does she have?
	Conflict—Karana/environment—survival

Figure 9.10 Fourth-Grade Book Club Anchor Chart: *Island of the Blue Dolphins*

Assessing Book Club Conversation and Student Learning

The first ten minutes of a book club meeting are generally spent retelling parts of the story or sharing favorite parts. Students also share any vocabulary words they marked, along with the page it's on. The group turns to that page, the student reads the word in context, and everybody discusses what it means. But inevitably, because we've had a lot of prior practice talking and conversing, a student will make an observation that launches the group into a deeper discussion.

When a group doesn't go deep, most likely one of two things is happening.

1. The students just aren't getting it. If they're not getting it, I need to teach, directly and explicitly. It's as simple as that.
2. There's not a lot of "meat" or depth to the book; it only lends itself to a literal reading. (That's why it's imperative to choose wisely!)

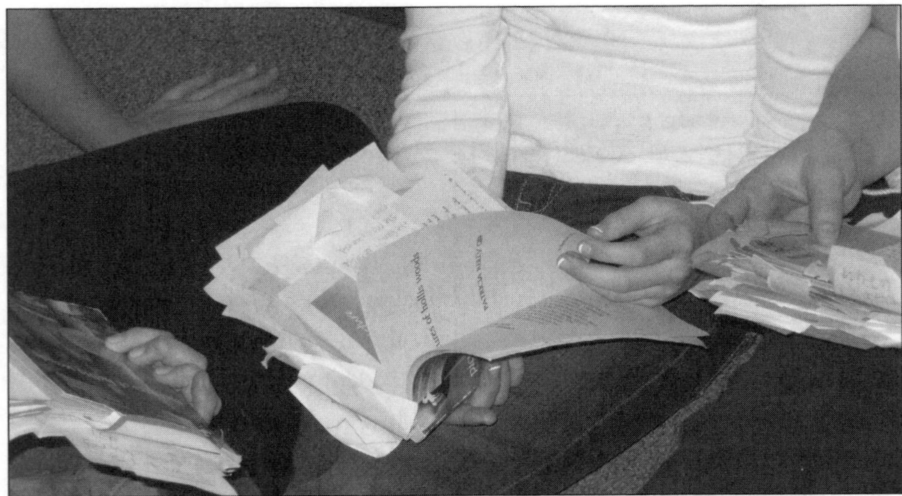

This is another reason I prefer that only one group meets at a time initially; I want to be able to monitor and facilitate if necessary.

I also take notes on the discussions and use these notes as an assessment. I don't have a rubric, but I make sure each child:

1. Comes to group prepared—book in hand and thinking *recorded*
2. Shares and brings up at least one "new learning"
3. Listens and participates in the discussion

When students finish reading the book, I have them remove the sticky notes (after first recording the page number to which it was affixed) and stick them in the book club section of their BLB. If a student used a bookmark, that also gets glued or taped into the BLB. And some students have written in their BLB to prepare for book clubs. All of these things are their (and my) record of their thinking.

Answers to Common Questions

HOW DO I MATCH BOOK CLUB "TALK" WITH THE READING COMPREHENSION STRATEGY I'M TEACHING?

I ask students to use the comprehension strategy we are focusing on to hold their thinking as they read. I also ask them to share those thoughts with the group first, so I can assess how well they do. After that, the book club conversation can go in whatever direction the kids want to take it!

WHAT IF I'M AFRAID TO GIVE UP CONTROL OF THE DIALOGUE? I FEEL SUCH PRESSURE TO GET MY STUDENTS FROM *A* TO *Z*, AND I DON'T TRUST THEIR INDEPENDENT CONVERSATION WILL DO IT.

Here's where tweaking comes in—and purpose. How do you envision your book clubs running? Do you want to be directing the discussion (more like guided reading)? Or do you want the group to be directing themselves? Without the proper foundation in place, book clubs are not going to operate smoothly. But if the students know how to talk and listen, are able to mark the text and hold their thinking, and then feel safe enough to share their thinking, all the pieces for successful book clubs are in place. Do they always run smoothly? Of course not. Sometimes I do need to step in, but I like to let the students have some leeway first. Remember, it takes a few minutes before the conversation shifts into high gear. When I'm eavesdropping on these initial "settling in" conversations, if I hear a student ask a question I know will springboard the group into a deeper discussion, I jump in, explicitly label it, and focus the kids on that question. I tell them that it will create rich discussion, my expectation being that students will begin to recognize and do this for themselves.

WHERE DO I SIT? RIGHT OUTSIDE THE CIRCLE OR A FEW FEET BACK?

Just outside the perimeter. If I'm in the circle, students focus on me. I don't want that. I want to be the observer, the recorder, and only occasionally the facilitator. Toward the end of the conversation, I ask to join the group and physically move my stool in. At that point I may restate key points, ask questions that the group didn't touch on, or teach a concept or a fact explicitly. Or I may simply ensure that the kids choose an appropriate amount of reading for the next week. Although they determine how far they will read before the next meeting, I expect them to read at least ten pages every school night as a minimum. Generally, the group opts to read more!

If a book club is running smoothly, I may get up and touch base with other students. I keep my ears open, however, and am always back before the group disbands. If a group requires a lot of intervention (or its members are reading significantly below grade level), I may become a more active participant. To let kids flounder is not okay. I expect my students to be growing as readers.

WHEN SHOULD I TRY HAVING MORE THAN ONE CLUB GOING AT A TIME?

As students become more familiar with book clubs and they need me less, I may hold two book clubs simultaneously, moving back and forth between them. The drawback is that the noise level increases and students working independently don't have as much quiet surrounding them. If every book club is humming along (usually by the third trimester), I have them all meet at the same time, while I circulate, eavesdropping, stopping and teaching when necessary, nudging them toward deeper thinking.

WHAT IS THE REST OF THE CLASS DOING DURING BOOK CLUBS?

Worksheets don't cut it. Period. Students who are not involved in book clubs should have *meaningful* work. Choice is a key component for keeping kids focused. If my total attention is focused on the book club, I have to trust that the rest of the class is working and using the time wisely. Again, the foundational lessons are critical for creating success. If I plan to conduct two book clubs during a literacy workshop, I know it's going to last at least an hour. Asking students (especially younger students, especially at the beginning of the year) to focus on a single activity for that long is asking a lot. So it's important to give students at least two activity choices and be available in between book clubs. That ten-minute break is crucial.

DO ALL BOOK CLUBS NEED TO LOOK THE SAME?

Just because I like to have one book club meet at a time, doesn't mean that's the best way. Many teachers have book clubs meet simultaneously as they move around the room teaching and assessing. It depends on your purpose, your expectations, how you use book clubs in your classroom.

When I have four book clubs and meet with each one separately, I spend two days a week on book clubs. That leaves three days for other literacy work. At the end of the year when I do have all book clubs meet simultaneously, I may spend only one day a week on them (two if the books are especially challenging or part of a larger study). Some teachers ask parent volunteers for help with book clubs outside the classroom, often in the hall or the library.

What works for you? And, once more, what is your purpose for the book club?

WHAT DO I DO WHEN THE BOOK CLUB IS DONE?

Often the various groups don't finish at the same time. Since my groups form based on student choice, I want to make sure they remain fluid. When a group ends, we have some sort of closure. It may be reflecting, it may be summarizing, it may be writing about the comprehension focus strategy. I leave what happens next up to the group.

Often the group wants to remain together, and the students choose another novel—often a sequel or another book by the same author—which usually means a trek to the bookroom. For example, when a group of fourth-grade girls finished reading *Esperanza Rising*, they chose *Becoming Naomi Leon* and went off to the bookroom to find enough copies of the book. Then they created their own launch chart without me.

Sometimes, members decide they want to take a break and concentrate on their independent reading until a new cycle of book clubs begins.

HOW CAN I ENTRENCH BOOK CLUBS WITHIN KIDS' LIVES?

The obvious way is by encouraging them to participate in book clubs outside the classroom. One year, some of my students participated in a mother–daughter book club. That inspired our parent–student book clubs. Students choose three books that they want to read and that they think their parents will enjoy, too. I send home a letter asking who's interested in participating. At least one parent has to agree to read the same book as the child. Once forms are returned, I distribute copies of the books, one for each participating student and one for the parent(s). These book clubs don't meet until every one has finished reading (we set a meeting date that allows enough time to finish!). But the goal is to encourage book talk at home. And it works. The culminating meeting is held in the evening. I order pizza, and we talk while we eat. The adults are always astounded at the children's capacity for absorbing, complex discussion.

Or how about meeting over the summer? When I move with my students to the next grade, they often want to continue book clubs over the summer. It takes some logistical doing, but we're able to set up groups and dates to meet and discuss novels (again completing the entire book before we meet). These meetings are generally held at a student's house, and we bring our lunches. Again, it's eat and talk.

The Kids Tell It Like It Is

I end this chapter with what a few of my students have said about their book club experiences. There's no better recommendation for book clubs' authenticity and effectiveness. Students are reading, working on comprehension, learning from their peers, and learning invaluable social tools. (How many adults do you know who you wish had learned to listen?!)

> My favorite part of reading is book clubs. I always enjoy talking about the book and visualizing, asking questions, using prior knowledge and determining importance in text. I will bring that with me the rest of my life.
>
> —Ryan, fifth grader

> I LOVED, LOVED book clubs. I thought I did really good in Island of the Blue Dolphins. Maybe I should have talked some more, but it's hard because everyone talks. I marked lots of stuff, but I didn't just slap it down any place. I thought our group was a really good group and we all worked together to get into deep conversations. Do you think I should write on the Post-it why I put it there? We really should work on going one at a time. I would like to keep the same group but get whole new books. Some suggestions for books are The Dear America Series, or some adventure or survival book. My favorite genres of books are adventure or survival. Really, there was nothing that I disliked about it and I really want to start again soon. I pay a lot more attention to what I read and I slow down and think about it.
>
> —Annie, fourth grader

Island of the Blue Dolphins was a very memorable book but the thing that made it most memorable was that I had a great group that was about the same reading level. I think it was great how Lilly brought in examples of the abalone and picture of the devilfish. I also thought that it was good that we could go through the really sad parts including when Rontu died and the exciting parts when the devilfish came and almost attacked them. Now that I've done this book club, I will start thinking about books differently. I would also like to try a different group. We want to read either Where the Red Fern Grows, Summer of the Monkeys, Tuck Everlasting, Witch of Blackbird Pond, or Crossing the Wire. Those all seem like amazing books like Island of the Blue Dolphins. It was pretty cool how [the lab teachers] got to see our first and last meeting. I love doing book clubs because you can express your feelings about the book and agree and disagree. I also like listening in on the other book clubs and hearing their thinking. I also like the freedom of someone not teaching us and we just kind of get to run them. But I don't really think that we need to change anything about the book clubs. It is almost like we are teaching Mrs. B.

—Maddie, fourth grader

I liked it when we had book clubs and when we would confer. I like having book clubs because we would all share our thoughts and we would disagree and agree. I think you learn more when you're in a group discussing the book together because you hear everybody's thoughts. Also, when you would confer with me because it would really make me think.

—Erin, fourth grader

EPILOGUE

Mentor texts. As I work to finish this book, I find myself sitting on my couch surrounded by mentor texts. I collected some of my favorite professional books and settled in to read the endings, because that's what writers do—when we're unsure of what to do, we look at examples. The only common denominator that I've come up with is that epilogues are short. Think about our kids; what's the hardest part of writing (besides starting)? It's ending. How do you wrap it up? In my case, how do I try to sum up a year of teaching reading and writing with final words that will make everything I've said lovely and neat, a gift box tied with a white satin ribbon?

When I confer with my students, I often tell them to go back to the beginning. So I did that, to the question that compelled me to write: "How did you get your kids this far?" I hope I've answered that question, but I know teaching and children are complex enough that I can't have answered it fully. And that's okay, because don't we always have lingering questions? Isn't that in part what helps us try something, nudge it, clip it, color it with our own personality and pedagogy, so the lesson or idea becomes *ours*?

So—tag, you're it. It's your turn. Make it your own, but come back to this book for guidance. Just as you return to favorite parts of a movie or replay certain scenes, revisit sections of this book that speak to you. Start with your core beliefs and then build. Have fun. Above all, remember your role of giving kids choice and earning their trust. Our children will become the readers and writers we want them to be if we remember they come into our classrooms wholly open to our belief in them.

APPENDIX

Mentor Texts with Suggestions for Reading and Writing Minilessons

Title and Author	Reading Lesson	Writing Lesson
Emily Michael Bedard	Schema Character	Poetry and poets connection
Anna's Table Eve Bunting	Schema Science connection (nature) Questions	Details Descriptive language "Zooming in"
The Memory String Eve Bunting	Schema Questions Inferences Problem/plot	Memoir Detail Organization
Bat Loves the Night Nicola Davies	Science integration What's important Sensory images Vocabulary	"Toggle" between the fictional story and the embedded facts Similes ("Its wings fall away, like the wrapper from a candy.") Strong verbs Present tense
Twilight Comes Twice Ralph Fletcher	Vocabulary Schema Sensory images	Organization Figurative language
"Autumblings" and "Winter Eyes" Douglas Florian (all his poetry is excellent)	Schema Sensory images Inferences	Poetry Concrete poetry Descriptive language

Title and Author	**Reading Lesson**	**Writing Lesson**
The Lotus Seed Sherry Garland	Questions Schema Inferences Vietnam connection	Family stories Strong verbs
Winter at Long Pond William T. George	Tracks in the snow, literally Life zones/science integration	Present tense Vivid details Memoir
Blizzard Carole Gerber	Comparison/contrast Schema Sensory images	Comparison/contrast Prepositions
I Feel Orange Today Patricia Godwin	Sensory images Schema	Language Sensory details
My Great-Aunt Arizona Gloria Houston	Character development Schema Visualization History connection	Character development Family stories And to begin sentences
Rose Blanche Roberto Innocenti	Questions Inferences Point of view (switches from first to third person) History integration	Details Sentence fluency: long sentences followed by a short one to make a point ("They all stood in front of long wooden houses. The sun was setting behind the hills. It was windy. I was cold.")
Desert Song Tony Johnston	Science integration (desert habitats) What's important Schema Sensory images	Beautiful descriptive language (poetic) Metaphors ("A pale, cold ribbon of moon, a snake leaves a trail in the sand as he slides along.") Figurative language Verbs
Cloud Dance Thomas Locker	Science integration (weather) Sensory images Organization (concluding nonfiction explanation)	Beautiful language Poetry conveying fact

(*continues*)

Title and Author	**Reading Lesson**	**Writing Lesson**
Water Dance Thomas Locker	Science integration (the water cycle / environment) Organization (concluding nonfiction explanation)	Personification Detail Rich language
Dream Weaver Jonathan London	Close look at the world Schema Sensory images	"Zooming in" Perspective Descriptive writing Verbs Present tense
Like Butter on Pancakes Jonathan London	Schema Sensory images	Organization (circular story) Plays on words ("the sun ticks, the birds talk") Personification Figurative language
Sled Dogs Run Jonathan London	Iditarod connection Problem/plot	Dialogue Language Facts embedded in fiction
The Moonflower Peter and Jean Loewer	Science connection (plants) Fiction/nonfiction Schema Questions Vocabulary	"Toggle" between fiction and nonfiction Beautiful, descriptive language Figurative language
Puddles Jonathan London	Schema Sensory images	Onomatopoeia Sensory details
Painting the Wind Patricia MacLachlan	Sensory images Schema Plot/problem	Detail
Snowflake Bentley Jacqueline Briggs Martin	What's important (fiction and nonfiction) Science integration (weather)	"Toggle" between fictional story and embedded facts Similes ("He said snow was as beautiful as butterflies, or apple blossoms.")
Canoe Days Gary Paulsen	Schema Sensory images	Figurative language Metaphors ("The canoe slides in green magic without a ripple"; "The water is a window into the skylake.")

Title and Author	Reading Lesson	Writing Lesson
Canoe Days Gary Paulsen		Similes ("Ahead is a mallard hen, her ducklings spread out like a spotted fan around her looking for skittering oar bugs to eat.")
Long Night Moon Cynthia Ryland	Visualization Science integration Vocabulary (succulent)	Descriptive language ("In June the Strawberry moon shimmers on succulent buds, on crisp new shoots, on quiet, grateful rabbits.") Present tense Similes
Night in the Country Cynthia Ryland	Schema Second person	Punctuation (ellipses) Onomatopoeia ("reek reek reek") Present tense Sensory detail (sound)
Snow Cynthia Ryland	Schema Sensory images Science integration (weather)	Present tense And to begin sentences Repetition
Home at Last: A Story of Migration April Pulley Sayre	Social studies connection (migration) Schema What's important Synthesis	Language Repetition ("home at last") Interesting punctuation Similes
Mojave Diane Siebert	Life zones connection First person Vocabulary	Personification Beautiful language Poetic nonfiction
"Fireflies at Midnight" Marilyn Singer	Inference (remove the title and allow students to infer what the poem is about from the text) (see Chapter 8) Vocabulary Science connection (animals)	Poetry Repetition ("Dead leaves / Dead crickets"; "Together we tow / Together we know") Language

(*continues*)

Title and Author	**Reading Lesson**	**Writing Lesson**
Three Pebbles and a Song Eileen Spinelli	Story line Plot Character development Relationships Vocabulary	Strong verbs (*twirled*, *skittered*) Onomatopoeia Dialogue
Hide and Seek Fog Alvin Tresselt	Schema Sensory images Vocabulary (*scowled*, *muffled*)	Descriptive writing Strong verbs Beautiful language Similes ("But out of doors the fog twisted about the cottages like slow-motion smoke.") Interesting punctuation
The Wreck of the Zephyr Chris Van Allsburg	Questions Inference What's important Synthesis Character development Problem	Organization Details Character
A Kitten Called Moonlight Martin Waddell	Character Plot Problem	Dialogue Story/memoir
Island Child Lisa Wallis	Schema Sensory images Inference	Memoir Rich, detailed language
"Color Me a Rhyme" Jane Yolen (all her poetry is exceptional; two other great ones are "Snow, Snow" and "Once upon Ice")	Science connection (nature) Sensory images Inferring Vocabulary	Language Details Specific words
Owl Moon Jane Yolen	Schema	Memoir Detail
Welcome to the Ice House Jane Yolen	Science connection (animal habitats) Vocabulary	Descriptive language Embedding facts in fiction Verbs

WORKS CITED

PROFESSIONAL BOOKS

Allen, P. 2009. *Conferring: The Keystone of Reader's Workshop*. Portland, ME: Stenhouse.

Allington, R. L. 2001. *What Really Matters for Struggling Readers: Designing Research-Based Programs*. New York: Addison-Wesley.

Anderson, B. 2003. *Daily Language Instruction, Grade 3: 30 Weeks of Editing and Proofreading Tasks*. Morrison, CO: Hogback Press.

Anderson, C. 2000. *How's It Going? A Practical Guide to Conferring with Student Writers*. Portsmouth, NH: Heinemann.

Atwell, N. 1987. *In the Middle: Writing, Reading, and Learning with Adolescents*. Portsmouth, NH: Heinemann.

———. 2007. *The Reading Zone*. New York: Scholastic.

Calkins, L., K. Montgomery, D. Santman, and B. Falk. 1998. *A Teacher's Guide to Standardized Reading Tests: Knowledge Is Power*. Portsmouth, NH: Heinemann.

Conrad, L., M. Matthews, C. Zimmerman, and P. Allen. 2008. *Put Thinking to the Test*. Portland, ME: Stenhouse.

Culham, R. 2010. *Traits of Writing: The Complete Guide for Middle School*. New York: Scholastic.

Daily Geography Practice. 2004. Various grade levels. Monterey, CA: Evan-Moor.

Daniels, Harvey. [1994] 2002. *Literature Circles: Voice and Choice in Book Clubs and Reading Groups*. 2d ed. Portland, ME: Stenhouse.

Davis, J., and S. Hill. 2003. *The No-Nonsense Guide to Teaching Writing: Strategies, Structures, Solutions*. Portsmouth, NH: Heinemann.

Fletcher, R. 1993. *What a Writer Needs*. Portsmouth, NH: Heinemann.

———. 2006. *Boy Writers: Reclaiming Their Voices*. Portland, ME: Stenhouse.

Fletcher, R., and J. Portalupi. 2001. *Writing Workshop: The Essential Guide*. Portsmouth, NH: Heinemann.

Graves, D. 1994. *A Fresh Look at Writing*. Portsmouth, NH: Heinemann.

Harvey, S. 1998. *Nonfiction Matters: Reading, Writing, and Research in Grades 3–8*. York, ME: Stenhouse.

Harvey, S., and A. Goudvis. 2000. *Strategies That Work: Teaching Comprehension to Enhance Understanding*. Portland, ME: Stenhouse.

———. 2007. *Strategies That Work: Teaching Comprehension to Enhance Understanding*, 2d ed. Portland, ME: Stenhouse.

Harvey, S., and H. Daniels. 2009. *Comprehension and Collaboration: Inquiry Circles in Action*. Portsmouth, NH: Heinemann.

Heard, G. 1989. *For the Good of the Earth and Sun: Teaching Poetry*. Portsmouth, NH: Heinemann.

———. 2002. *The Revision Toolbox: Teaching Techniques That Work*. Portsmouth, NH: Heinemann.

Keene, E., and S. Zimmermann. 1997. *Mosaic of Thought: Teaching Comprehension in a Reader's Workshop*. Portsmouth, NH: Heinemann.

———. 2007. *Mosaic of Thought: The Power of Comprehension Strategy*. 2d ed. Portsmouth, NH: Heinemann.

Lane, B. 1993. *After* The End: *Teaching and Learning Creative Revision*. Portsmouth, NH: Heinemann.

———. 2003. *Reviser's Toolbox*. Shoreham, VT: Discover Writing Press.

Lane, B., and G. Bernabei. 2001. *Why We Must Run with Scissors*. Shoreham, VT: Discover Writing Press.

Miller, D. 2002. *Reading with Meaning: Teaching Comprehension in the Primary Grades*. Portland, ME: Stenhouse.

———. 2008. *Teaching with Intention*. Portland, ME: Stenhouse.

Morgan, B. 2005. *Writing Through the Tween Years: Supporting Writers, Grades 3–6*. Portland, ME: Stenhouse.

Nagy, W. E. 1996. *Teaching Vocabulary to Improve Reading Comprehension*. Urbana, IL: National Council of Teachers of English.

Newkirk, T. 2002. *Misreading Masculinity*. Portsmouth, NH: Heinemann.

Overmeyer, M. 2005. *When Writer's Workshop Isn't Working*. Portland, ME: Stenhouse.

Pearson, P. D., and M. C. Gallagher. 1983. "The Instruction of Reading Comprehension." *Contemporary Educational Psychology* 8 (3): 317–44.

Pearson, P. D., J. A. Dole, G. G. Duffy, and L. R. Roehler. 1992. "Developing Expertise in Reading Comprehension: What Should Be Taught and How Should It Be Taught?" In *What Research Has to Say to the Teacher of Reading*, 2d ed., ed. J. Farstup and S. J. Samuels. Newark, DE: International Reading Association.

Perkins, D. 1995. *School Smarts: Better Thinking and Learning for Every Child*. New York: Free Press.

Ray, K. W. 1999. *Wondrous Words: Writers and Writing in the Elementary Classroom*. Urbana, IL: National Council of Teachers of English.

———. 2006. *Study Driven: A Framework for Planning Units of Study in the Writing Workshop*. Portsmouth, NH: Heinemann.

Ray, K. W., with L. Laminack. 2001. *The Writing Workshop: Working Through the Hard Parts (And They're All Hard Parts)*. Urbana, IL: National Council of Teachers of English.

Ray, K. W., with L. B. Cleaveland. 2004. *About the Authors: Writing Workshop with Our Youngest Writers*. Portsmouth, NH: Heinemann.

Robb, L. 2010. *Teaching Middle School Writers*. Portsmouth, NH: Heinemann.

Routman, R. 1996. *Literacy at the Crossroads*. Portsmouth, NH: Heinemann.

———. 2003. *Reading Essentials: The Specifics You Need to Teach Reading Well*. Portsmouth, NH: Heinemann.

———. 2005. *Writing Essentials: Raising Expectations and Results While Simplifying Teaching*. Portsmouth, NH: Heinemann.

Snowball, D., and F. Bolton. 1999. *Spelling K–8: Planning and Teaching*. York, ME: Stenhouse.

Spandel, V. 2001. *Creating Writers: Through 6-Trait Writing Assessment and Instruction*. New York: Addison Wesley Longman.

Spandel, V., and R. Culham. 2010. *Traits of Writing*. Portsmouth, NH: Heinemann.

Tomlinson, C. A. 1999. *The Differentiated Classroom: Responding to the Needs of All Learners*. Alexandria, VA: Association for Supervision & Curriculum Development.

Tovani, C. 2000. *I Read It, but I Don't Get It: Comprehension Strategies for Adolescent Readers*. Portland, ME: Stenhouse.

———. 2004. *Do I Really Have to Teach Reading? Content, Comprehension, Grades 6–12*. Portland, ME: Stenhouse.

Wilhelm, J. D. 2001. *Improving Comprehension with Think-Aloud Strategies: Modeling What Good Readers Do*. New York: Scholastic.

Zimmermann, S., and C. Hutchins. 2003. *Seven Keys to Comprehension: How to Help Your Kids Read It and Get It!* New York: Three Rivers Press.

CHILDREN'S BOOKS AND TRADE TITLES

Ada, Alma Flor. 1994. *Dear Peter Rabbit*. New York: Aladdin.

———. 1998. *Yours Truly, Goldilocks*. New York: Atheneum.

Avi. 1986. *S.O.R. Losers*. New York: HarperCollins.
———. 1990. *Something Upstairs*. New York: HarperTeen.
———. 1990. *True Confessions of Charlotte Doyle*. New York: Scholastic.
———. 1991. *Windcatcher*. New York: Avon.
———. 1994. *The Barn*. New York: Scholastic.
———. 1994. *Smuggler's Island*. New York: HarperCollins.
———. 1994. *"Who Was That Masked Man, Anyway?"* New York: HarperCollins.
———. 2001. *The Good Dog*. New York: Atheneum.
———. 2001. *The Secret School*. New York: Sandpiper/Harcourt.
———. 2004. *Midnight Magic*. New York: Scholastic.
Babbit, Natalie. 1975. *Tuck Everlasting*. New York: Farrar, Straus & Giroux.
Barraclough, Susan. 2007. *Bugs*. Phoenix: Amber.
Blume, Judy. 2003. *Fudge-a-Mania*. New York: Macmillan.
Brown, Margaret Wise. 1949. *The Important Book*. New York: HarperCollins.
———. 1991 (reissue). *Goodnight, Moon*. New York: HarperCollins.
Bryant, Jen. 2008. *A River of Words: The Story of William Carlos Williams*. Cambridge, UK: Eerdmans Books for Young Readers.
Buckey, Sarah Masters. 2004. *The Curse of Ravenscourt: A Samantha Mystery* (American Girl Mystery series). Middleton, WI: American Girl Publishers.
Bunting, Eve. 1989. *The Wednesday Surprise*. New York: Clarion.
———. 1995. *Smoky Night*. New York: Harcourt Brace.
———. 1998. *So Far from the Sea*. New York: Clarion Books.
Burnett, Frances Hodgkins. [1911] 2002. *The Secret Garden*. New York: Gramercy/Random House.
Christelow, Eileen. 2006. *Letters from a Desperate Dog*. New York: Clarion.
Cleary, Beverly. [1981] 1992. *Ramona Quimby Age 8*. New York: HarperCollins.
Clements, Andrew. 2002. *Things Not Seen*. New York: Philomel.
———. 2006. *Things Hoped For*. New York: Philomel.
Creech, Sharon. 2001. *Love That Dog*. New York: HarperCollins.
Cronin, Doreen. 2000. *Click, Clack, Moo: Cows That Type*. New York: Simon & Schuster.
———. 2002. *Giggle, Giggle, Quack*. New York: Simon & Schuster
Danneberg, Julie. 2003. *First Year Letters*. Watertown, MA: Charlesbridge.
Day, Alexandra. 1985. *Good Dog Carl*. New York: Scholastic.
Deedy, Carmen Agra. 2000. *The Yellow Star*. Atlanta: Peachtree Publishers.
Dicamillo, Kate. 2000. *Because of Winn-Dixie*. Cambridge, MA: Candlewick.

———. 2001. *The Tiger Rising*. Cambridge, MA: Candlewick.

———. 2006. *The Tale of Desperaux*. Cambridge, MA: Candlewick.

Dixon, Franklin W. 2005. *Running on Fumes: Undercover Brothers*. New York: Aladdin.

Dr. Seuss. 1948. *Thidwick the Big-Hearted Moose*. New York: Random House.

Fletcher, Ralph. 1995. *Fig Pudding*. New York: Clarion.

———. 1996. *The Writer's Notebook: Unlocking the Writer Within You*. New York: HarperCollins.

Friedman, T. 2005. *The World Is Flat: A Brief History of the Twenty-first Century*. New York: Farrar, Straus & Giroux.

Funke, Cornelia. 2004. *Dragon Rider*. Translated by Anthea Bell. New York: The Chicken House/Scholastic.

———. 2010. *Thief Lord*. New York: The Chicken House/Scholastic.

Gardiner, John Reynolds. 1980. *Stone Fox*. New York: HarperCollins.

George, Jean Craighead. 1972. *Julie of the Wolves*. New York: Harper Trophy.

Grogan, John. 2005. *Marley and Me*. New York: HarperCollins.

Gross, Gwen. 1985. *Knights of the Round Table*. New York: Random House.

Haddix, Margaret Peterson. 2001. *Among the Imposters*. New York: Simon & Schuster.

———. 2008. *Found*. New York: Simon & Schuster.

Hesse, Karen. 1996. *The Music of Dolphins*. New York: Scholastic.

Hiassenon, Carl. 2005. *Flush*. New York: Random House.

Hobbs, Will. 1989. *Bearstone*. New York: Atheneum.

———. 2006. *Crossing the Wire*. New York: HarperCollins.

Hunter, Erin. 2003. 2008. *Warriors: The New Prophecy* (series) Boxed Set, Volumes 1–6. New York: HarperCollins.

Innocenti, Roberto. 1985. *Rose Blanche*. Mankato, MN: Creative Paperbacks.

James, Simon. 1996. *Dear Mr. Blueberry*. Fullerton, CA: Aladdin.

Johnston, Tony. 1994. *Amber on the Mountain*. New York: Dial Books for Young Readers.

Kinney, Jeff. 2007. *Diary of a Wimpy Kid*. New York: Amulet Books.

Kipling, Rudyard. [1894] 1994. *The Jungle Book*. New York: Everyman's Library Children's Classics/Alfred A. Knopf.

Kitchen, Bert. 1992. *Somewhere Today*. Cambridge, MA: Candlewick.

Korman, Gordon. 2000. *Swindle*. New York: Scholastic.

Larson, Kirby. 2010. *The Fences Between Us*, vol. 1 in Dear America series. New York: Scholastic.

Lowry, Lois. 1988. *All About Sam*. Boston: Houghton Mifflin.

———. 1989. *Number the Stars*. Boston: Houghton Mifflin.

MacGowan, Christopher, ed. 1986. *Poetry for Young People: William Carlos Williams*. New York: Sterling.

MacLaughlin, Patricia. 1985. *Sarah, Plain and Tall*. New York: HarperCollins.

Martin, Ann M. 2005. *A Dog's Life: The Autobiography of a Stray*. New York: Scholastic.

Milan, Cesar. 2007. *Cesar's Way: The Natural, Everyday Guide to Understanding and Correcting Common Dog Problems*. New York: Three Rivers Press.

Mills, Claudia. 2002. *7 × 9 = Trouble*. New York: Farrar, Straus & Giroux.

O'Dell, Scott. [1960] 1988. *Island of the Blue Dolphins*. Boston: Houghton Mifflin Harcourt.

Paulsen, Gary. 1987. *The Crossing*. New York: Orchard.

———. 1987. *Hatchet*. New York: Atheneum.

———. 1990. *Canyons*. New York: Delacorte.

———. 1996. *Brian's Winter*. New York: Delacorte.

———. 2001. *Guts*. New York: Delacorte.

———. 2003. *How Angel Peterson Got His Name*. New York: Wendy Lamb Books/Random House Children's Books.

Pirsig, Robert M. 1974. *Zen and the Art of Motorcycle Maintenance*. New York: William Morrow and Co.

Polacco, Patricia. 1994. *Pink and Say*. New York: Philomel.

———. 1996. *Aunt Chip and the Triple Creek Dam Affair*. New York: Philomel.

———. 1998. *Thank You, Mr. Falker*. New York: Philomel.

Rahaman, Vashanti, and Lori McElrath-Eslick. 1997. *Read for Me, Mama*. Honesdale, PA: Boyds Mills Press.

Raskin, Ellen. 1978. *The Westing Game*. New York: Scholastic.

Rawls, Wilson. 1989. *Summer of the Monkeys*. New York: Doubleday.

———. 1996. *Where the Red Fern Grows*. New York: Delacorte.

Riordan, Rick. 2005. *The Lightning Thief*. New York: Hyperion.

Ritter, John H. 2003. *The Boy Who Saved Baseball*. New York: Philomel.

Ryan, Pam Muñoz. 2000. *Esperanza Rising*. New York: Scholastic.

———. 2004. *Becoming Naomi Leon*. New York: Scholastic.

Sachar, Louis. 1998. *Holes*. New York: Scholastic.

Selznick, Brian. 2007. *The Invention of Hugo Cabret*. New York: Scholastic.

Siamon, Sharon. 2001. *Sky Horse*. Vancouver, BC: Whitecap Books.

Silverstein, Shel. 1994. *Where the Sidewalk Ends*. New York: HarperCollins.

Speare, Elizabeth George. [1958] 1997. *The Witch of Blackbird Pond*. Boston: McDougal Little.

———. 1983. *Sign of the Beaver*. Boston: Houghton Mifflin.

Teague, Mark. 2002. *Dear Mrs. LaRue: Letters from Obedience School*. New York: Scholastic.

———. 2004. *Detective LaRue: Letters from the Investigation*. New York: Scholastic.

Tolkien, J. R. R. 2005. *Lord of the Rings*. Boston: Houghton Mifflin.

Van Allsburg, Chris. 1979. *The Garden of Abdul Gasazi*. Boston: Houghton Mifflin.

———. 1983. *The Wreck of the Zephyr*. Boston: Houghton Mifflin.

———. 1986. *The Stranger*. Boston: Houghton Mifflin.

Winter, Jeanette. 2005. *The Librarian of Basra*. New York: Harcourt.

Wollard, Kathy. 1993. *How Come? Every Kid's Science Questions Explained*. New York: Workman.

———. 1999. *How Come? Planet Earth*. New York: Workman.

Woodson, Jacqueline. 2009. *Peace, Locomotion*. New York: Putnam Juvenile.

Wright, Betty Ren. 1999. *The Dollhouse Murders*. New York: Scholastic.

Yee, Wong Herbert. 2003. *Tracks in the Snow*. New York: Henry Holt.

INDEX